Ecologies of Urbanism in India

Ecologies of Urbanism in India

Metropolitan Civility and Sustainability

Edited by Anne Rademacher and K. Sivaramakrishnan

香 港 大 學 出 版 社
HONG KONG UNIVERSITY PRESS

**Hong Kong Institute for the
Humanities and Social Sciences**
(Incorporating the Centre of Asian Studies)

This publication has been generously supported by the Hong Kong Institute for the Humanities and Social Sciences, and grows out of a conference convened by the "Environmental Sustainability, Political Ecology, and Civil Society" research group in the Institute's Inter-Asia Program.

Hong Kong University Press
The University of Hong Kong
Pokfulam Road
Hong Kong
www.hkupress.org

© Hong Kong University Press 2013

ISBN 978-988-8139-76-7 *(Hardback)*
ISBN 978-988-8139-77-4 *(Paperback)*

British Library Cataloguing-in-Publication Data
A catalogue record for this book is available from the British Library.

10   9   8   7   6   5   4   3   2   1

Printed and bound by Goodrich Int'l Printing Co., Ltd. in Hong Kong, China

Contents

Illustrations

Figures

Tables

Foreword

As a Chinese anthropologist, I am honored to write a foreword for this remarkable volume on urban ecology issues in contemporary Indian cities. I have known the editors, Anne Rademacher and K. Sivaramakrishnan, since they were doctoral students in the Department of Anthropology at Yale University. We have embarked on parallel intellectual and ethnographic journeys in East and South Asia, and share a deep commitment to the development of interdisciplinary studies of a broadly defined 'Asia.' In pursuing our research interests, we have moved from rural to urban sites; from forests, rivers, and rice fields to global cityscapes. In the process, we have found many conventional analytical distinctions increasingly difficult to maintain. The volume they have put together, with colleagues who have done meticulous historical and ethnographic work in India, reflects critical rethinking of conceptual categories.

We are accomplices in an intellectual enterprise to reconceptualize 'Asia' by highlighting connections—in geographies, institutions, cultural meanings, and the movement of material goods and people. We would like to bring back classic social theorists to challenge the positivist social science paradigms based on bounded, empirically quantifiable units such as city and countryside, nature and built environments, polity and society, local and global scales. We focus on processes of 'structuring' involving meaningful, historically situated, interpretative actions of human agents that are contingent and full of power implications.

Their project has been supported by Yale University and by the Hong Kong Institute for the Humanities and Social Sciences which is a research entity I helped set up at the University of Hong Kong in 2001. The institute highlights an interdisciplinary, inter-institutional and inter-Asian agenda, and supports multi-year research groups pursuing creative themes. It brings together colleagues from around the world to share expertise on evolving topics and to build a critical community of scholars who are willing to cross multiple boundaries.

Environmental Sustainability, Political Ecology and Civil Society, is one of these research groups that display tremendous intellectual rigor and collegiality. Key players began a brainstorming session at Yale in 2009, followed by a three-day workshop and site visits at the University of Hong Kong, and a panel at the Association for Asian Studies meeting in March 2010. With collective enthusiasm and record speed, they delivered a publishable manuscript. Although the panels were focused on cities in India, colleagues and students with East Asian and Middle Eastern interests were invited to share insights and experiences. In June 2012, Anne and Shivi continued with the momentum generated by their project in a workshop on "Sustainability and Citizenship in Asian Cities." This workshop was part of the third conference in a series jointly organized by the Social Science Research Council, the National University of Singapore and the Hong Kong Institute for the Humanities and Social Sciences on the theme of "Inter-Asian Connections."

This volume, entitled *Ecologies Of Urbanism In India: Metropolitan Civility And Sustainability*, focuses on India's major cities with complex historical layers of sociality that are both connected and comparable to many pre-and postcolonial cities. In the twenty-first century, they are sites for intense fluidities in a dynamic Asian region and emergent nodes of a much-transformed global system. They are rich sources of ethnographic materials for us to use in trying to understand new urbanisms in which an increasing proportion of the world's population will find themselves. These studies are timely, and provide tremendous value for analysis and comparison.

In a recent review of two books on China's urbanisms today (http://cross-currents.berkeley.edu/e-journal/inaugural-issue/history-chinas-urban-post-modern), I pose key questions parallel to those of our authors in this volume. Let me paraphrase. Decades of global market flows, population migrations, digital technology, and accelerated interconnectedness have resulted in remarkable urban transformations in this century. Today, eight of the world's ten mega-cities (with populations over 10 million) are in Asia. In what Ananya Roy and Aihwa Ong (2011) termed an inter-referencing Asian urban renaissance, city building has reached revolutionary scale, intensity, and audacity. What are the distinctive features of this dramatic moment?

Who are the major players? What cultural meanings and lifestyles are visibly forged? How are these processes intertwined with nationalistic aspirations, social divisions, and political contestations? What analytical insights and theoretical reflections can we gain from this historical juncture of an urban postmodern that links Asia and the globe? These are issues in the minds of scholars across the disciplines.

Anne and Shivi have gone far in connecting diverse perspectives and promoting conversations. They also deliver results. This brief summary of the history and themes of this book is an appreciation for their collective efforts and a call to move forward.

Helen F. Siu
Yale University
February 16, 2012

References

Roy, Ananya, and Aihwa Ong, eds. 2011. *Worlding Cities: Asian Experiments and the Art Of Being Global*. Malden, MA: Wiley-Blackwell.

Siu, Helen F. 2011. Review of *The Great Urban Transformation: Politics of Land and Property in China*, by You-tien Hsing.

Preface and Acknowledgments

This project owes its origins to a small workshop, called "Citizenship, Civility, and Environmental Sustainability across Urban Asia," convened at Yale in January 2009 in the Department of Anthropology. Many of the contributors in this volume, and a few others, met to discuss the relationship between the making of urban society and the urban environment. How, we asked, do these intersect? We were particularly interested in Asia, where dramatic urban growth made this inquiry especially timely. As our group was comprised entirely of scholars working in India, we decided to focus on the Indian experience in its historical complexity and geographical diversity. Even within India, we limited ourselves in initial deliberations to two of its most important cities—Delhi and Mumbai—with their strikingly different modern histories of urbanization.

The discussions were lively and fruitful; they persuaded us to move forward as a research network that would meet periodically to continue to share ideas and writing. From work in these Indian cities, and other metropolitan centers as well, we found our discussions increasingly organized around four themes. The first we identified as 'the political ecology of the city.' We considered how, in the spirit of that scholarly tradition, natural resource claims in urban contexts may resonate in particular ways with questions of citizenship, civility, informality, and equity. A second theme addressed the political mobilization of urban middle classes around environmental concerns such as urban health, aesthetics, recreation, and conservation. Here we asked, how do middle-class sensibilities constitute ideologies of belonging to the city, and construct 'natural' spaces in the city? We then identified a third set of issues related to green corporatism and green design, which addressed ideas of nature and aspirations for the ecological remaking of cities. Questions of sustainability in urban infrastructure, architecture, and planning were central. Finally, in a cluster of questions related to civil society and ideas of nature in the city, we explored issues associated with nature in the city—safety, access to recreation and leisure space, public health—and other understandings of nature that differentiate the city from the countryside.

With these themes defined, we agreed to meet a year later for a full conference at the University of Hong Kong. Research papers, grouped according to these thematic clusters, were presented to the group for intensive discussion. It was here that we were able to begin a series of discussions with scholars whose expertise lay outside the urban experience in India. This broadened and enriched our understanding of what we were coming to regard as the ecologies of urbanism in Indian cities. By the end of the Hong Kong conference, we were committed to both a publication that would assemble many of the papers that were discussed, and also future meetings, where we hoped for even more systematic comparative exchange drawing on urban ecology from other parts of Asia.

The Hong Kong conference also helped us realize that our interest in contemporary urbanization and its ecological dimensions could benefit from engagement with urban history in India. To this end, we convened a panel at the annual meeting of the Association for Asian Studies later that year. This panel explored how the histories of Indian urbanism illuminate the themes we pursued in Hong Kong. The current volume has come thereby to embrace a strong historical perspective, with several papers by historians and others who have taken a historical view of planning and urban infrastructure.

This volume draws together many of the papers presented in Hong Kong, and two historical pieces presented at the Association for Asian Studies meeting. All the papers were further revised in light of comments we shared with each other, and submitted to an extended virtual discussion before this manuscript took its final shape. At this point, we are happy that the volume now contains papers not only about Delhi and Mumbai, where we started, but also about Bengaluru and Chennai. We realize that the next frontier for our collective enterprise is the ecologies of urbanism in smaller Indian cities and towns, as well as a more systematic placement of that experience in a wider Asian experience, from China to South East Asia, and other parts of South Asia.

From its very inception three years ago in the small workshop in New Haven, this project has been blessed with the generous financial support of the Hong Kong Institute for the Humanities and Social Sciences. Even more important has been the moral and intellectual support provided by Helen Siu, then director of the institute, who brought our conference to Hong Kong, took active part in it, watched over the development of this book, and has now kindly written its foreword.

Yale University also provided financial support for this project at various points. The Department of Anthropology supported our workshop in New Haven, and the South Asian Studies Council at the MacMillan Center, Yale University, made it possible to bring scholars from India to the Association for Asian Studies meeting. We were able to accomplish a great deal at our conference in Hong Kong precisely because the Hong Kong Institute for the Humanities and Social Sciences, especially Emily Ip and Jascha Yu, took great care with the details and made us comfortable during our stay. Their team not only facilitated the meeting, but was a source of boundless energy as we explored the urban environment of Hong Kong even as we discussed urban India.

Like any such volume, it has not been possible to reflect the full range of papers presented and the full extent of discussions that has occurred in our meetings. We owe, however, a deep debt of gratitude to all those who joined our deliberations in New Haven, Hong Kong, and Philadelphia. Amita Baviskar and Shekhar Krishnan were with us from the beginning in New Haven. They traveled with us to Hong Kong and their contributions greatly enriched our discussions. Their work does not appear in this present volume. Roshni Udyavar Yehuda and Lalit Batra presented papers in Hong Kong but are likewise not included in this volume. The Hong Kong conference panels also benefited from comments provided by George Lin, Solomon Benjamin, and Sarah Liao.

Over the last three years, this project has been fortunate to be continuously supported by a series of talented research assistants, graduate students in the Department of Anthropology at Yale University. Their efforts and ideas have been integral to our success on many levels. Min Lieskovsky worked as the research assistant for the New Haven workshop, and traveled with us the following year to Hong Kong to join the team of students working with us there. Thereafter, Amy Zhang worked as our research assistant as we moved from the conference into the virtual discussion groups that would later yield the chapters in this book. Amy Zhang and Aniket Aga helped us find many of the secondary materials we read as we wrote our own introductory chapter and stayed in touch with our colleagues through another round of revisions.

Very soon after the Hong Kong conference, as we planned for this book, it won the interested attention of Michael Duckworth, publisher at Hong Kong University Press. We are grateful for his enthusiasm for this project and we thank the anonymous reviews whose extremely positive comments persuaded the editorial committee at the press to accept this work for publication.

We are very grateful to Aniket Aga for all his patient and thorough work as we prepared the manuscript for publication.

Anne Rademacher and K. Sivaramakrishnan
New Haven
February 2012

Contributors

Nikhil Anand is Assistant Professor of Anthropology at Haverford College, Haverford, Pennsylvania.

Karen Coelho is Assistant Professor, Madras Institute of Development Studies, Chennai, India.

Sapana Doshi is Assistant Professor of Geography at University of Arizona, Tucson.

D. Asher Ghertner is Assistant Professor of Geography at Rutgers University, New Brunswick, New Jersey.

Vinay Gidwani is Associate Professor of Geography and Global Studies at University of Minnesota, Twin Cities.

William J. Glover is Associate Professor of Architecture and History, and Associate Director of the International Institute at University of Michigan, Ann Arbor.

Shubhra Gururani is Associate Professor of Anthropology and Associate Director of the York Center for Asian Research, York University, Toronto, Canada.

Janaki Nair is Professor, Center for Historical Studies, Jawaharlal Nehru University, New Delhi, India.

Anne Rademacher is Assistant Professor of Metropolitan Studies and Environmental Studies, and Director of the Metropolitan Studies Program, Department of Social and Cultural Analysis, New York University, New York.

Nithya V. Raman is an independent researcher and writer based in Chennai, India.

Awadhendra Sharan is Associate Fellow, Center for the Study of Developing Societies, Delhi, India.

K. Sivaramakrishnan is Dinakar Singh Professor of India and South Asian Studies, Professor of Anthropology, Professor of Forestry & Environmental Studies, Co-Director of the Program in Agrarian Studies, and Chair of the South Asian Studies Council at Yale University, New Haven, Connecticut.

1
Introduction: Ecologies of Urbanism in India

Anne Rademacher and K. Sivaramakrishnan

Ecology and Urbanism

As analysts turn to the urban question in India, estimates of the scale and rapidity of urban change in India multiply. One predicts that by 2030 nearly 600 million Indians will live in cities, and in them 70 percent of all net new employment will be generated (Sankhe et al. 2010). For India's young and mobile population, cities are undeniable magnets—for resources, and for their aspirations.

Transforming Indian cities into sustainable environments is the single greatest opportunity that governments, entrepreneurs, and innovators face in the coming decades. In this project, we consider that same transformation as a scholarly opportunity to re-imagine engagement with the Indian city. Positioned at the crossroads of urban studies and environmental studies, contributors to this volume seek to understand how rapidly proliferating and resource-intensive urbanism affect everyday lived environments and the ecological processes that undergird them. To do this, we employ an urban ecologies analytic that attends both to ideas of nature in the city, and to the dense networks of livelihoods and intimate connection that make urban life possible.

Urban ecologies can be explored through familiar ideas and dynamics that unfold in urban landscapes, including improvement, planning, infrastructural organization, political struggles over resources and amenities, and the aesthetics of nature. Such analytics are often deployed with an explicit concern for synergizing urban environmental and social processes in more sustainable ways. Concepts from ecological theory also inform urban analysis, and are often so deployed. Ecological footprints, for instance, are widely used to convey the amount of land needed to support the resources ingested, and wastes extruded, by cities over time. Urban expansion, similarly, is widely discussed in terms of patch dynamics and edge effects within ecological complexes as a way of mapping the density and rapidity of urban material inputs and outputs (see Collins et al. 2000). Likewise, concepts from social theory are brought to bear on understanding urban ecologies; Erik Swyngedouw's ideas about circulation and metabolisms provide one example. Here, one sees a generative connection between historical materialism and the hybrid socio-natures produced in the biophysical–technological complexes that gird cities, and facilitate flows within and across them. As Swyngedouw writes,

> the creation of urban space as space of movement of people, com-modities, and information radically alter(s) the choreography of the city . . . connections are lost, identities reconfigured, and attachments broken down. Yet, at the same time, the accumulation of movement, and of capital, also signal(s) an intensified and accelerated accumulation of new urbanized natures. (2006, 112)

Another common approach to urban ecologies is grounded in considered examinations of urban nature itself. Here, it is useful to contrast earlier views of cities as destroyers of nature and harmonious rural life with a new regard for managed urban nature and cities as ecosystems. Parks, gardens, and tree-lined boulevards brought designed, controlled nature into critical purview, while the acknowledgement of cities as themselves ecological systems challenged ideas of nature as located everywhere *but* in cities. The gathering critique of modernist planning since the 1970s fostered new intersections between urban design and biophysical science. Urban nature now plays a role in creating public spaces that 'green' the city by providing recreation, oxygen, and enhanced private property values. As Gandy argues,

> the urbanization of nature—and the concomitant rise of a metropolitan sensibility toward nature—encompasses not just new approaches to the technical management of urban space such as improved housing and sanitation but also extends to different kinds of cultural interaction with nature as a source of leisure. (2006, 64)

To this point we add that nature also serves as a source of authority and legitimation; in its intimate mingling with what human activity builds as its urban ecumene, nature becomes a key repository for ideas of history and belonging.

In this volume, we draw from these varied analytical frames to address 'ecologies of urbanism' in India. We do so through explorations based largely in two major Indian cities, Delhi and Mumbai. Both immensely important to contemporary India, and each representing different historical conjunctures that produced them as urban locations in Indian landscapes, these cities are symbolic of two major patterns of Indian urbanism—one in the hinterland, the other coastal.

Writing of how imperial New Delhi was designed and built when the British moved the colonial capital from Calcutta to Delhi in 1911, Khuswant Singh remembers that the city's chief architect and designer, Edwin Lutyens chose the village of Malcha on Raisina Hill for its elevation and proximity to stone that could be quarried in the Ridge. He describes his partner in designing New Delhi, Herbert Baker, standing on this hill, looking down on "the vast collection of ruins of cities, tombs and monuments lying below" wondering if the epicenter of the new capital was well chosen (K. Singh 2010, 4). A certain deep, if not admired, history of Delhi, recalling the series of Sultanates that made it their capital, and the monumental landscape of Mughal rule, was visible from such a vantage point, and this is better known. But there is more, ancient and prehistoric, that marks Delhi as an urban site, less visible for its dislocation and submergence in the magnificent architecture of medieval and modern Delhi, but woven all the same into contemporary urban nature in the form of pillars, fragments of old sculpture, and abandoned shrines to lesser gods (U. Singh 2010, 23–26).

If Delhi stands on many millennia of history, and specifically a history of serving as the capital of many kingdoms and empires, Mumbai (earlier Bombay) is very much a colonial city, and its fort, white and native enclaves, slums, and suburbs have a distinct quality even as they reveal a set of patterns that one might also see in Kolkata (Calcutta) or Chennai (Madras)—all ports and presidency cities of modern India, forged in the colonial encounter with the British Empire.[1] As Gyan Prakash writes, "the physical form of the city invites reflection on its colonial origin . . . in fact, the Island City occupies land stolen from the sea," and it "bears the marks of its colonial birth and development" (Prakash 2010, 26–27). Unlike Delhi, Mumbai's built environment has no monuments to a deep past, but it does testify to land reclamation and occupation in the construction of a vast empire of colonial commerce (ibid.). To an ecologist, Mumbai appears a product of deforestation, concretization, and encroachment that has deeply transformed Bombay's coastal, littoral, and intertidal ecosystems. An urban ecosystem is dependent for most of its primary needs—like air, water, and food—on the immediate environment, and increasingly, on more distant areas. The supply of these ecosystem services depends crucially on landform, land use, and the preservation of biophysical conditions that generate these services. In Mumbai, given the constriction of usable contiguous land by surrounding water bodies, the pressure for space has given land gain such prominence that landforms have taken a back seat (Srivastava and Mukherji 2005, 3908).

Arguably, the ecological ruptures through which contemporary Mumbai was made over the last 150 years were more dramatic and certainly of a faster pace than those that shaped Delhi and New Delhi over several centuries. But as two of the fastest growing metropolitan centers in India after the First World War, Delhi and Mumbai experienced several similar processes of change as well. And in that regard, by the later part of the twentieth century, they also found themselves on a comparable trajectory. As Delhi and Mumbai now refashion themselves as global cities, we find it useful to use the broad scheme outlined by Manish Chalana, who identifies three forms of modernism at work in Indian cities: the first colonial (Lutyens' Delhi), the second nationalist (Le Corbusier's Chandigarh), and the third global— the latter associated with the deepest and most radical transformation of cityscapes and city use patterns (Chalana 2010).

Authors in this volume investigate urbanism, nature, and ecological sustainability in major Indian cities, primarily Mumbai and Delhi, but also Chennai and Bengaluru. As mega-cities like these take new shape throughout Asia, they leave unprecedented ecological imprints on those who live in them, and on the hinterlands around them. Fecund yet stressed, nature in these cities seems typified by polluted air, unsafe and inadequate water, crowded tenements, choked highways, and mounting quantities of industrial and consumer waste. Yet in these same cities, urban nature is encountered anew in shining gated communities, new city parks, greenways, zoos, and growing pet industries. Although marked by a proliferation of life in myriad forms, urban sustainability in Asian cities is suspended in the growing tensions between humans and non-human nature, and between different classes and social groups that include historical settlers, new immigrants, itinerants, and occasional travelers.

It is in this twenty-first-century context, when for the first time in human history the majority of the world's population resides in cities (UN 2003), that scholarly work urges a complete rethinking of 'the urban' as an object of study (e.g., Amin and Thrift 2002; Low 1996). The proportion of the world's population that lives in cities has grown since the Industrial Revolution, from about 3 percent of the world living in urban places in 1800, to about 13 percent in 1900, over 40 percent in 1980, and 47 percent in 2000. That latter figure equaled about 2.9 billion people. Since 1950, urban growth in less developed parts of the world has been about 1.62 percent per year, compared to 0.65 percent in countries regarded as most developed (Smart and Smart 2003, 265). In a couple of decades India is predicted to join other regions of the world in finding more people in cities than in the countryside. The projected expansion of urban built and social environments, especially in and around large metropolitan centers in India, comes in the wake of high rates of GDP growth, particularly over the last decade. While India's urban population, as a proportion of total population, has increased gradually but significantly, from about 10.87 percent in 1901 to 27.78 percent in 2001, it has since topped 30 percent of the total population in the last ten years. This trend is expected to accelerate in the coming decades.

Rethinking Urban Contexts

In the midst of such sweeping change, scholarly and policymaking arenas resonate with uncertainty and concern over the pace, magnitude, and primary geographic location of contemporary urbanization. Major, rapid-growth cities of the southern hemisphere, often shorthanded as 'cities of the global South,' are typically framed as mired in varying combinations of intractable poverty, environmental disorder, and a present or expected 'urban explosion'[2] with potentially catastrophic socio-environmental implications.[3] Dawson and Edwards (2004, 6) capture the perceived urgency of this predicament when they write, "the megacities of the global South embody the most extreme instances of economic injustice, ecological unsustainability, and spatial apartheid *ever confronted by humanity*" (emphasis added).

A sense of historical exceptionalism tends to accompany such anxieties, and attendant appeals for new thinking about the conceptual content of 'the urban,' urbanism, and urbanization are a result. These appeals are often couched in the language of sustainability, a malleable, almost ubiquitous, and yet enormously powerful modifier when applied to conventional concepts and practices in cities. In this volume, we engage and problematize the social life of sustainability thought and practice by exploring urban ecologies in Indian cities. In doing so, we aim to understand more fully the stakes, form, and meanings of the socio-environmental transformations that animate the everyday lives lived in them, and the multiscaled processes of which they are a part. We take particular interest in the sense of historical exceptionalism that urban sustainability praxis often implies, arguing that despite its future-focused orientation, the processes through which specific cities were initially formed continue to influence urbanization's meaning and implications. Contributors to this volume explore the ways that history shapes contemporary urban socio-ecological life, noting its modern guises and underlining its enduring traction. At the same time, they take seriously the aspirations for deep and lasting socio-environmental transformation that sustainability thought and practice so often imply.

One need not look far for historical threads that join past and present articulations of urban sustainability, particularly for echoes of perceived and pending chaos in the cities of the global South. Recall, for example, the now classic description of Delhi with which the demographer Paul Ehrlich opened his extremely influential, if later roundly critiqued, 1968 volume *Population Bomb*. Locating his dismal outlook on urbanism's immediate future precisely in India, he wrote,

> I have understood the population explosion intellectually for a long time. I came to understand it emotionally one stinking hot night in Delhi a few years ago. My wife and daughter and I were returning to our hotel in an ancient taxi. The seats were hopping with fleas. The only functional gear was third. As we crawled through the city, we entered a crowded slum area. The temperature was well over 100, and the air was a haze of dust and smoke. The streets seemed alive with people. People eating, people washing, people sleeping. People visiting, arguing, screaming. People thrusting their hands through the taxi window, begging . . . People, people, people . . . It seemed that anything could happen . . . (Ehrlich 1968, 1)

Past echoes like this in no way discount the real material, social, and environmental stresses that accompany twenty-first-century urbanization, nor do they undermine the importance of asking whether, and how, contemporary urban settings might be rethought and reinvented as more sustainable, "livable cities" (Evans 2002). They do, however, suggest that diagnoses of urban problems that are grounded in historical exceptionalism may risk missing key explanatory variables. It is this assertion that compels some of the contributors to this volume to invoke historical analysis as a mode for understanding the contemporary 'unprecedented' nature of Indian urbanization. Their approach is surprisingly unconventional. In fact, the general sense of an urgent and exceptional urban predicament is perhaps nowhere more visible than at the interface of urban environments and societies, the site of urban ecologies. Indeed, the past decade and a half has witnessed a shift from largely passive or discipline-specific attention to something called 'urban ecology' to the inclusion of this concept in an inventory of our most pressing *transdisciplinary* global concerns.[4]

Special urban issues of scholarly journals ranging from *Social Text* (2004) to *Science* (2008) supplement a wealth of literature on the contemporary global urban condition intended for a more popular readership. Recent titles like *Planet of Slums* (Davis 2006), *Shadow Cities* (Neuwirth 2006), and *Maximum City* (Mehta 2004) have both constructed and reinforced understandings of a global, and yet simultaneously Southern, twenty-first-century urban crisis marked by seemingly intractable poverty, marginality, uncontrolled growth, and environmental degradation.

It may be the case that, in a manner similar to the way that an overarching aspiration for something called 'development' focused scholarly, policy, and popular analytics on the 'dysfunctional' polities and economies of the global South in the late twentieth century (cf. Crush 1995; Escobar 1994; Ferguson 1994; Greenough and Tsing 2003), environmental improvement, and in particular an aspiration called 'sustainability,' anchors our attention to, and in turn reproduces, a 'global South' in the early twenty-first. We contend in this volume that this is a question worthy of exploration, for it underscores the importance of maintaining a historical orientation that simultaneously illuminates enduring processes and exposes those that are truly without precedent.

We notice that in some ways, the surge in attention to particular aspects of global urbanization continues longstanding engagements with, and concerns over, the future of cities, modernization, and social life (AlSayyad 2003, 8). The category of the urban has long stood for concentrated sites of wealth,

opportunity, social diversity, and state bureaucratic activity; it continues
to represent the possibility of social mobility, accessing basic services, and
engaging in certain forms of cultural life. As is the case today, cities are
also historically associated with particular kinds of social inequality, quite
notably specific class formations, patterns of segregation, and affinities
linked to the expansion of transnational industrial capitalism. It is primarily
through these analytical associations that cities have also served as sites—
both imagined and enacted—of potentially powerful and far-reaching social,
political, and cultural transformation.

Likewise, urbanization has a long analytical history as the primary lens
through which we view and understand the physical growth of cities and the
material processes associated with that growth, while urbanism captures
a distinction between the social, economic, and political life of cities and
that of their rural hinterlands. The meaning and content of the categories
of 'urban' and 'rural' change over time and across place, and their mutual
social production has long been recognized as distinct from fixed, essentialist
definitions of the city and the countryside (e.g., Ferguson 1999; Lefebvre
1991; Williams 1973).

Within anthropology, scholars compelled by an interest in the relationship
between urban life and the reproduction of community, kinship networks,
and social mobility looked to cities to conduct early work in 'community
studies,' network analyses, and the reproduction of wealth and poverty (e.g.,
Bott 1957; Gluckman 1971; Lomnitz 1977; Mitchell 1969; Stack 1974, 1996;
Werbner 1984). Mid and late twentieth-century scholarship in the emergent
multidisciplinary arena of urban studies refined the "urban question" by
investigating the interface of urban contexts and transnational capitalism
(Castells 1977; Harvey 1989; Sassen 1991). They eventually popularized the
idea of the "global" (Abu-Lughod 1999) or "world" (Hannerz 1996) city, the
"global circuits" (Sassen 2002) on which it could be mapped, and the power of
cities as organizing centers for capital and politics (Sassen 1991).

Attendant questions of scale and state power (Brenner 1998), the future
relevance of nation-states (Chatterjee 1986), emergent forms of citizenship
(Holston and Appadurai 1999), and questions about the future of social
movements (Mayer 2000) all elaborated on parallel processes of globalization
and urbanization. In this volume, cities like Delhi and Mumbai remind
us that the global aspect of urbanization must be grounded in regional
environmental and social processes; these, in turn, have no single pattern.

We explore two significantly different historical patterns of urbanization here; one is a modern commercial port city that formed in just 200 years through dense settlement on the western coast of India. The other is a much older urban formation in the north Indian plains; its history involves the rise and fall of urban settlement over a much longer period.

One way to explore and account for these multiple patterns is to address the interface between environmental change and urban transformation. Such an inquiry enjoys a long and complex genealogy that easily warrants its own much more detailed account. A very general sketch recognizes that in the social sciences, 'urban ecology' has sometimes stood for the relationship between a human social community and its larger social whole; it has also indicated attention to human social life at a variety of scales and the relationship between those social scales and the natural cycles, systems, and processes with which they interact and through which they forge material and cultural lifeworlds. Of longstanding interest is the question of how human social actors organize social life in response to, and for engagement with, changes in the natural environment, and vice versa.

Yet another strain of socio-environmental scholarship focuses on the social production and implications of mutually separate conceptual spheres, such as 'society' and 'nature,' or 'the city' and 'the environment.' Taking inspiration from critical theoretical work on the concept of "nature-cultures" (e.g., Demeritt 1994; Haraway 1989, 1991, 1997; Latour 1993, 1999; Swyngedouw 1996; Zimmerer 2000), some anthropologists have begun to produce ethnographic analyses that engage the social life of environmental knowledge, perception, and problem definition, in cities. Anthropology has tended to foreground issues like the politics of place (Baviskar 2003; Gregory 1998a, 1998b; Hansen 2001; Hayden 1995), concerns over segregation and citizenship (Caldeira 2001; Holston and Appadurai 1999; Low 2003), urban governmentality (Chakrabarty 2002; Chatterjee 2006; Joyce 2003; Scott 1998), and cultures of consumption and class formation (Davila 2004; Davis 2000; Liechty 2003; Mankekar 1999; Mazzarella 2003; O'Dougherty 2002).

However, many social scientists who draw on ethnographic theory and practice, including contributors to this volume, recognize the need to apply anthropological forms of analysis to the twenty-first-century urban sustainability predicament described above. In this volume such issues are illuminated in case studies that explore the ecological dimensions of urban features like infrastructure. The discussion of waste, for instance, points to the tension between waste as a crucial source of livelihood and its role in urban strategies for realizing more sustainable energy production. In a similar vein, urban ecological perspectives show how riparian ecological improvement can simultaneously recover nature and sever crucial ties on which everyday urban social life and work depend. Tensions such as these are increasingly central to urbanization itself.

When one considers the environmental dimensions of contemporary urbanization, it is perhaps the scholarly tradition of political ecology that brings the most instructive inspiration to this volume. This body of work offers rich insight into questions of environmental knowledge and practice (e.g., Blaikie and Brookfield 1987; Brosius 1999a, 1999b; Bryant 1992; Bryant and Bailey 1997; Escobar 1996, 1998, 1999; Peet and Watts 1996), the cultural politics of conservation, development, and statemaking (e.g., Baviskar 1995; Fairhead and Leach 1996; Ferguson 1994; Mosse 2003; Sivaramakrishnan 1999), modern ecology and territoriality (e.g., Brosius and Russell 2003; Saberwal 1999; Vandergeest and Peluso 1995), the formation of environmental subjects (Agrawal 2005), and the historical production of ideas and imaginaries of nature itself (Grove 1989; Peet and Watts 1996; Raffles 2002; Williams 1980). Nevertheless, significant openings remain for a better understanding of these issues in contemporary urban contexts. It is with this in mind that we assemble the works in this volume.

Our work suggests that an urban political ecology in India would have similar concern for social stratification, power, and unequal access to natural resources and ecological services. It would likewise confront the precarious lives of the poor in conditions of environmental degradation. But our work also indicates that contemporary urbanism raises new kinds of questions about networks, neighborhoods, enclaves, and communities, highlighting the different ways that city dwellers are embedded in dense urban webs, yet remain connected to more distant locations beyond the city.

With these elaborations on existing scholarly considerations in mind, our analytical approach to sustainability, civility, and urbanism in India employs the idea of multiple 'urban ecologies.' In singular form, the phrase is not new; the long and diverse scholarly histories of 'urban' and 'human' ecology are sufficiently rich and complex to warrant the separate and more detailed histories that others have capably undertaken. Many genealogies of urban ecology in the social sciences point to the Chicago School of the early twentieth century, which famously analyzed urban social life, difference, and change through an analytical map of concentric urban 'niches' radiating outward from a central core (e.g., AlSayyad 2003). Indicators such as class and occupation then determined an individual or collective's location in the series of rings; movement across them became a method for capturing and expressing urban social change.

More recently, critical geographers have vigorously engaged and elaborated on urban ecology theory (e.g., Gandy 2002; Kaika 2005; Smith 1984; Swyngedouw 1996, 1999), calling attention to 'flows' and global economic processes that often warrant reconceptualizations of the urban scale. A notable limitation of this innovative work, however, is its tendency to miss many of the specificities of everyday urban environmental knowledge production, transfer, and application that are the rich contribution of work in environmental anthropology, political ecology, and, most recently, ethnographic science studies.

In this volume, we address the ways that struggles over the environment and quality of life in urban centers are increasingly framed in terms of their future place in a geography of global sustainability, and the future relationship between cities and their changing hinterlands. In these struggles, nature, with its imputed attributes of simplicity, purity, health, balance, cultural anchoring, and spiritual appeal, often grounds imaginaries of, and aspirations for, urban ecological, cultural, and social well-being. We are, therefore, interested in social nature, urban or rural, as a contested site and a constituent of imagined sustainable lives in Asian cities and their domains of influence.

Our analytic, that of urban ecologies, assumes the presence of multiple, simultaneous, and overlapping representations of the urban nature–urban culture interface. Each represents competing visions, ideas, and stakes of urban environmental change. Their corresponding efforts to ensure, create, or imagine ecological stability are often infused with, and shaped by, aspirations for political, social, or cultural stability; to promote particular urban ecologies may also involve the reproduction or contestation of cultural ideas of belonging to certain social groups, including the city, the nation-state, the region, and the realm called the 'global.'

These issues highlight the ongoing methodological and conceptual challenges of studying urban ecologies and their attendant socio-natural processes. Their multiple forms and practices in contemporary cities demand an adaptive analytical framework that can assess biophysical change while attending to the production of the categories, histories, and meanings that legitimize them in social life. We would like to advance the view that "a city is a process of environmental production, sustained by particular sets of socio-metabolic interactions that shape the urban in distinct, historically contingent ways" (Swyngedouw 2006, 114).

Analyses will inevitably capture moments in otherwise dynamic processes, since, like their biophysical counterparts, social categories and histories are never fully fixed and stable. Yet understanding why, after fervent efforts including measured policy interventions and scientific prescriptions, certain forms of undesirable environmental change continue unabated demands attention to such snapshots; through them, we discern the form and content of the claims to moral order through which certain ecological logics are rendered legible, powerful, and active.

Complex and multiple forms of social exclusion often accompany particular experiences of the environment, and the ways that social groups try to preserve or recreate certain environmental experiences. Specific *social* expectations, whether made explicit or simply implied, nearly always accompany urban environmental interventions. We may usefully ask what kinds of communities, affinity networks, and polities do actors imagine or intend when they advocate for particular urban ecological practices, policies, and outcomes? How do those expectations shape the range of responses that are considered reasonable, acceptable, and moral, and how do those expectations influence metrics of environmental failure and success? These considerations are critical aspects of urban ecologies, as they signal social processes that constantly engage, and sometimes rework, the structures within which specific knowledge forms, claims to identity and territory, and narrations of history are acknowledged and legitimized, while others are not.

Urban ecologies, particularly in the form of sustainability aspirations and practices, may also be studied for their perceived emancipatory power. Ideas and practices of urban environmental sustainability often fold together hope for positive change and engagement with powerful material and discursive tools understood as imbued with the capacity to effect that change. In this sense, practices of urban ecology imply a capacity to reproduce belief in the very possibility of change, that is, to operate socially as facilitators of the capacity to aspire (Appadurai 2004). Urban environmental change narratives are often infused with aspirations for broader socio-environmental transformation, and it is precisely these aspirations, and the belief that they can and will be realized, that give those narratives powerful social traction (Rademacher 2011).

Environmental Sustainability

Many policymakers and environmental practitioners find their anxieties about the urban future potentially assuaged through innovations in the fields of ecosystem science and environmental design (WRI 1996; UN 1996; UN-HABITAT 2001). They look to two emergent movements: one, the rise of distinctive *urban* ecosystem ecology within the ecosystem sciences (e.g., Grimm et al. 2003; McKinney 2002; Parlange 1998; Pickett and Cadenasso 2002; Pickett et al. 2001; Rebele 1994), and two, the rise of green design technologies and interventions worldwide (Buchanan 2005; Gissen 2003; Leach 1997; Williamson et al. 2002). The two are interrelated, insofar as urban ecosystem ecology often provides the scientific basis for particular green technological interventions, and urban environmental problems and particularities often shape urban ecosystem sciences research (e.g., McKinney 2002; *Science* 2008). This synergy produces new conceptualizations of what constitutes sustainable 'urban nature' and how best to assess its order, functionality, and quality. It also foregrounds the set of environmental problems that urban areas are thought to face, folding within them demographic, economic, and cultural assumptions that are often taken as automatic, self-evident, and universal. As noted above, these are sometimes distinctly located in a new and unprecedented historical era called the twenty-first century.

While the scientific dimensions of ecology give us essential tools with which to compare cases of environmental degradation, and to render commensurate and intelligible common environmental conditions in cities around the world, multiple urban ecologies suggest the need to engage the context, and the context-generating power, of urban ecology enacted in place. It emphasizes social knowledge production and its hierarchies, and suggests that the meanings of urban ecology defy any single, ordered way of knowing, or changing, nature. Experiences of urban ecological change are real and often unprecedented, but the urban nature and social dynamics in which they are experienced in everyday life form mosaics of moral logic, aspiration, and struggles over power. These require us to bring the places and situated practices of urban ecology more fully into focus, and to ask not only how change is occurring, but also when and how dominant environmental narratives sharpen or obscure the full contours of those changes.

We therefore propose a dual frame for understanding urban nature, in which it is both a bundle of enablers and imagined values for particular forms of urban social life, and, simultaneously, a set of overlapping institutions, processes, and interdependencies through which urban material and cultural life are continually produced, defined, and organized. Such a frame leads us to think about environmental sustainability in India in a way that recognizes the presence and influence of multiscaled processes and multiple histories.

It also underlines the point that urban ecology is as much a question of social life as it is an assessment of the quality and vitality of biophysical systems. This point is not always self-evident, as biophysical scientific accounts of nature, whether in the city, suburb, or countryside, usually assume an authoritative posture among competing accounts of environmental problems. Assembling such accounts is typically the domain of natural scientists, engineers, and planners—those producers of knowledge whose work most directly translates into prescriptions for management and intervention (Mitchell 2002, 30). Their modes of inquiry and the languages through which they convey their diagnostics tend to occupy a privileged place among the many ways of experiencing the socio-natural environment.[5] Yet these same approaches often yield an incomplete understanding of why people undertake specific forms of action in relation to their environment.

Indeed, science is in many ways essential for expressing and understanding environmental processes and change. In the ecosystem sciences, urban ecology marks a specific sub-discipline wherein cities are theorized and modeled as hosts to specific combinations of stresses, disturbances, and structures that affect nutrient cycling, hydrological processes, air and soil quality, vegetative cover, and a range of other parameters (McDonnell and Pickett 1990; Pickett 1997; Sukopp et al. 1990; Walbridge 1998). By engaging with urban contexts, urban ecosystem ecology has also highlighted important limitations of the rural-centric ecology that has historically regarded cities as antithetical to natural space, and human social activity as a *de facto* perturbation of natural systems. It has in many ways driven a rethinking—albeit confined to particular epistemological parameters—of human–nature interactions, and roundly challenged the supposition that nature can be scientifically understood as separate from human activity (e.g., Grimm et al. 2003; McKinney 2002; Pickett and Cadenasso 2002;

Pickett et al. 2001; Rebele 1994). The result is a set of scientific models that explicitly link human and natural components of singularly conceived urban ecosystems.[6] These models, however nascent, invite studies of human sociality into scientific mappings of ecosystems in a way that demonstrates the extent to which modern science is itself transforming.[7]

In its fullest sense, the urban ecologies analytic that we employ in this volume spans a vast disciplinary terrain that requires combinations of natural and social science analytics to capture. As Auyero and Swistun (2009) have recently shown, and as our contributors elaborate here in cases from India, ethnographic evidence suggests a constant tension between the production and control of 'valid' knowledge—that is, facts about biophysical processes—and the meanings that are attributed to the everyday life realities shaped by those same facts. We are concerned with the production of meaning because it is closely associated with human agency and action; meaningful accounts of the past, present, and future motivate purposeful human action. 'What urban ecology means,' across actors, times, and places, is thus an extremely important entry point for understanding how and why individuals and collectives engage the environment and one another as they do. It is reasonable to expect that purposeful action on behalf of the urban environment or specific ideas of urban social life—or both—may be driven by processes not captured or conveyed through scientific facts.

Yet let us underscore that the urban environment is never an exclusively social construct. Biophysical settings, including dense urban landscapes, are not infinitely malleable, regardless of our recognition that social forces are crucial for delineating the form and content of environmental categories (Benton 1989; Gupta and Ferguson 1992; Mosse 1997). As Sivaramakrishnan has argued elsewhere (1999, 282), any concept of nature is, in fact, "produced through the interaction of biophysical processes that have a life of their own and human disturbance of the biophysical." Thus nature is conceived out of this interaction between the human and the biophysical. Sivaramakrishnan continues, "Human agency in the environment, mediated by social institutions, may flow from cultural representations of processes in 'nature' but we cannot forget the ways in which representations are formed in lived experience of social relations and environmental change" (ibid.). Understanding how biophysical constraints and social imaginings converge on a given landscape, then, is fundamental to studying ecology as the set of experience and action (Peet and Watts 1996; Redclift and Benton 1994) that constitute an important part of a fuller analytic of urban ecology.

Citizenship and Nature in Histories of Indian Urbanism

How does one maintain an active and generative tension between dynamic ecological processes and human experience when considering the urban question in India? To answer this, we begin with Rotenberg's (1996) contention that the identity of a city also structures residents' urban experience, adding urban identity to place and time as universal sources of metropolitan knowledge. Sennett's (1994) interest in embodied urban experience is further instructive here. These are admittedly universalizing characterizations, but they also provide provocative means for perceiving cities, as bundles of processes that link social experience and social structure (Low 1996, 401). To return to our framing question, the work assembled in this volume draws on analytical categories of urban citizenship and civility, which for us invoke the question of rights, their formulation, and their negotiation in law, government and social conflict.

We agree with John Gledhill that "the politics of citizenship was about rights in the positive sense that people struggled to have more and new rights" even as modern nation-states were being formed (Gledhill 2005, 85). And we recall the valuable distinction between political and civil rights, which T. H. Marshall (1950) argued constitute defenses against abuses of power by states. In this sense, social rights are those that require active intervention by states to equalize citizen opportunities.[8]

A characteristic of late twentieth-century urbanism in many parts of the world is the fracturing of neighborhoods and kinship-based community. A sharp separation of spaces of wealth and poverty is enforced in new urban forms, in part by private security and in part by state policing. These can generate a market conviviality that makes vending, buying, and traveling to the market one of the few activities that infuses urban living with thick interaction and social spontaneity that are otherwise mostly sucked out.[9] And as Smart and Smart (2003, 271) note, increased inter-urban competition further complicates the picture when we look at any particular urban experience. In this context, diverging trajectories for the economic prospects of residents raise crucial issues for urban governance and citizenship. We might usefully ask: is economic redistribution counterproductive in an era of urban entrepreneurialism (Gregory 1998a, 1998b; Jessop 2002)? How are development coalitions constituted and maintained (Logan et al. 1997)? What are the implications of increasing inequality and disenfranchisement for the civility of urban society (Holston 1999)?

If citizenship is articulated in a language of rights, and calls our attention to political struggles, social movements, and litigation in the urban public sphere, civility refers to the contested realm of style, taste, personhood, and cosmopolitanism in India's growing, and largely urban, middle classes. These two streams of public engagement converge in specific environmental experiences, and form the basis of each author's contribution. Contributors therefore examine the ecologies of urban India in light of infrastructural development, varied connections and destabilizations of the city as an imagined or experienced place, struggles over rights and resources in the city, and the crafting of aspiration to new forms of urban life among planners, residents, and investors.

Using urban India as its focal geography, the authors further explore questions germane to understanding the dynamics of social nature in contemporary urban settings. They address intersections between urban social processes and assessments of urban environmental order and disorder, asking: how are relationships between urban environments and urban societies made, remade, and rendered *meaningful* in contemporary cities? How do biophysical properties, rules, and histories of nature converge to enable social actors to construct new identities and demarcate political spaces?

We therefore frame this collection of studies of urban ecologies in India through two intersecting analytics. One requires an examination of the way nature functions as a set of properties and amenities, endowments in short, that biologically, physically, and spatially render urban life possible. The other explores the institutions and processes through which urban life creates and relies on webs of interdependence; connections and flows that concentrate life in cities and sustain such concentration through increasing internal regulation and proliferating external linkages.

As noted earlier, the cases are drawn chiefly from Mumbai and Delhi. These South Asian mega-cities have attracted considerable global attention for their demographic, economic, and political dynamics. Yet, like all cities, they have distinct, layered, and regionalized histories. Delhi, for instance, has a long pre-colonial, colonial, and postcolonial heritage as the seat of empire, the headquarters of regional polity, or the nation-state capital. Mumbai, a much newer city and commercial center, is a key historical and contemporary node in Indian Ocean flows and connections.[10] In the twenty-first century, in separate but comparable ways, these are now mega-cities of India's post-industrial aspirations. They serve as examples of how knowledge industries shape megalopolises, and they are fruitful urban settings within which to explore questions of urban social nature.[11]

We should clarify that 'nature' in this volume captures processes and relationships that invoke and involve resources, histories, and collective aspirations. The transformative power of these processes and relationships reflects the extent to which they embody intense economic interests, political contests, moral evaluations, and biophysical experiences. With these conceptual and terminological definitions in hand, let us turn in some detail to the histories of urbanism in Delhi and Mumbai.

Before Delhi there was Shahjahanabad. There, neighborhoods of caste and occupation were less commonly the pattern of settlement; it was more that retainers settled in clusters around their patrons or amirs (Spodek 1980, 258). Delhi remained a city of military encampment in the early colonial period, and issues of regional security shaped the way urban walled and open space was utilized until the colonial capital was moved there, just before the First World War (Gupta 1971).[12] Dramatic population increase, densification of urban living space, insufficient potable water supply, and massive drainage and sewerage difficulties were the major urban problems in colonial India (Mann 2007, 2), and Delhi was no exception in facing these predicaments. Urban governance until the end of the nineteenth century was preoccupied with public health, and disease in the city was frequently attributed to the 'corruption' of air due to decaying vegetation, lack of natural light, and the cramped and poorly ventilated housing that seemed to dominate the *mohalla* landscape of pre-colonial urban settlement (Sharan 2006, 4905).

There was soon a Delhi Improvement Trust, and similar entities followed in Bombay and Calcutta. Regulation of smoke nuisances in Calcutta had already pioneered the idea of urban improvement by mitigating air pollution (see Anderson 1995). Piped water supply began to take the place of canal and well water in some parts of Delhi by 1890, and avenues and parks began to separate European quarters from native settlement, bringing Delhi into conformity with models already in place for colonial settlement patterns in the port cities of the Bombay, Calcutta and Madras Presidencies, the oldest

British provinces of colonial India. Public defecation and polluting industries also drew the occasional ire of the colonial government in Delhi, Bombay, and Calcutta (Sharan 2006, 4906). When the new capital of British India was inaugurated in 1931, New Delhi was born, and certain implications associated with this had to be faced. As the municipal government was inaugurated, municipal services focused on New Delhi to the neglect of Old Delhi, as the walled city and adjacent suburbs were now called (Mann 2007, 28). The urban landscape in these two parts of Delhi began to diverge, as one was planned and beautified through active state intervention, and the other languished in crumbling visible memorials to older *mohallas* and patterns of self-organization.

The afforestation of the Central Ridge was part of the enormous changes that altered the environment and the ecology of the region. By 1913, twenty-five villages and their agricultural land had been acquired, many stretches of low-lying land were filled up, and several hillocks were leveled (Mann and Sehrawat 2009, 557). This led to an urban forest on the Ridge by the 1930s, creating an English prospect on an Indian landscape and thereby crafting new vistas of power and government.[13] Delhi in the 1950s was reshaped by partition, the arrival of refugees, and a round of planned development that now looked to the United States for inspiration. By that time, the city that planners encountered was one deeply embedded in the regional economy, drawing upon resources and providing goods, but above all attracting people, both migrants and refugees. For the development of Delhi as a metropolis, slums and industry became the chief environmental concerns. As Sharan (2006) notes, apart from some cotton mills, very few industries had come to Delhi in the years between the great wars. Refugees brought new commerce and manufacturing, especially to Old Delhi, where they mingled industry with residence and created new anxieties about pollution and nuisance, which generated a new wave of efforts to relocate them elsewhere. It appears the politics of sanitation dominated Indian town planning and municipal politics until after Independence, most prominently during the 'Emergency' (1975–77) with its notorious clearance and resettlement schemes for Delhi.[14]

Urban planning was initiated by the Delhi Development Authority (DDA) in 1957, following what Sundaram (2004) rightly calls classic modernist urban design principles: enumeration, classification, zoning, and slum management. He also observes that, as the city rapidly expanded in areas of housing and commerce through the 1980s and 1990s, planned development lost both efficacy and popular support and Delhi sprawled (Sundaram 2004, 65). Notably, though, this expansion was mediated through a series of non-legal informal arrangements by the urban poor, small businesses, and affluent house owners wanting to expand private space beyond legal norms. Included as well, of course, were private builders and contractors.

Despite complex informal arrangements and processes, slums and the relocation of industries remained major issues in environmental struggles in Delhi.[15] But to those older, even colonial concerns, we can add the growing interest in amenities like parks, as well as the gating of residential colonies to privatize access roads, increase safety, and exclude itinerants.[16] The building of planned Delhi was thus mirrored in the simultaneous emergence of unplanned Delhi. As Baviskar notes, "in the interstices of the Master Plan's zones, the liminal spaces along railway tracks and barren lands acquired by the DDA, grew the shanty towns built by construction workers, petty vendors, and artisans, and a whole host of workers" (Baviskar 2003, 91).

Between 1951 and 2001, the population of the National Capital Region of Delhi grew from 1.7 million to 13.8 million (Census of India), and about half of the population now lives in informal settlements, shanties, or *jhuggis* (Delhi Development Authority 2000 cited in Sivam 2003). The repertoire of responses that poor people have in such situations has grown out of available legacies of protest and mobilization, but also has a distinctive urban flavor. In Delhi, the poor have used their votes, relatives, and moral claims on employers to contest this; they have also formed effective neighborhood associations, and most recently, a coalition of slum-dwellers' organizations, trade unions, and NGOs. Baviskar argues that such "multiple practices, simultaneously social and spatial, attempt to democratize urban development even as they challenge dominant modes of framing the environment–development question" (2003, 97). It is important to remember, though, that civic urbanism and associated forms of resistance arise not only from internal fractures in civil space; they also reflect awareness among the leaders of such movements that informal social relations are also vulnerable to predation and cooptation by states and powerful financial interests (Gledhill 2005, 90).

In this regard, looking at contemporary struggles in Mumbai, there is much to find in parallel to contemporary Delhi. The efforts of governments to fashion global cities has led to the massive transfer of urban land to private developers and this has mainly affected the urban poor. In Mumbai, it has meant that slums, squatter settlements, and defunct industrial lands in the city center have been targeted. In this context, we may ask: how have cities become strategic sites for the enactment of new kinds of citizenship?

Since big cities concentrate both the most advanced service sectors and a large marginalized population, they often become a setting in which new citizenship practices can emerge. For Saskia Sassen (2006), the struggles of the poor over rights to the city do not necessarily bring power, but the presence of struggle itself has generated "operational and rhetorical openings" for new political subjects to emerge. James Holston (2008) argues that when the gap between substantive and formal citizenship becomes intolerable, people search for insurgent spaces within which they become active citizens. Partha Chatterjee (2006) seems to develop similar arguments with his ideas on political society, even as they stop short of describing such insurgent populations as active citizens.

Grounding general formulations of the emergence of urban citizenship in actual social experience requires us to locate the political structures through which power works across any city. Urban renewal in Mumbai, for instance, was initiated neither by national-level reforms nor by actions of the municipal government, but by the policies and programs of the state government, the middle rung of India's three-tiered federalist structure. A combination of mass protest and court filings have marked the response to slum clearance and textile mill land reallocation drives, and these actions have prevented large-scale privatization of land. They have also enabled a constant reworking of the decision-making process of central city redevelopment, and facilitated some gains for the urban poor (Weinstein and Ren 2009, 415–426). These few positives have to be put in perspective, however. Mariam Dossal's moving account of the aftermath of the disastrous floods that crippled Mumbai in 2005 provides an example. As she reminds us, since the plague of the 1890s, plans to improve Bombay and Mumbai had foundered in the face of traders and developers who had grown stronger with rising real estate values in the city. "To give back the city to its citizens, to protect its environment, urban heritage, cosmopolitan culture, and vibrant economy," she writes, "will require Herculean efforts on the part of all those who care about this city and all that it has stood for" (Dossal 2005, 3900).

Chopra (2007, 109) writes that colonial Bombay was the product of the fragmentation of two modes of urbanism: one colonial and one local. While the former sought architectural regularity, the latter offered stability of purpose, though there were also intersections of style and spatial design.

So, she writes, "colonial urban interventions acted to punctuate or envelop parts of the city with facades that hid or fronted the inner city. One entered through the gates and lanes between these facades only to be transported into a different world" (2007, 123).

In 1898 the Bombay Improvement Trust was the first such trust to be founded in India, in response to the threat of plague and disease in one of the country's foremost ports (Kidambe 2001, 60). Here began a process of social and slum reform that mirrored practices in other colonial cities at the turn of the last century, not least because key colonial figures of influence in these institutions, such as J. P. Orr, were familiar with these concerns from several other Indian cities (Legg 2008).

It is in this context that we can see a colonial approach to urban citizenship where political representation and participation rights were closely tied to class privilege. To enable the growth of industrial enterprise in Bombay, the colonial government was interested in working out property and trading rights and facilitating freedoms of movement and residence—albeit within a grid of imperial and racialized spaces—and this encouraged modern urban markets more than the development of public civic consciousness. As Hazareesingh (2000, 803) notes, "while the rules of the market-place ensured inter-community rivalries, the values of caste emphasized communitarian obligations to promote particular group interests, largely impervious to any wider notion of collective urban solidarity." Even during the colonial period, Patrick Geddes challenged this pattern of urbanism and cast urban citizenship as primarily an engagement in the local arena. If water supply and health were basic civic entitlements, he was quick to observe that urban poverty was a serious impediment to the achievement of minimal urban citizenship. Homes and affordable public transport would assure not only amenities, but also the cultivation of the spirit that was conducive to the proper exercise of citizenship.[17] By 1920, an expanded public sphere of press, political, and voluntary groups was questioning the hitherto untroubled hegemony of the market sphere of urban civil society, guaranteed by the limited colonial framework of legal rights (Hazareesingh 2000, 812).

As was the case in Delhi, Calcutta, or Madras, urban sanitation became the most readily available point of entry for urban government in Bombay. The City Improvement Trust concerned itself primarily with improving sanitation and hygiene as anxiety grew about overcrowding and filth in the old city. In addition to making limited improvements there, building spacious east–west boulevards to bring sea breezes, and moving some people into suburbs were also part of the urban improvement plans that began to take shape in the early twentieth century (Rao 2007, 45–49). The native town in Bombay was similar to the others in that it was heterogeneous, with blurred boundaries between residential and work-related spaces. But Bombay was unique in that it developed apartment dwelling for the middle classes long before such dense and segregated housing emerged in other Indian cities.

Earlier *wadis* and *mohallas* developed around the idea of the multifunctional street and the emotional centers provided by temples, water tanks, mosques, and bazaars. This stood in contrast to the grid of residences or commercial complexes built around intersecting streets that mainly served as channels of communication (Rao 2007, 28–29). Despite the ecological limitations posed by Bombay's location on a series of interlinked, and gradually landfilled islands, and the socio-economic obstacles created by the lack of transparency in land markets, urban consolidation made its presence steadily known across the burgeoning metropolis. A series of redevelopment efforts were mooted and partially carried out; many involved building high-rise complexes. But for both *jhuggi* and *chawl* residents, although relocation into high-rise apartments might ensure better services, it was invariably at the expense of earlier forms of conviviality. Chalana writes, "the drastic rearrangement of life in a vertical high-rise . . . lead[s] to social isolation and the breakdown of community and economic networks . . ." (Chalana 2010, 33). But as *chawl* and *wadi* came to be replaced by apartment and neighborhood, urban planning powerfully altered notions of community as well, and led the formation of Bombay's modern middle class and its unique forms of modern urbanism (Rao 2007, 184–187).

The emergence of an urban middle class, and its associated aspirations and desires, is closely connected to urban spatial configurations, new ecologies of urban life, and elaborations of ideas of urban nature. This point is adumbrated by Leela Fernandes when she argues that lifestyle issues related to consumption in the public sphere have come to dominate the self-fashioning of the urban middle class. This, she says, stands in opposition to work and community-based living in distinct neighborhoods. She writes,

> Historically . . . metropolitan cities in India did not develop into strict class-segregated spaces. While cities like Mumbai, Delhi and Calcutta have certainly reproduced spatial distinctions between wealthier, middle-class and poorer, working-class neighborhoods, such distinctions

have historically been disrupted by the presence of squatters, pavement-dwellers and street entrepreneurs such as tailors, shoe repairmen and hawkers. (Fernandes 2004, 2420)

The push to shape new global cities in a compact between rising middle class expectations of urban civility and governments keen to attract service industries and host world spectacles like international sports events, remakes urban ecologies in a manner less tolerant of these disruptions. The result is a form of spatial purification, named beautification, and cleaning, to purge the city of the poor (Fernandes 2004, 2421).

In this form of new urban civility, civic activism is deeply ambivalent about consumerism, the decline of 'community,' and exclusionary ways of defining citizenship. A technocratic associational elite tends to define a consumer citizen, while the rise of neighborhood associations reinforces a particular model of urban living (Harriss 2007; Nair 2005). Resisting neat class-based assumptions, Anjaria (2009, 393) observes that an unlikely "grouping of powerful builders, corrupt state officials, and small-scale hawkers as urban villains suggests the uneven and contradictory nature of urban reconfiguration."[18] And such a reconfiguration, puzzled out of civic action on diverse issues like environmental sustainability, social justice, urban governance, and the rights of the working poor, projects citizenship as that which aligns with a public and future-oriented spirit for the conservation of the city as heritage site. Notably, this variegated and contradictory civility cannot be contained in any narrative that sees urban government as moving from welfare and guardianship to profit and world recognition (cf. Smith 2002), or encompassed by neat ideas about civic governmentality or technocratic urban citizenship (cf. Roy 2009).

This point comes across elegantly in Arjun Appadurai's examination of the urban public sphere in Mumbai. Writing about the Society for the Protection of Area Resource Centres (SPARC), the National Slum Dwellers' Federation (NSDF), and Mahila Milan, all organizations born in the 1970s and 1980s, Appadurai (2002, 24) notes, "movements among the urban poor, such as the one I document here, mobilize and mediate these contradictions. They represent efforts to reconstitute citizenship in cities. Such efforts take the form, in part, of what I refer to as *deep democracy*." He underlines the fact that in Mumbai the growth of aspirations to global city status, with its corresponding privatization of urban resources and marginalization of the poor, is also productive of new forms of activism that unite middle classes and the most disenfranchised among the poor through the work of specialized NGOs and their broader alliances. These are alliances that make local democracy more effective because of the translocal cultural capital that is brought to bear through urban civic networks. Participation in transnational social movements is a particularly crucial dimension in the adoption of a global worldview. The nature of citizenship is affected by affiliation with distant individuals, groups, or causes (Smart and Smart 2003, 275).[19]

Inchoate yet powerful middle classes have a central role in the formation of new urban ecologies that are considered and depicted in many ways in the various chapters in this volume. How they do that and more, illuminating the many questions and themes highlighted by us, will be briefly anticipated in the next section of this introductory chapter.

Ecologies of Urbanism

The volume begins with a set of contributions that use historical approaches to understand questions of the Indian 'urban,' the shifting concept and uses of 'environment,' and the mutual constitution of rural and urban contexts over time in South Asia. Taken together, these chapters ground the volume's analytical approach in temporal, spatial, and historical specificities; separately, each author—Nair, Sharan, and Glover—offer historically grounded and empirically rich explorations of Indian urbanism, the environment, and the rural–urban continuum, respectively. In an extended consideration of the vagaries and outcomes of urban planning and its legal manifestation in Bengaluru, Janaki Nair wonders why cities elude the most persistent efforts of capital and state to render them in a fashion amenable to their mutually interested workings. Her answers focus on the messy complexities of the urban public sphere where rights are articulated, and civility imagined and defended. It is her insight that the failures of planning do not create illegible landscapes that benefit the urban poor in particular. As her account of improvement activities in Bangalore, inaugurated by a law passed in 1945, reveals, illegal construction and the politics of regularization are at least as old as modern urban planning itself, which was a force shaping the urban ecologies of Bengaluru from the very first decade of independent India.

The politics she examines is that of urban settlement and its systematic lack of conformity to extant urban regulation. Janaki Nair locates these struggles in the wider context of the relationship between government and sovereignty. As she notes, colonial government established a pattern of framing rules for urban civility that were left in their implementation to the working of multiple competing sovereign powers that operated in the localities where urban life was actually regulated or eluded control. The fractured nature of the colonial public created the conditions for contemporary urban public spheres to be stratified and segmented, leaving space open for cross-cutting coalitions, a space only enlarged and enlivened by the working of democratic politics in the municipality and the city.

The limits of urban planning and their particular antecedents are also the subject of Awadhendra Sharan's discussion of the management of air quality in Delhi. He vividly describes the early days of master planning in Delhi, and the emergence of fine distinctions between noxious and non-conforming industries. Once again, a distinct trajectory is found for the way illegality is carefully delimited against other forms of regulatory violation and the ways in which lines are drawn around the admissible conditions of urban civility. Air pollution in Delhi also drew the Supreme Court into the struggles over its definition and management. The growth of public interest litigation and the issue of the environment of Delhi, the very seat of the highest government agencies, each left their stamp as the contestation developed. And as science was marshaled with considerable adroitness by all parties in the dispute over pollution and its causes in industry and transport, the courts elaborated a different principle—one of risk mitigation—that sidestepped the politics of constructing scientific authority in the service of an exalted standard of urban civility named the precautionary principle. The story that Sharan tells, therefore, takes us beyond looking for patterns of social antagonism in the city to the modes of elaboration by which urban ecology is itself constructed and deployed in sophisticated public debate.

A chapter by Will J. Glover anchors these two more contemporary questions about urban planning practices to a historical analysis of key colonial and postcolonial notions of the relationship between material built forms and sociality. Glover traces historical connections between intellectual movements in colonial era sociology and planning, and suggests that underlying assumptions in the new town planning approaches that became a locus of bureaucratic attention in the postcolonial period were and remain socially "conservative." This is true, he argues, insofar as they anticipate "a kind of society putatively based on the collective rather than the individual, on people's organic habits and psychological needs rather than on independent will and the restless search for the 'new' " (this volume, 26).

In an interesting complement to the essay by Janaki Nair, Shubhra Gururani analyzes the discourse of planning and the spectacle of unplanned development in Gurgaon, a rapidly growing urban formation on the edges of Delhi, and an emerging center for information technology industries, high-end shopping, and luxury. She describes the malleability of planning and policy in practice, showing how the letter of policies and plans rarely determine their form in everyday life. Calling this opposition between legal guidelines and technically illegal official practices "flexible planning" (this volume) she shows how flexibility takes the form of exemptions built into plans. She contends that the political economy of urban development necessitates this approach due to the varied ways in which private enterprise and civic organizations are included in urban futures. That several interests beyond welfarist concerns of government are at play in any major urban project is intrinsically destabilizing of any planned activity, as intense negotiations and the pursuit of divergent priorities characterize the process of urban development at every stage.[20]

While planning itself unfolds, in her essay, as inherently fluid and unpredictable, Gururani is also mindful of Gurgaon's location, both in relation to the prosperous agrarian areas of Faridabad that benefited from the Green Revolution, and the rich and dense urban universe of Delhi that moved to encompass Gurgaon in its outer reaches. In a sense, across the regional scale, Gurgaon was caught between agrarian and urban identities and it took that uncertainty into recent decades of vertical and opulent urbanism. As Gururani pithily describes it, land development policies in Delhi, and the expulsion of major private developers from Delhi, coincided with a series of enabling Haryana laws to open Gurgaon to large private builders and their imagined cities.

Urban infrastructure makes the urban agglomeration work as a town or city. It creates grids of transmission lines, roads, and pipes and channels that bind the city into a self-regulating unit. But urban infrastructure also produces space and in doing so delineates relations of power that shape the flow of resources and human mobility through and across the city. All the papers in this group are interested in this production of space and the associated relations of power. The papers are also concerned with socio-economic changes in the cities—Delhi, Mumbai, Chennai—that are characterized by terms like privatization, rights, and mobility affecting people and resources.

Coelho and Raman remind us that if land and water are the physical infrastructure of urban life, spatial patterning and services, variably defined, might be thought of as the social infrastructure of urban concentration. In this account, slums come under a different kind of analytical scrutiny. They are an urban necessity, for they mark the process of continuous property creation in the city; they represent property that is valued differently in different historical moments thereby generating the logic by which slums appear in some places, are destroyed or dislocated, and are rebuilt elsewhere. Their erasure may be read as urban renewal or reclamation, their reappearance as a sign of urban decay. Yet they are hard to place outside any putative urban center, and in that sense, along with land, water, waste, and energy, slums are part of the infrastructure of the city.[21]

Coelho and Raman also make the important suggestion that the provision of infrastructure changes dramatically in agency and scope as economic and state regimes move to different logics of organization. Thus, concerns for public health, safety, and reliable transportation networks, often key motivators for public provision of the infrastructure of sanitation or roadways, can be replaced by concerns about unfettering enterprise, or easing the flow of finance capital into the city. In the latter case the infrastructure development reveals a spatial pattern and regimes of access that create mechanisms to enable specific kinds of investment. Such shifts can have a direct influence on urban ecology, for land may become water, where once water more often became land, or, at least, a place to dump waste from land. What is fascinating about this reversal is that it alters the material landscape, but also signals a new regime of values in which water in marshes, artificial lakes, and tanks, is revalorized in historic locations for newly acquired sensibilities.

From an ecological perspective Coelho and Raman also note that the poor live in the most ecologically unstable, and hazardous, areas where they are most exposed to the vagaries of climate events and natural calamities. They are also, often, living in proximity to toxic urban waste streams. While such living conditions pose dangers that are often poorly understood even by those who might wish to help such poor urban dwellers, those who live in them are also threatened by reclamation and beautification projects that would displace and relocate the poor rather than improve their access to amenities.

Coelho and Raman deftly juxtapose these harsh material conditions against the urban aesthetic at work, and the related social imaginaries of urban living, in schemes of river restoration, waterfront development, and the creation of green enclaves in the city.

These harsh realities and the notions of formality and informality that undergird them are then taken up in a study of municipal waste management and collection in Delhi by Vinay Gidwani. Waste, after all, can be understood in terms of its producers, for whom it is a consequence of having more than they can consume. Waste can also be understood in terms of its collectors, for whom it is a source of survival and possibly accumulation. This distinction, though heuristically clarifying at one level, can at another level obscure the ways in which waste is a part of the urban economy of materials and signs. Therefore, for some, it is both a product of their actions and a collectible in their business.

Taking as a starting point the recent consolidation of private waste management services in Delhi, Gidwani examines how earlier private sector operations are either supplanted or absorbed in newer forms of waste management service. He links this to the broader issue of understanding urban transformations as struggles over values. He argues that "the exclusionary urbanism and renewed enclosure of the common that is transforming contemporary cities in the global South [in this case, Delhi] is repeating with difference a centuries old class war against 'waste'" (this volume). By attending to the sociality of urban waste management in Delhi, he thus identifies important connections between middle class aspirations to develop Delhi into a 'global city' and the enduring social relations that undergird the consumption patterns of everyday life . Changes such as those Gidwani considers in the waste management sector can be seen in processes of industrialization more generally; the displacement of artisanal forms and labor-intensive modes are a prominent facet of everyday urban ecologies in Delhi.

From here, contributions by Anand and Rademacher, Doshi, and Ghertner address different dimensions of the relationship between contemporary urban ecological processes and the forms of housing deemed environmentally sound within them. Through contemporary studies from Mumbai and Delhi, these authors explore how complex caste, class, and gender asymmetries are reproduced or reconfigured in practices of housing advocacy, 'improvement,' and formalization. Anand and Rademacher's detailed account of the everyday experience of the contemporary housing initiatives of the Slum Rehabilitation Authority (SRA) in Mumbai is complemented by Doshi's study of the complex and uneven effects of this relocation scheme. While Doshi's accounts are not stories of absolute dispossession, they nevertheless involve complex caste, class, and gender asymmetries produced and reproduced in this otherwise widely lauded policy for reworking informal housing landscapes in Mumbai.

Ghertner then turns our analytical attention to questions of informal housing management in Delhi, offering a rich ethnographic and theoretical discussion of the everyday cultural politics of remaking Delhi as a world-class city. He shows how discursive framings of informal housing, particularly its occupants as a 'nuisance,' inflect everyday symbolic, discursive, and legal constructions that are at work in the city. In turn, he argues, the boundaries between legality and illegality are shaped and reinforced in everyday life. Resident welfare associations, assisted by media and government agencies like the local police, produce a more aggressive and exclusionary account of what belongs and does not belong in the neighborhood, in Ghertner's account.

Across the chapters in this volume, we see the emergence of a set of conflicts that involve not merely the material conditions of urban life— security, green spaces, municipal services, unimpeded mobility through the city—but also the very people, mostly slum dwellers, who might undermine these conditions. Thus, discussions of metropolitan civility and sustainability reference contention not only in terms of matter, but also people, who are deemed out of place, a disruption to the ecologies of urbanism imagined by different groups in the city.

Notes

1. See Preeti Chopra (2007) for a basic schematic account of the development of colonial port cities distinguishing native town and European quarter, the former dense and unplanned, the latter spacious, green, and well designed.
2. See, for example, the film by the same name, produced and distributed by the National Geographic Society as part of its *Journey to Planet Earth* film series: http://www.pbs.org/journeytoplanetearth/about/urbanexplosion.html, accessed August 10, 2012.

3.   Studies of the cities of the 'global north,' in turn, tend to focus on issues of over-consumption, greenhouse gas emissions, and other conditions associated with relative wealth. At both poles of the binary, our expectations and priorities are pre-conditioned by the categories North and South.

4.   See, for example, World Resources Institute (1996), which introduced 'the urban environment' as a comprehensive set of global problems for its audience of poli-cymakers and academics. For more recent representations of the city as an eco-system and an environmental problem, see Alberti (2003); Collins et al. (2000); Parlange (1998); Pickett et al. (1997); Pickett et al. (2001). See also *Science* (2008) special issue.

5.   All forms of knowledge emerge within particular sets of social relations and institutional dynamics. Knowledge is not simply the revelation of facts; it is itself productive and reproductive of specific social and power relationships. Some useful elaborations of expert knowledge in political ecology and science and technology studies include Blaikie (1985); Bocking (2004); Brookfield (1999); Bryant (1998); van Buuren and Edelenbos (2004); Collingridge and Reeve (1986); Davis and Wagner (2003); Dimitrov (2003); Jasanoff and Martello (2004); Mitchell (2002).

6.   Attempts to conceptualize how natural and social factors come together in cities include the Burch–Machlis human ecosystem model (Machlis, Force, and Burch 1997; Pickett et. al. 1997), which posits that human–non-human "hybrid" char-acteristics (Pickett et. al. 1997, 189) are found in most urban ecosystems. Unlike previous models that suggested reciprocal interconnections between a human and a natural ecosystem (Boyden 1993), this model uses more fluid nature–culture categories, suggesting that, "some [ecosystem] components, fluxes, regu-lators, and processes in [urban] systems retain many of their 'natural' behaviors, whereas others may be entirely altered or constructed by humans" (Pickett et al. 1997, 189). The Burch–Machlis model also explicitly recognizes what it terms "key hierarchies" (Pickett et al. 1997, 189) in social organization (wealth, educa-tion, status, property, and power), and the difficulty of representing these at a variety of spatial scales. Thus urban ecology has become the theoretical terrain in which longstanding disciplinary divisions between the natural and social sciences have begun, perhaps by necessity, to dissolve.

7.   In this way, disciplinary urban ecology complicates the conventional Latourian critique of modern science and its "purification rituals" (Latour 1993).

8.   In essence, citizenship has been argued to include civil rights like freedom of speech, freedom from assault, and equal treatment under the law; political rights such as participation in the exercise of political power through elections; and social rights like entitlements to a modicum of material and social welfare guaranteed by the state. See Janoski (1998, 28–33); and for the original ideas he builds on, see Marshall (1950).

9.   It is also important to remember, as Helen Siu notes in writing of Guangzhou, "although drawn into a fast-forward mode of market-oriented gain, residents of

village enclaves in Guangzhou seem surprisingly grounded and dispossessed" (Siu 2007, 345).

10. We draw the distinction tentatively here, but earlier writing on Indian urbanism quite emphatically distinguishes inland and port cities as two separate patterns of urban settlement and growth in India. Rhoads Murphey (1977) and John Brush (1970) point to the sharp differences in organization, function, ecology, and cityscape of colonial port cities and the Hindu or Muslim cities of the Indian hinterland.

11. We are mindful here of Manuel Castells' (1996) network society thesis that focuses on how a new space of flows draws producers of information goods everywhere into powerful communication networks. And as Ravi Sundaram (2004, 64) notes, elite urban enclaves service/house these classes, simultaneously marginalizing other forms of labor in the city.

12. Anthony King (1976) traces the ideas of the cantonment, the civilian quarter, and the old city, as Indian urban forms were adapted and overlaid with colonial ones through the nineteenth and twentieth centuries.

13. The development of the Ridge as a colonial urban forest is sometimes forgotten in the more recent struggles to conserve the Ridge, as NGOs in Delhi fight to restrict industrial and residential development in the green spaces of Delhi, claiming as postcolonial natural heritage the landscapes that were part of the planned development of colonial Delhi.

14. See Tarlo (2003) for a close examination of the resettlement colonies of East Delhi, a striking product of this spectacular effort to clean Delhi in the mid-1970s.

15. Most slums are located on land owned by DDA, the Municipal Corporation of Delhi (MCD), the New Delhi Municipal Council (NDMC) and Indian Railways. This is a reflection of the biggest urban problem—the absence of equitable land distribution. In virtually all metropolises in India nearly two-thirds of the people live on one-tenth of the urban land. The Draft National Slum Policy seeks to freeze this by describing slums as "under-serviced areas," and does away with the promise of equitable land supply (Navlakha 2000, 4471).

16. Taneja (2008) shows how different interests in amenity and heritage rub up against each other in Delhi. He describes the development of a public golf course getting tangled with the heritage of Prithivraj Chauhan in a time of growing Hinduized reconstruction of the built heritage of Delhi.

17. Geddes developed these ideas in a number of ways. See, for instance, Geddes (1965[1915], 1972). See also R. Guha, Scottish Internationalist, *The Hindu*, January 21, 2007.

18. In this reconfiguration, the point being made here is that, middle class NGOs do not clearly identify particular classes as the main or only enemy of their vision of a sustainable city. This allows for issue-based alliances to blur and destabilize class conflict.

19. Michael Smith (2001) sees contemporary cities as being profoundly changed by the "rise of translocalities" (places separated by national borders but united

through social and cultural affiliations with groups, categories, networks, and amenities) where the politics of transforming and defending place are generated in the friction between bounded jurisdictions and translocal coalitions.

20. Even before the myriad forces and concerns we see in Gurgaon at the end of the twentieth century became prominent, in the case of planning for New Bombay earlier in the twentieth century, similar departures from ideals in actual accomplishments can be noticed. See Shaw (1999) for a detailed analysis of the uncertainties of this planning exercise in much earlier times.

21. Then there is the most interesting case of providing services in slums and linking them into infrastructure networks without giving them legal status that might destabilize property regimes in the city. For a discussion of this aspect, see McFarlane (2008, 6–12).

References

Abu-Lughod, J. 1999. *New York, Chicago, Los Angeles: America's Global Cities*. Minneapolis, MN: University of Minnesota Press.

Agrawal, A. 2005. *Environmentality: Technologies of Government and the Making of Subjects*. Durham, NC: Duke University Press.

Alberti, M., J. M. Marzluff, E. Shulenberger, G. Bradley, C. Ryan, and C. Zumbrunnen. 2003. Integrating Humans into Ecology: Opportunities and Challenges for Studying Urban Ecosystems. *Bioscience*, 53: 1169–1170.

AlSayyad, N. 2003. Urban Informality as a "New" Way of Life. In *Urban Informality: Transnational Perspectives from the Middle East, Latin America, and South Asia*, ed. A. Roy and N. AlSayyad. 7–32. Lanham, MD: Lexington Books.

Anderson, M. R. 1995. The Conquest of Smoke: Legislation and Pollution in Colonial Calcutta. In *Nature, Culture, Imperialism: Essays on the Environmental History of South Asia*, ed. D. Arnold and R. Guha. 293–335. Delhi: Oxford University Press.

Anjaria, J. S. 2009. Guardians of the Bourgeois City: Citizenship, Public Space, and Middle-Class Activism in Mumbai. *City & Community*, 8 (4): 391–406.

Appadurai, A. 2002. Deep Democracy: Urban Governmentality and the Horizon of Politics. *Public Culture*, 14 (1): 21–47.

———. 2004. The Capacity to Aspire: Culture and the Terms of Recognition. In *Culture and Public Action*, ed. V. Rao and M. Walton. 59–84. Stanford, CA: Stanford University Press.

Ash, A., and N. Thrift. 2002. *Cities: Reimagining the Urban*. Cambridge: Polity Press.

Auyero, J., and D. A. Swistun. 2009. *Flammable: Environmental Suffering in an Argentine Shantytown*. New York: Oxford University Press.

Baviskar, A. 1995. *In the Belly of The River: Tribal Conflicts over Development in the Narmada Valley*. New Delhi: Oxford.

———. 2003. Between Violence and Desire: Space, Power, and Identity in the Making of Metropolitan Delhi. *International Social Science Journal*, 55 (175): 89–98.

Benton, T. 1989. Marxism and Natural Limits: An Ecological Critique and Reconstruction. *New Left Review*, I/178 (November–December): 51–86.

Blaikie, P. 1985. *The Political Economy of Soil Erosion in Developing Countries*. London: Longman.

Blaikie, P., and H. Brookfield. 1987. *Land Degradation and Society*. London: Methuen.

Bocking, S. 2004. *Nature's Experts: Science, Politics, and the Environment*. Piscataway, NJ: Rutgers University Press.

Bott, E. 1957. *Family and Social Network: Roles, Norms, and External Relationships in Ordinary Urban Families*. London: Tavistock.

Boyden, S. V. 1993. The Human Component of Ecosystems. In *Humans as Components of Ecosystems: The Ecology of Subtle Human Effects and Populated Areas*, ed. M. A. Pickett. 72–78. New York: Springer-Verlag.

Brenner, N. 1998. Global Cities, "Glocal" States: Global City Formation and State Territorial Restructuring in Contemporary Europe. *Review of International Political Economy*, 5 (1): 1–37.

Brookfield, H. 1999. A Review of Political Ecology: Issues, Epistemology, and Analytical Narratives. *Zeitschrift Fur Wirtschaftsgoegraphie*, 43: 131–147.

Brosius, J. P. 1999a. Comments on Escobar's "After Nature: Steps to an Antiessentialist Political Ecology." *Current Anthropology*, 40: 16–17.

———. 1999b. Green Dots, Pink Hearts: Displacing Politics from the Malaysian Rain Forest. *American Anthropologist*, 101 (1): 36–57.

Brosius, J. P., and D. Russell. 2003. Conservation from Above: An Anthropological Perspective on Transboundary Protected Areas and Ecoregional Planning. *Journal of Sustainable Forestry*, 17 (1–2): 39–65.

Brush, J. 1970. The Growth of the Presidency Towns. In *Urban India: Society, Space and Image*, ed. R. Fox. 91–114. Durham, NC: Duke University.

Bryant, R. L. 1992. Political Ecology: An Emerging Research Agenda in Third World Studies. *Political Geography*, 11 (1): 12–36.

———. 1998. Power, Knowledge and Political Ecology in the Third World. *Progress in Physical Geography* 22: 79–94.

Bryant, R. L., and S. Bailey. 1997. *Third World Political Ecology*. London: Routledge.

Buchanan, P. 2005. *Ten Shades of Green: Architecture and the Natural World*. New York: Architectural League of New York.

Caldeira, T. 2001. *City of Walls: Crime, Segregation, and Citizenship in São Paulo*. Berkeley, CA: University of California Press.

Castells, M. 1977. *The Urban Question: A Marxist Approach*. Cambridge, MA: MIT Press.

———. 1996. *The Rise of the Network Society, the Information Age: Economy, Society and Culture*. Vol. I. Cambridge, MA; Oxford, UK: Blackwell.

Chakrabarty, D. 2002. *Habitations of Modernity: Essays in the Wake of Subaltern Studies*. Chicago: The University of Chicago Press.

Chalana, M. 2010. Slumdogs vs. Millionaires: Balancing Urban Informality and Global Modernity in Mumbai, India. *Journal of Architectural Education*, 63 (2): 25–37.

Chatterjee, P. 1986. *Nationalist Thought and the Colonial World: A Derivative Discourse?* New Delhi: Oxford University Press.

———. 2006. *Politics of the Governed: Reflections on Popular Politics in Most of the World.* New York: Columbia University Press.

Chopra, P. 2007. Refiguring the Colonial City: Recovering the Role of Local Inhabitants in the Construction of Colonial Bombay, 1854–1918. *Buildings & Landscapes: Journal of the Vernacular Architecture Forum*, 14: 109–125.

Collingridge, D., and C. Reeve. 1986. *Science Speaks to Power: The Role of Experts in Policy Making.* New York: St. Martin's Press.

Collins, J., A. Kinzig, N. Grimm, W. Fagan, D. Hope, J. Wu, and E. Borer. 2000. A New Urban Ecology: Modeling Human Communities as Integral Parts of Ecosystems Poses Special Problems for the Development and Testing of Ecological Theory. *American Scientist*, 88 (5): 416–425.

Crush, J., ed. 1995. *Power of Development.* New York: Routledge.

Davila, A. 2004. *Barrio Dreams: Puerto Ricans, Latinos, and the Neoliberal City.* Berkeley, CA: University of California Press.

Davis, A., and J. R. Wagner. 2003. WHO knows? On the Importance of Identifying "Experts" When Researching Local Ecological Knowledge. *Human Ecology*, 31 (3): 463–489.

Davis, D. 2000. *The Consumer Revolution in Urban China.* Berkeley, CA: University of California Press.

Davis, M. 2006. *Planet of Slums.* New York: Verso.

Dawson, A., and B. Edwards. 2004. Introduction: Global Cities of the South. *Social Text*, 22 (4 81): 1–7.

Demeritt, D. 1994. Ecology, Objectivity and Critique in Writings on Nature and Human Society. *Journal of Historical Geography*, 20 (1): 22–37.

Dimitrov, R. S. 2003. Knowledge, Power, and Interests in Environmental Regime Formation. *International Studies Quarterly*, 47 (1): 123–150.

Dossal, M. 2005. A Master Plan for the City. *Economic & Political Weekly*, 40 (36): 3897–3900.

Ehrlich, P. 1968. *Population Bomb.* New York: Ballantine Books.

Escobar, A. 1994. *Encountering Development.* Princeton, NJ: Princeton University Press.

———. 1996. Constructing Nature: Elements for a Poststructuralist Political Ecology. In *Liberation Ecologies: Environment, Development, Social Movement*, ed. R. Peet and M. Watts. 46–68. London: Routledge.

———. 1998. Whose Knowledge, Whose Nature? Biodiversity, Conservation, and the Political Ecology of Social Movements. *Journal of Political Ecology*, 5: 53–82.

———. 1999. After Nature: Steps to an Antiessentialist Political Ecology. *Current Anthropology*, 40 (1): 16–17.

Evans, P., ed. 2002. *Livable Cities? Urban Struggles for Livelihood and Sustainability*. Berkeley, CA: University of California Press.

Fairhead, J., and M. Leach. 1996. *Misreading the African Landscape: Society and Ecology in Forest-Savanna Mosaic*. Cambridge: Cambridge University Press.

Ferguson, J. 1994. *The Anti-Politics Machine: Development, Depoliticization, and Bureaucratic Power in Lesotho*. Minneapolis, MN: University of Minnesota Press.

———. 1999. *Expectations of Modernity: Myths and Meanings of Urban Life on the Zambian Copperbelt*. Berkeley, CA: University of California Press.

Fernandes, L. 2004. The Politics of Forgetting: Class Politics, State Power and the Restructuring of Urban Space in India. *Urban Studies*, 41 (12): 2415–2430.

Gandy, M. 2002. *Concrete and Clay: Reworking Nature in New York City*. Cambridge, MA: MIT Press.

———. 2006. Urban Nature and the Ecological Imagination. In *In the Nature of Cities: Urban Political Ecology and the Politics of Urban Metabolism*, ed. N. C. Heynen, M. Kaika, and E. Swyngedouw, 62–72. London; New York: Routledge.

Geddes, P. 1965 [1915]. *Reports on Re-Planning of Six Towns of Bombay Presidency*. Bombay: Government of Maharashtra Urban Development and Public Health Department.

———. 1972. Selection from "Cities in Evolution." In *Patrick Geddes: Spokesman For Man and the Environment*, ed. M. Stalley. 190–200. New Brunswick, NJ: Rutgers University Press.

Gissen, D. 2003. *Big and Green: Toward Sustainable Architecture in the Twenty-First Century*. Princeton: Princeton Architectural Press.

Gledhill, J. 2005. Citizenship and the Social Geography of Deep Neo-Liberalization. *Anthropologica*, 47 (1): 81–100.

Gluckman, M. 1971. Preface. In *Family and Social Network*. 2nd ed. E. Bott. xiii–xxx. New York: New Press.

Greenough, Paul, and A. Tsing, eds. 2003. *Nature in the Global South: Environmental Projects in South and Southeast Asia*. Durham, NC: Duke University Press.

Gregory, Steven. 1998a. *Black Corona: Race and the Politics of Place in an Urban Community*. Princeton, NJ: Princeton University Press.

———. 1998b. Globalization and the "Place" of Politics in Contemporary Theory: A Commentary. *City and Society: Annual Review*, 10 (1): 47–64.

Grimm, N. B., L. J. Baker, and D. Hope. 2003. An Ecosystem Approach to Understanding Cities: Familiar Foundations and Uncharted Frontiers. In *Understanding Urban Ecosystems: A New Frontier for Science and Education*, ed. A. R. Berkowitz, C. H. Nilon, and K. S. Hollweg. 95–114. New York: Springer.

Grove, R. 1989. *Green Imperialism: Colonial Expansion, Tropical Island Edens and the Origins of Environmentalism 1600–1860*. Cambridge: Cambridge University Press.

Gupta, A., and J. Ferguson. 1992. Beyond "Culture": Space, Identity, and the Politics of Difference. *Cultural Anthropology*, 7 (1): 6–23.

Gupta, N. 1971. Military Security and Urban Development: A Case Study of Delhi, 1857–1912. *Modern Asian Studies*, 5 (1): 61–77.

Hannerz, U. 1996. *Transnational Connections*. New York: Routledge.

Hansen, T. B. 2001. *Wages Of Violence: Naming and Identity in Postcolonial Bombay*. Princeton, NJ: Princeton University Press.

Haraway, D. J. 1989. *Primate Visions: Gender, Race, and Nature in the World of Modern Science*. New York: Routledge.

———. 1991. *Simians, Cyborgs, and Women: The Reinvention of Nature*. New York: Routledge.

———. 1997. *Modest Witness at Second Millennium. Female Man Meets Onco Mouse: Feminism and Technoscience*. New York: Routledge.

Harriss, J. 2007. Antimonies of Empowerment: Observations on Civil Society, Politics and Urban Governance in India. *Economic and Political Weekly*, 42 (26): 2716–2724.

Harvey, D. 1989. *The Condition of Postmodernity: An Enquiry into the Origins of Cultural Change*. Cambridge: Blackwell.

Hayden, D. 1995. *The Power of Place: Urban Landscapes And Public History*. Boston, MA: MIT Press.

Hazareesingh, S. 2000. The Quest for Urban Citizenship: Civic Rights, Public Opinion, and Colonial Resistance in Early Twentieth-Century Bombay. *Modern Asian Studies*, 34 (4): 797–829.

Holston James. 1999. The Modernist City and the Death of the Street. In *Theorizing the City: The New Urban Anthropology Reader*, ed. S. Low. 245–276. New Brunswick, NJ: Rutgers University Press.

———. 2008. *Insurgent Citizenship: Disjunctions of Democracy and Modernity in Brazil*. Princeton, NJ: Princeton University Press.

Holston, J., and A. Appadurai. 1999. *Cities and Citizenship*. Durham, NC: Duke University Press.

Janoski, T. 1998. *Citizenship and Civil Society: A Framework of Rights and Obligations in Liberal, Traditional and Social Democratic Regimes*. Cambridge: Cambridge University Press.

Jasanoff, S., and M. L. Martello, ed. 2004. *Earthly Politics: Local and Global in Environmental Governance*. Cambridge, MA: MIT Press.

Jessop, B. 2002. Liberalism, Neoliberalism, and Urban Governance: A State-Theoretical Perspective. *Antipode*, 34: 452–472.

Joyce, P. 2003. *The Rule of Freedom: Liberalism and the Modern City*. London: Verso.

Kaika, M. 2005. *City Of Flows: Modernity, Nature, And The City*. London: Routledge.

Kidambe, P. 2001. Housing the Poor in a Colonial City: The Bombay Improvement Trust, 1898–1918. *Studies in History*, 17 (1): 57–79.

King, A. 1976. *Colonial Urban Development: Culture, Social Power and Environment*. London: Routledge and Paul.

Latour, B. 1993. *We Have Never Been Modern*. Trans. C. Porter. Cambridge, MA: Harvard University Press.

———. 1999. *Pandora's Hope: Essays on the Reality of Science Studies*. Cambridge, MA: Harvard University Press.

Leach, N. 1997. *Rethinking Architecture: A Reader in Critical Theory*. London: Routledge.

Lefebvre, H. 1991. *The Production of Space*. Cambridge: Blackwell.

Legg, S. 2008. Ambivalent Improvements: Biography, Biopolitics, and Colonial Delhi. *Environment and Planning A*, 40 (1): 37–56.

Liechty, M. 2003. *Suitably Modern: Making Middle Class Culture in a New Consumer Society*. Princeton, NJ: Princeton University Press.

Logan, J. R., R. B. Whaley, and K. Crowder. 1997. The Character and Consequences of Growth Regimes: An Assessment of 20 Years of Research. *Urban Affairs Review*, 32 (5): 603–630.

Lomnitz, L. A. 1977. *Networks And Marginality: Life in a Mexican Shantytown*. New York: Academic Press.

Low, S. M. 1996. The Anthropology of Cities: Imagining and Theorizing the City. *Annual Review of Anthropology*, 25: 383–409.

———. 2003. *Behind the Gates: Life, Security, and the Pursuit of Happiness in Fortress America*. New York: Routledge.

Machlis, G., J. E. Force, and W. Burch, Jr. 1997. The Human Ecosystem Part I: The Human Ecosystem as an Organizing Concept in Ecosystem Management. *Society and Natural Resources*, 10 (4): 347–367.

Mankekar, P. 1999. *Screening Culture, Viewing Politics: An Ethnography of Television, Womanhood, and Nation in Postcolonial India*. Durham, NC: Duke University Press.

Mann, M. 2007. Delhi's Belly. *Studies in History*, 23 (1): 1–31.

Mann, M., and S. Sehrawat. 2009. A City with a View: The Afforestation of the Delhi Ridge, 1883–1913. *Modern Asian Studies*, 43 (2): 543–570.

Marshall, T. H. 1950. *Citizenship and Social Class*. Cambridge: Cambridge University Press.

Mayer, M. 2000. Urban Social Movements in an Era of Globalization. In *Urban Movements in a Globalizing World*, ed. P. Hamel, H. Lustiger-Thaler, and M. Mayer. 141–156. London: Routledge.

Mazzarella, W. 2003. *Shoveling Smoke: Advertising and Globalization in Contemporary India*. Durham, NC: Duke University Press.

McDonnell, M., and S. Pickett. 1990. Ecosystem Structure and Function along Urban–Rural Gradients: An Unexploited Opportunity for Ecology. *Ecology*, 71 (4): 1232–1237.

McFarlane, C. 2008. Sanitation in Mumbai's Informal Settlements: State, "Slum" and Infrastructure. *Environment and Planning A*, 40 (1): 88–107.

McKinney, M. L. 2002. Urbanization, Biodiversity, and Conservation. *Bioscience*, 52 (10): 883–890.

Mehta, S. 2004. *Maximum City: Bombay Lost and Found*. 1st ed. New York: Alfred A. Knopf.

Mitchell, J. C. 1969. *Social Networks in Urban Situations*. Manchester: Manchester University Press.

Mitchell, T. 2002. *Rule of Experts: Egypt, Technopolitics, Modernity*. Berkeley, CA: University of California Press.

Mosse, D. 1997. The Symbolic Making of a Common Property Resource: History, Ecology, and Locality in a Tank-Irrigated Landscape in South India. *Development And Change*, 28 (3): 467–504.

———. 2003. *The Rule of Water: Statecraft, Ecology, and Collective Action in South India*. New Delhi: Oxford University Press.

Murphey, R. 1977. *The Outsiders: Western Experience in India and China*. Ann Arbor, MI: University of Michigan Press.

Nair, J. 2005. *The Promise of the Metropolis: Bangalore's Twentieth Century*. New Delhi: Oxford University Press.

Navlakha, G. 2000. Urban Pollution: Driving Workers to Desperation. *Economic & Political Weekly*, 35 (51): 4469–4471.

Neuwirth, R. 2006. *Shadow Cities: A Billion Squatters, a New Urban World*. 1st ed. New York: Routledge.

O'Dougherty, M. 2002. *Consumption Intensified: The Politics of Middle Class Daily Life in Brazil*. Durham, NC: Duke University Press.

Parlange, M. 1998. The City as Ecosystem. *Bioscience*, 48 (8): 581–582.

Peet, R., and M. Watts, eds. 1996. *Liberation Ecologies: Environment, Development, Social Movements*. New York: Routledge.

Pickett, S. T. A., W. R. Burch Jr., S. E. Dalton, T. W. Foresman, J. M. Grove, and R. Rowntree. 1997. A Conceptual Framework for the Study of Human Ecosystems in Urban Areas. *Urban Ecosystems*, 1 (4): 185–199.

Pickett, S. T. A., and M. L. Cadenasso. 2002. The Ecosystem as a Multidimensional Concept: Meaning, Model, and Metaphor. *Ecosystems*, 5 (1): 1–10.

Pickett, S. T. A., M. L. Cadenasso, J. M. Grove, C. H. Nilon, R. V. Pouyat, W. C. Zipperer, and R. Costanza. 2001. Urban Ecological Systems: Linking Terrestrial Ecological, Physical, and Socioeconomic Components of Metropolitan Areas. *Annual Review Of Ecology And Systematics*, 32: 127–157.

Prakash, G. 2010. *Mumbai Fables*. Princeton, NJ: Princeton University Press.

Rademacher, A. 2011. *Reigning the River: Urban Ecologies and Political Transformation in Kathmandu*. Durham, NC: Duke University Press.

Raffles, H. 2002. *In Amazonia*. Princeton, NJ: Princeton University Press.

Rao, N. 2007. *"House, But No Garden": Apartment Living in Bombay, 1898–1948*. Chicago, IL: University of Chicago.

Rebele, F. 1994. Urban Ecology and Special Features of Urban Ecosystems. *Global Ecology and Biogeography Letters*, 4: 173–187.

Redclift, M., and T. Benton, ed. 1994. *Social Theory and the Global Environment*. London: Routledge.

Rotenberg, R. 1996. The Metropolis and Everyday Life. In *Urban Life*, ed. G. Gmelch and W. P. Zenner. 60–81. Prospect Heights, IL: Waveland.

Roy, A. 2009. Civic Governmentality: The Politics of Inclusion in Beirut and Mumbai. *Antipode*, 41: 159–179.

Saberwal, V. K. 1999. *Pastoral Politics: Shepherds, Bureaucrats, and Conservation in the Western Himalaya*. Oxford: Oxford University Press.

Sankhe, S., I. Vittal, R. Dobbs, A. Mohan, A. Gulati, J. Ablett, S. Gupta, A. Kim, S. Paul, A. Sanghvi, and G. Sethy. 2010. *India's Urban Awakening: Building Inclusive Cities, Sustaining Economic Growth*. New York: McKinsey Global Institute.

Sassen, S. 1991. *The Global City: New York, London, Tokyo*. Princeton, NJ: Princeton University Press.

———. 2002. *The Global City: New York, London, Tokyo*. 2nd ed. Princeton, NJ: Princeton University Press.

———. 2006. *Territory, Authority, Rights: From Medieval to Global Assemblages*. Princeton, NJ: Princeton University Press.

Science. 2008. Special Issue: Cities. 319 (5864). February 8.

Scott, J. C. 1998. *Seeing like a state: How Certain Schemes to Improve the Human Condition Have Failed*. New Haven, CT: Yale University Press.

Sennett, R. 1994. *Flesh And Stone: The Body and the City in Western Civilization*. New York: Norton.

Sharan, A. 2006. In the City, Out of Place: Environment and Modernity, Delhi 1860s to 1960s. *Economic and Political Weekly*, 41 (47): 4905–4911.

Shaw, A. 1999. The Planning and Development of New Bombay. *Modern Asian Studies*, 33 (4): 951–988.

Singh, K. 2010. My Father the Builder. In *Celebrating Delhi*, ed. M. Dayal. 1–14. New Delhi: Penguin and Ravi Dayal Publishers.

Singh, U. 2010. Discovering the Ancient in Modern Delhi. In *Celebrating Delhi*, ed. M. Dayal. 15–27. New Delhi: Penguin and Ravi Dayal Publishers.

Siu, H. F. 2007. Grounding Displacement: Uncivil Urban Spaces in Postreform South China. *American Ethnologist*, 34 (2): 329–350.

Sivam, A. 2003. Housing Supply in Delhi. *Cities*, 20: 135–141.

Sivaramakrishnan, K. 1999. *Modern Forests: Statemaking and Environmental Change in Colonial Eastern India*. Oxford: Oxford University Press.

Smart, A., and J. Smart. 2003. Urbanization and the Global Perspective. *Annual Review of Anthropology*, 32: 263–285.

Smith M. P. 2001. *Transnational Urbanism*. New York: Blackwell.

Smith, N. 1984. *Uneven Development: Nature, Capital, and the Production of Space*. Oxford: Blackwell.

———. 2002. New Globalism, New Urbanism: Gentrification as Global Urban Strategy. *Antipode*, 34 (3): 427–450.

Social Text. 2004. Special Issue: Global Cities of the South. 22 (481).

Spodek, H. 1980. Studying the History of Urbanization in India. *Journal Of Urban History* 6 (3): 251–295.

Srivastava, S., and D. Mukherji. 2005. Emerging Cityscapes and Environmental Issues. *Economic & Political Weekly*, 40 (36): 3905–3909.

Stack, C. 1974. *All Our Kin: Strategies for Survival in a Black Community*. New York: Harper and Row.

———. 1996. *Call to Home: African Americans Reclaim the Rural South*. New York: Basic Books.

Sukopp, H., Hejný, S., and Kowarik, I., eds. 1990. *Urban Ecology. Plants and Plant Communities in Urban Environments*. Hague: Academic Publishing.

Sundaram, R. 2004. Uncanny Networks. *Economic & Political Weekly*, 39 (1): 64–71.

Swyngedouw, E. 1996. The City as a Hybrid: On Nature, Society, and Cyborg Urbanisation. *Capitalism, Nature, Socialism*, 7 (1): 65–80.

———. 1999. Modernity and Hybridity. *Annals Of The Association Of American Geographers* 89: 443–465.

———. 2006. Circulations and Metabolisms: (Hybrid) Natures and (Cyborg) Cities. *Science as Culture* 15 (2): 105–121.

Taneja, A. V. 2008. History and Heritage Woven in the New Urban Fabric: The Changing Landscapes of Delhi's "First City". Or, Who Can Tell the Histories of Lado Sarai? In *Patterns of Middle Class Consumption in India and China*, ed. C. Jaffrelot and P. van der Veer. 157–169. Los Angeles, CA: Sage.

Tarlo, E. 2003. *Unsettling Memories: Narratives of the Emergency in Delhi*. Berkeley, CA: University of California Press.

United Nations. 1996. Habitat Agenda and Istanbul Declaration on Human Settlements Summary: Road Map to the Future. United Nations Department of Public Information. DPI/1846/HAB/CON.

UN-HABITAT. 2001.*The State of World Cities*. New York: United Nations Habitat.

UN Population Division. 2003. *World Urbanization Prospects: the 2003 Revision*. New York: United Nations Population Division.

van Buuren, A., and J. Edelenbos. 2004. Why is joint knowledge production such a problem? *Science and Public Policy*, 31 (4): 289–299.

Vandergeest, P., and N. Peluso. 1995. Territorialization and State Power in Thailand. *Theory and Society*, 24 (3): 385–426.

Walbridge, M. 1998. Growing Interest in Urban Ecosystems. *Urban Ecosystems*, 2 (1): 3.

Weinstein, L., and X. Ren. 2009. The Changing Right to the City: Urban Renewal and Housing Rights in Globalizing Shanghai and Mumbai. *City & Community*, 8, (4): 407–432.

Werbner, R. P. 1984. The Manchester School in South-Central Africa. *Annual Review of Anthropology*, 13: 157–185.

Williams, R. 1973. *The Country and the City*. New York: Oxford University Press.

———. 1980. Ideas of Nature. In *Problems in Materialism and Culture: Selected Essays*. 67–85. London: NLB.

Williamson, T. J., A. Radford, and H. Bennetts. 2002. *Understanding Sustainable Architecture*. London: Spoon Press.

World Resources Institute [WRI]. 1996. *World Resources 1996–1997*. Washington DC: World Resources Institute, United Nations Environment Programme, United Nations Development Programme, The World Bank.

Zimmerer, K. 2000. The Reworking of Conservation Geographies: Nonequilibrium Landscapes and Nature Society Hybrids. *Annals of the Association of American Geographers*, 90 (2): 356–369.

2
Is There an 'Indian' Urbanism?

Janaki Nair*

An urban "community" in the full meaning of the word, appears as a general phenomenon only in the Occident. (Weber 1958, 80)

Why has the law, and planning law in particular, been so pliable an instrument in the governance of cities? Indeed, if the law is understood historically as part of the ideological apparatus of the bourgeoisie in its desire for control of urban spaces, has it run its course in the Indian city or is it yet to achieve its true potential (see McAuslan 1980)? With this as my opening question, I would like to go further and ask what the rich materials of history, particularly of the colonial period, can contribute to an understanding of the problems of the contemporary Indian city. Is there a specifically 'Indian urbanism' with longer roots in the ways city space was conceived and used, and spatial practices determined? Is India imprisoned in the older sociological categories that were laid out by Max Weber in his study of the medieval Western city (Weber 1958, 80),[1] or can one theoretically account for the apparent regeneration of some historical features of Indian urbanism in the contemporary city? While a critical and sophisticated body of work, largely by sociologists, geographers, and anthropologists (and the contributions to this volume are fine examples of this) have contributed to the analysis of, and generated new categories for understanding, the predicaments of the contemporary Indian city, equally complex historical understandings of cities in modern India, especially in the colonial period, have remained at a remove from these conversations. In bringing the two sets of methodologies/

* I would like to thank Anne Rademacher and K. Sivaramakrishnan for inviting me to reflect on this theme for the AAS panel in Philadelphia, 2010. P. K. Datta, Mary John, and A. R. Vasavi also made comments on the first draft of this chapter, though all responsibility for this reworking remains mine.

chronologies/discourses together in this brief discussion, my intention is to begin an inquiry into the prospects of law as an instrument for increasing not only the predictability of urban life and the legibility of Indian cities, beyond small enclaves of successful planning, but also principally in achieving a more just and equal urban order.

This discussion is largely focused on the city of Bengaluru, but many of the claims about, and descriptions of, its historical trajectory will intersect with the experiences of most other Indian cities. Two simultaneous and apparently contradictory developments in twenty-first-century Bengaluru have prompted these reflections on the shape and governance of contemporary Indian cities. One is the establishment in 2008 of a new task force for Bengaluru, and the other is the passage of the Karnataka Town and Country Planning and Certain Other Laws (Amendment) Bill 2010, which regularizes unauthorized constructions in the state of Karnataka. Reading these recent developments together, I would like to ask two kinds of questions. One is about our understanding and characterization of law as it operated in the urban Indian setting, and the other is about the nature of institutional arrangements for city governance which are manifested in an apparently persistent and irreconcilable clash of interests between the corporate (economic) and the political realms. I will develop my argument in relation to these questions in five sections. I begin with a discussion of the hopes posed by the new initiatives in Bengaluru (Section 1); an examination of prevailing critiques and understandings of planning in the Indian setting (Section 2); and an exploration of Bengaluru's own tangled histories of defining and permitting illegalities (Section 3). In the following sections, I turn to the more general uses of history in understanding modern city governance (Section 4); and finally discuss whether taking both this history and contemporary developments into account could yield an insight into the prospects of extending democratic practice and achieving equality (Section 5).

Renewed Hopes and a New Future for Planning?

In 2008, the newly-elected government of Karnataka, led by the Bharatiya Janata Party (BJP), set up the Agenda for Bengaluru's Infrastructure and Development Task Force (ABIDe), one of eleven new task forces that were formed at that time (Daksh 2009).[2] Under its convener, Rajeev Chandrasekhar, Rajya Sabha Member of Parliament (MP), former chairman of BPL Mobile, and also former chief of the Federation of Indian Chamber of Commerce and Industry (FICCI), the new task force shared a great deal with its previous incarnation, the Bangalore Agenda Task Force (BATF) in its composition and goals. Set up in 1999, the BATF, an experiment in urban governance involving several important leaders of the IT and IT-enabled 'new economy,' was an attempt to realize the dream of a 'world class' city by 2004, which would compete favorably with the shining example of Singapore in its infrastructure, governance, and budgeting practices. As the BATF chairman, Nandan Nilekani, also the head of Infosys Technologies, later recalled,

> The BATF was a coalition of industry, civil organizations and the Karnataka state government, to upgrade Bangalore's infrastructure and public governance systems. The PPP (Public Private Partnership) focused on employing corporate expertise and industry best practices in building efficient delivery of civic systems, and enabling internal capacity building in state infrastructure.

It need come as no surprise that this dazzling future was not realized, nor that the task force itself, a 'para-statal' and indeed extra-constitutional body, was disbanded by the new government in 2004 (Ghosh 2005). The bourgeoisie, alas, did not make the city in their own image (see Chatterjee 2004).[3]

The constitution of ABIDe is thus the triumph of hope over experience. Despite some distinctions in the language and architectures of these two successive managerial efforts, they represent a continued desire by the state to forge anew its relationship to the private sector, and an acknowledgement that private–public partnerships can take on city wide development plans for the growth of the city. It also signifies the renewed yearning of the new bourgeoisie for control of the city.

The second significant scheme announced by the Karnataka government has met with both dread and anticipation from the people of Bengaluru. The *Akrama Sakrama* (roughly, 'regularizing the irregular') Scheme refers to the Karnataka Town and Country Planning and Certain Other Laws (Amendment), Bill 2010. Based on the Karnataka Town and Country Planning (Regularization of Unauthorized Development or Constructions) Rules 2007, it amended the Karnataka Town and Country Planning Act, 1961. It was first stayed by the Karnataka High Court in 2008; an unsuccessful attempt was made to reintroduce it as an ordinance prior to the municipal elections scheduled in 2009;[4] it was finally passed by the legislature in July 2010 and awaits the governor's approval at the time of writing.[5] It regularizes constructions that have been built in violation of building bylaws or planning uses, by the payment of a 'one-time' penalty to the government. The law also sets limits as to how much and what types of illegal development and construction will be accepted for regularization.[6]

As many as 700,000 properties in Bengaluru alone, and 500,000 in cities elsewhere in Karnataka, are expected to be regularized, generating up to Rs. 10,000 crore (Rs. 100 billion) for municipal bodies. The measure would additionally generate grateful support for the current BJP regime from those who yearn for state legality, while successfully asserting their right to the city.

The new scheme was opposed by a number of divergent interests and groups: by those protesting the high cost of 'converting' their illegalities into legal structures, and by those who claimed that the acceptance of 50 percent violation would only encourage rent seeking intermediaries to offer their services in getting higher violations regularized.[7] It was also opposed by law-abiding citizens, those who saw the government's action as the end (or the 'graveyard') of public planning itself. At the same time, the new rules were welcomed with relief by the large numbers who had invested in properties over the last few decades, in anticipation of eventual legalization.

In other words, the optimism with which successive task forces plan agendas and hope to impose urban order via *the instrumentalities of planning (law)* on the one hand, is equally matched, on the other hand, by periodic political 'regularizations' which extend and encourage the continued evasion and undermining of municipal laws and planning norms, which in turn *constitute new laws based on practice*. The shrill and routine derision of the political process by the corporate elite and the middle class is equally matched by the routine handwringing of the administration in its inability to assert itself against the perceived disorders of the city. It is as if the ritual anger at the violation of the law is balanced by a ritualized obeisance to its (albeit always deferred) observation. Yet the two processes in fact work in tandem—continuously renewed hopes based on the implementability of planning law are pitted against those who hope that a new law will legitimize existing illegalities.

In an Indian city where the bourgeoisie is so clearly in the ascendant, and the bureaucracy such a willing accomplice, there is as yet no urban order that reflects its exclusive power. Nilekani and others have obliquely reflected on the gap between economic power and its urban administrative/political correlates: "We have a unique situation in India in general, *and Bangalore in particular*, which is that there are so many people who are doing great stuff and doing it for the world, then why can't they also contribute to the country? [read: city]" (Nilekani 2007).[8]

ABIDe holds out a promise of change despite the legacy of BATF's notable failures. Let us turn briefly to the distinctions between the BATF and its newest incarnation, ABIDe—while the former attempted to supersede the municipal political structure, ABIDe is careful not to undermine the political process, pointing instead to technocratic failures, namely, the lack of a comprehensive plan which takes the region into account, and allots its resources for development goals (ABIDe 2008). One of the persistent critiques of the BATF was its disregard for issues dealing with the urban poor (Ghosh 2005); ABIDe has listed the problems of the urban poor among its concerns.

Such differences between the two task forces are superficial at best. If the BATF, for instance, looked to cement a corporate brand identity for the future (through a strategy of 'development by design' and the branding of Bangalore with its brash slogan "Bangalore Forward"), ABIDe has found it useful to hark back to the city's founding moments, and anachronistically "Bring[s] Back a Bengaluru of Kempe Gowda's Dreams" (http://abidebengaluru.in/attachments/1/original/plan_bengaluru_2020_agenda.pdf). It is difficult to decide which is the richer irony, the desire for a city run by a twenty-first-century managerial elite using corporate chieftains and their 'best practices,' or the choice of a warrior chieftain from the sixteenth century with modest claims to city building as a suitable emblem of the sprawling megalopolis that has been throttled by cars and illegal construction.

Despite the more cautious tone of the new initiatives, they appear to reiterate old goals—ABIDe's Plan 2020 unfurled plans for infrastructure and governance that are strikingly similar to those of BATF. In its ambition to think for, and plan the city, ABIDe matches the BATF. An important change proposed by ABIDe is the Bangalore Region Governance Act which envisages filling in the 'missing piece' in the architecture so far, namely regional planning. Meanwhile, a "comprehensive new Bengaluru Legislation" will "supersede and encompass all previous acts such as Bengaluru Municipal Legislations, covering a Bruhat Bengaluru Area of 800 square km and a region of 8000 square km"(ABIDe 2009, 9).

The demand for legislation that will supersede all previous legislation is recurrent, a recent plea being made by the Kasturirangan Committee in August 2008, in its report on proposed reforms to urban governance structures. The committee recommended the immediate formation of a Metropolitan Planning Committee in fulfillment of Article 243 ZE of the constitution (Report of the Expert Committee 2008). To quote, "The Committee . . . decided that it would be appropriate to recommend the inclusions of the entire territorial jurisdiction of the BMRDA [Bangalore Metropolitan Region Development Authority] currently comprising the three revenue districts of Bangalore Urban, Bangalore Rural, and Ramanagaram into the BMA [Bangalore Metropolitan Authority]" (Report of the Expert Committee 2008, 4.16). Do these totalizing visions represent merely an expansion of scale, or a tectonic shift in the language of governance and planning?

Clearly, the language of these initiatives reveals that more, rather than less, planning is seen as the panacea to the city's ills, with considerable optimism being pinned on the implementability of planning law. Is this optimism justified? Does the history of urbanization and city growth in the Bengaluru setting suggest that the modality of planning will triumph beyond the pockets or enclaves where it currently flourishes, amidst widespread violations of the planning law beyond?

Critiques of Planning

The insistence of every new urban design or task force on the techniques of appropriate planning, and the hopes pinned on an assertive planning law as its principle modality is striking. Yet how successfully will planning meet the expectations of its advocates as a transformative tool? Legions of commentators, bureaucrats, historians, and urban planners have acknowledged the failure of planning while emphasizing a series of alternative futures. There continue to be optimists who detect a temporal lag between those sites where planning has succeeded and India, and who broadly conclude that the abysmal state of Indian cities represents a historical stage prior to the eventual success of planning. In this view, it is only a matter of time before planning achieves its objects—India today is what Britain was in the nineteenth century (Tindall 2000, 2–5). In another optimistic view, one particularly held by technocrats, planning could succeed where there is less *political* interference, and when competing and overlapping jurisdictions are eliminated in order to strengthen the law, unifying and thereby clarifying tenures in the city space. Several interventions over the last few decades have strongly argued for taking politics out of the governance of cities and handing it over to a managerial elite (Ravindra 1997). This is also the widely held desire of civil society organizations, which see the venality of politicians as obstructing the process of planned order (Citizens' Action Forum 2008; Idiculla 2009), although an increasing number of resident welfare associations (RWAs) and Community Based Organisations (CBOs) are putting forward their less 'corruptible' candidates as the alternative, thus far without too much success.

Among scholars, there is less optimism about the transformative potential of master planning, which is seen as impacting directly on the opportunities provided by a multiplicity of legal tenures and certain grey areas of planning law for survival and even accumulation among the urban poor, particularly in the 'informal sector.' Solomon Benjamin, for instance, has seen master planning as "regressive" and localized power networks that checkmate its powers as the only "good news" for the pro-poor local economies that manipulate local political alliances in "stealth like ways" (Benjamin 2000, 48).[9]

Yet, the recent history of Bengaluru has revealed that the advantages of illegalities have been reaped not just by the poor. The success of smaller IT firms at least is accounted for by their willingness to evade corporation bylaws and planning modalities (Nair 2005). Are these the inevitable if painful consequences of 'economies in transition'?

Recent reflections by economists and political scientists alike have brought the narrative of 'economies in transition' into question, instead suggesting a structural linkage between what has for so long been characterized as the 'informal sector.' Kalyan Sanyal's (2007) recent challenge to the narratives of capitalist development, derived from unreconstructed notions of Marxist 'transitional' stages, has strenuously argued for the necessary *heterogeneity* of postcolonial economies. The 'need economy' in this optic, is a 'castaway economy'; rather than representing a residue of a pre-capitalist economic order, it is a structural feature of capitalist development in the postcolonial setting (Sanyal 2007). This formulation has been further elaborated by Partha Chatterjee in what he has called the sphere of "non-corporate" capital, structurally linked to, and therefore servicing, the large interests of capital (Chatterjee 2008, 53–61). Together, these arguments posit a "castaway economy" outside the domain of the transformatory capability of capital. If we extrapolate from this line of reasoning, the Indian city is fated to escape vigorous re-inscription by corporate capital.

In none of these latter critiques is the realm of planning law squarely discussed, except as a route for capitalist accumulation within the city. Indeed, to the extent that rampant illegalities and violations of planning are discussed at all, it is as a sign of the survival strategies of the urban poor, as a sign of the source of possible "resistance" using political resources (Fernandes and Varley 1998).[10]

Some sociologists and geographers, however, such as Madhu Sarin writing on Chandigarh (Sarin 1982) and Amita Baviskar writing on Delhi have noted that, to use the words of the latter, "the development of slums . . . was not a violation of the plan, it was an essential accompaniment to the plan, its Siamese twin" (Baviskar 2003: 91). Ananya Roy has framed the issue more sharply as "why India cannot plan its cities" to argue for an "idiom of planning" that reveals more than a mere detection of the failure of planning. In her view, this idiom consists of ". . . insurgent claims to land [that] have been nurtured and fostered by systems of unmapping, deregulation and informality" (Roy 2009, 81). Further insights into the systematic nature of these processes take Roy's definition of these processes as "calculated informality" (Roy 2009, 82–3) forward. For instance, Shubra Gururani notes the "carefully orchestrated flexibility" or the "flexible planning" of entire new city developments such as Gurgaon, which incite illegalities from the poor, the indigenous bourgeoisie, and international finance capital at one and the same time (Gururani this volume).

Contemporary Bengaluru similarly allows us the opportunity to rethink the attractions of, and the limits to, planning precisely because of the dominance of its middle class and their habitual violations of the law (see Rao and Tewari 1979). I have outlined elsewhere the importance of understanding the question of illegalities on a broad spectrum, one end of which is composed of the state itself, and fully includes the illegalities of the middle class (Nair 2005, 166–199). Although I concluded that exploration with the suggestion of a broad coalition of state and non-state forces that constitute the governing power structures in cities, the coherence of this coalition was asserted rather than fully demonstrated (see also Nair 2008a, 16–17).[11] A schematic representation would serve as a helpful reference to the discontinuous, uneven, and discrepant registers which mark the stages of Bengaluru's protracted 'passage' to its contemporary form.

The Pliability of the Law: SAKRAMA 2011

The schematic representation of the stages through which Bengaluru has passed in the modern period, as presented in Table 2.1, help us to identify not only the uneven temporalities of change between different registers (i.e., the economy, the built form, and the practice of municipal power), but also those elements that have remained more stable than others (e.g., the divided nature of the city, first on occupational/caste grounds, then racial, and finally class, with significant overlaps between these forms of power in the city; the relatively weak hold of state law through all periods). While the stages through which the process of industrialization actually passed are quite distinct, other elements run through several stages, their residual effects being reshaped or reaffirmed by the demands of each new phase.

How recent, for instance, is the process of 'regularization'? Some investigations have dated its origins in the 1991 amendments to the Karnataka Land Revenue Act, 1964, which permitted regularization of structures on government lands. In fact, there has been a long history of such interventions by the state in Bengaluru. K. N. Venkatrayappa notes that between 1892 and 1921, when the city was only gradually expanding, the supply of housing stock largely kept pace with demand. This relatively balanced demand and supply continued until about 1940 (Venkatrayappa 1957, 49). The next decade saw a near-doubling of the population (i.e., a 91 percent increase) due to wartime industrial development (e.g., the Hindustan Aircraft Factory, the Radio and Electric Manufacturing Company), the expansion of educational institutions, and flight from coastal areas threatened by war. While admitting that the state alone could no longer provide housing, the Bangalore Development Committee of 1954 noted with some dismay the origins of 'private planning':

> Under Section 25 of the City of Bangalore Improvement Act, 1945, the formation of layouts by private persons was absolutely prohibited. By an amendment effected in 1952, provision has been made to allow private layouts with the express sanction in writing of the Trust Board subject to such conditions as the Board may specify. This relaxation was apparently intended to promote the growth of additional housing of suitable type by encouraging private enterprise to come forward and contribute towards the relief of the acute shortage of housing accommodation in Bangalore . . . [however] layouts proposed by private individual owners are generally on small and often isolated pieces of land, and the sole

Table 2.1
Schematic histories: Bengaluru's modern existence

Historical Stages	Physical/Material Form	Spatial Practice	Economic Structures	Legal/Institutional Form	Modality of Power
Indigenous Modern (Bengaluru in the time of Tipu Sultan, late 18th century)	Walled city; segregated space for castes; mixed use	Predictability and legibility; undifferentiated sacred and civic; pedestrian or animated modes of transport; organic growth	Proto-industrial	Desegregated authorities; caste panchayats	Reciprocity; limited urban powers
Colonial Modern (Bangalore in the 19th and early 20th centuries)	Racially and hierarchically divided city space; east–west zonation; segregated space for residence/occupations	Inorganic; partially planned; new separation of sacred and civic	De-industrialized, dependent urbanization	Two municipalities; municipalization of caste	Limited representation; restricted municipal powers; discrepancy between social and political power
National Modern (Bengaluru's public sector period, 1950s–1980)	Unified city; enclaves of public planning (industrial townships); the rise of the unauthorized/irregular revenue layout	Partial state planning; zonal laws flouted by 'informal sector'; violence and sacralities as strategies for claiming space	Industrialization via public sector; growth of the informal sector; phase of patriotic production	Planning as pedagogy; provision of housing through post hoc legalization; illegalities of state and private agencies	State apparatuses; trade unions; rate-payers associations; caste as capital in representational politics
Global Modern (post 1980s Bengaluru)	Urban sprawl; decentered, placeless production; gated communities	Zoning laws flouted by formal and informal sectors; privatized public space; city as the space of 'flows'; rampant automobilization	Postindustrial; private sector, new economy including expansion of 'producer' services; phase of patriotic consumption	Planning as commodity (private consumption); provision of housing through post hoc legalization; illegalities of state and private bodies; rights discourse trumped by patronage networks	Private–Public partnerships; task forces; resident welfare associations; caste as capital in representational politics; discrepancy between economic (globalized networks) and political (local networks) power

object of forming the layouts is profiteering. In such layouts, reserving space for unremunerative purposes like parks and playgrounds is impracticable. The sites are often disposed of before all the amenities are actually provided and the moment the sites are sold out, the original layout owner falls out of the picture, and the purchasers are put to serious inconvenience regarding proper drainage, water supply, etc. . . . It is therefore advisable to prohibit the formation of private layouts, particularly in respect of those outside the limits of the Corporation . . . *If layout of any such extension is considered necessary, it should be taken up as a public undertaking by the City Improvement Trust Board.* (Report of the Bangalore Development Committee 1954, 42–43, emphasis added)

These pleas went unheeded in successive reports, until the gravity of the situation was pointed out by the 1997 Committee on Urban Management (Ravindra et al. 1997, 93–95).The committee identified the plethora of laws acting as a brake on house construction in planned and legal ways, without hazarding a guess on what proportion of housing was provisioned in this manner. Indeed, the history of the intervening period has been a continuous expansion of the scale of planning authority (first the Bangalore Development Authority 1976, then the Bangalore Metropolitan Region Development Authority 1985), without undermining or replacing existing authorities. "While repeatedly professing the need for central planning authority for better coordination and provision of civic services, it is indeed sad and unbelievable as to why none of the governments over the past 16 years thought it fit to implement the 74th amendment to the constitution and constitute the Metropolitan Planning Committee as mandated therein," states the Citizens' Action Forum (2008) booklet.

Civic activists have noted the resigned pragmatism of the state, which admitted the following in 1987:

Looking to the large number of unauthorized constructions, which have already come up over the years in/near-about big urban centers as also the acute shortage of housing in most of the large cities and towns, however, Government are of the view that it would be incorrect to look at all unauthorized developments of the past as an unmixed evil. On the contrary, some of these developments have helped in alleviating the housing shortage in large cities/towns of the State at least to a limited extent. Demolition of all the unauthorized constructions will also pose an uphill task for the State machinery, besides amounting to some kind of wastage of national wealth. (Government letter No. HUD 36 MNX 86, October 12, 1987, as cited in Citizens' Action Forum 2008, Section 6)

Indeed, as the CAF booklet points out, the new plan for 2015 expands to include a range of transformations that are already underway, endorsing for instance the "mutation corridors" or roads along which usage has already changed from residential to commercial purposes (Citizens' Action Forum 2008, Section 6).

If the estimates of illegalities to be regularized are any indication (700,000 out of 1.2 million properties in Bengaluru alone), the periodic expression of indignation by technocrats and advocacy groups is surprising. It is clear that rather than being an indication of the failure of planning, or indeed its limits, the systematic nature suggests that this is the norm, namely, the *very way* in which housing stock is being added, at low cost to the state. This is *in situ* planning, which allows every 'regularization' scheme to be announced as a one-off, final acceptance of what has already taken root on the ground. Therefore, as I have suggested previously, the map is not the territory; the legibility and knowability of a place do not correspond to the formal knowledge systems. New ethnographic research on the production of knowledge about the water supply systems in Mumbai and systems for maintenance suggests that there is a profound gap between the personalized knowledge of individual junior engineers and the impersonal, and therefore verifiable, map as a source of data on the city. Indeed, "agents of the state conceal, or avoid a calculated and comprehensive . . . knowledge of the system" (Anand 2011, 193). If anything, the gap is nurtured and fostered to block the transparency of the plan/law/map, though not always to ensure some form of rough justice. It is, as Veena Das has stated, "the very instruments of surveillance such as surveys and verifications of documents" that provide opportunities for "brokers to emerge from within the community and become the new face of the State" (Das 2010, 23).

Further to this, can we detect, in the systematic nature of the invitation to subvert the law, a production of *dependence* on the state rather than independence from its strictures? 'Regularization' will constantly appear as a favor bestowed on violators rather than as a right demanded from the state, thereby allowing for a continuous process of negotiation between the political class and the citizenry, whether middle class or poor. Is it indeed, as at least one bureaucrat has lamented, a case of private interests being given precedence over public interest? Or is it the very structure and function of the law that facilitates 'illegal activity'? "A law designed and administered to curb illegality," says Patrick McAuslan, "which did not at the same time ensure an adequate supply of low income plots would . . . cause instability—lawlessness of another kind" (McAuslan 1998, 28). Indeed, as McAuslan suggests, citing the case of Karachi, the resolution offered by unauthorized construction relieves public agencies of their obligations to provide housing, while simultaneously posing no threat to vested interests, and therefore to the system itself.

How then is this process, so well entrenched in the present day, squared with the larger requirements and ambitions of the new economy leaders? What are the chances of a singular logic triumphing in the space of the city, as is being demanded by a wide range of interests and groups? It is here perhaps that the method of the historian, with her concern for the long roots of these vested interests, may have some lessons to offer.

The Pliability of Law: Lessons of Colonial History

In a recent article that examines the pliability of criminal law in Indian cities, the historian Rajnarayan Chandavarkar has considered routine violations of the law (Chandavarkar 2007). He begins by querying the wisdom of the long-held skepticism about the "rule of law" as representing no more than "a cover for limited cliques of dominant groups to pursue their own particular interests." Suggesting that this skepticism be revised in the light of the intolerable strains on city life produced by the widespread espousal of criminality and violence among all sections of society, Chandavarkar raises a critique of the sphere identified by Partha Chatterjee as "political" society, which encompasses this realm of urban violence (Chatterjee 2001, 176). Arguing for a return to history, and particularly the history of the colonial period, to uncover the persistence of domains of power from which the colonial state "averted its gaze" (Chandavarkar 2007), Chandavarkar concludes that these norms of colonial statecraft were generated by "the problems of managing, controlling and governing labour" (ibid.). Disciplinary mechanisms of local structures of power thus dominated and indeed overwhelmed "public order" (ibid.). Propertied elites, merchants, and industrialists, he suggests, "created their own private arrangements for protection and policing" in the colonial city, with pernicious consequences for the prospects of a consensually formed public order. The result was the creation of enclaves and social arenas characterized by the "arbitrary exercise of social power" (ibid.).

A similar analysis of modern Mumbai by Thomas Hansen detects at least three "repertoires of power" that have resulted from such practices and have continued into the postcolonial period. There is thus, the "legal sovereignty of the state, the moral sovereignty of the nation, and the multiple forms of informal sovereignty based on local big men and everyday violence" (Hansen 2005, 141). He too talks of this form of sovereignty emerging from the specificities of colonial rule, which traced a trajectory quite different from its metropolitan counterparts. "In spite of this apparent determination to assert the sovereignty of the colonial state, its relationship with its subjects was never direct in terms of the bio-politics developed in Europe, where the unit and object of intervention was carefully counted and registered individuals" (Hansen 2005, 120). Despite the fact that colonialism broke the "majesty and marginality of the state in pre-colonial India" (ibid.), a pervasive, perhaps irrational, awe of the state continues its hold on the popular imagination, alongside awe for the Robin Hood of the Indian slums.

The colonial city, as Partha Chatterjee (2009) reminds us, was the place where a range of liberal techniques developed in the imperial center, relating to water supply, sewage, avenues and parks, street lighting, even libraries, and municipal government were indeed applied, although the "rule of freedom" was crucially constrained by the "rule of colonial difference" (Chatterjee 2009, 312). Planning, and planning law in particular, was compromised from its historical outset by the specific arrangements of governance under colonial rule, with important legacies for the present day. Any understanding of the place of planning law in the shaping of contemporary Indian cities and urban practices, or even a "public sphere," must therefore necessarily account for widespread violations, and not only by the poor or marginalized of the city, but also by those classes that benefit from the exercise of what Hansen calls "repertoires of power." Only by schematically correlating the stage of development to built forms, spatial practices, and legal/institutional orders, as I have attempted in Table 2.1, may we clear a space for an understanding of the new institutional arrangements that are being forged in the city today.

Anthony King's analysis of colonial urban development noted that planning apparatus and vested interest in the nineteenth century "were one and the same thing" with the planning authority playing either "a negative or delaying function" (King 1976, 24). The British were able to introduce "comprehensive and positive planning theory . . . many decades before this became feasible in the metropolitan society" (ibid.). If this is true of the areas that the British occupied, what of the other side of the racial divide? Most studies of Indian cities in the colonial period provide evidence of British reliance on 'natural leaders,' old power networks, in *mohallas* for instance, as the basis for the new *thanas* (after the Police Act of 1862), or for council borders, in cities as widely dispersed as Bombay, Madras, Lucknow, Delhi, Kanpur, Bangalore, or Surat (Balachandran 2008; Chandavarkar 1994; 1998, 108–117; Gooptu 2001, 74–76, 105–109; Gupta 1981, 28; Heynes 1991, 112–114; Joshi 2003, 15–61; Masselos 2007, 125–149; Mukherjee 1970; Oldenburg 1984, 114). The repeated reliance on and reinforcement of diffused power networks throughout the colonial period led to the emergence of a colonial political order which was composed of a coalition of interests, rather than one reflecting a singular exercise of state power.

In order to legitimize their system of 'governance,' which extended and strengthened local powers, the colonial authorities drew on a variety of reasons for the inoperability of impersonal law in the Indian setting. There were innumerable commentators on the incorrigibly 'illegal' Indian whose capacity to resist or escape the law (or indeed escape modernity itself) was a cultural trait, or at least a form of resistance. Yet there were times when British administrators such as Bombay's Arthur Crawford, who threw up his hands at the sheer impossibility of law enforcement in the city in the 1870s, admitted that some urban failures were due to severe constraints on finances rather than stubbornly resilient habits of caste or Indian predispositions (Dossal 1997, 202–204). Yet more resilient features of a collective addiction to dirt/disorder continued to be recalled not only in the more ambitious theorization of the city form, as in the work of Max Weber, but by town planners such as H. V. Lanchester who detected an "Indian way of being" (2007, 41).[12] The Indians' obstinate adherence to dirt and disorder, and disregard for anything like recognizable planning, was traced to the power of communities and their adjudicatory powers.[13]

Such readings ignore the very specific ways in which these local power structures were nurtured in the time of the colonial modern. How were caste-specific uses of space, and caste orders themselves, given a new lease of life in the colonial city? I refer to this process in the nineteenth century as the 'municipalization of caste' (see Table 2.1), of a deference to caste norms in spatial practice, and caste authority in social control, which, while it may not have had the same depth and meaning as in the village, and indeed may even have been based on entirely new sources of power in the city, continued to be recognized within the new municipal orders that emerged after the 1860s (Nair 2010). I cite just one of instance of this early (seventeenth century) reliance on existing power networks for the governance of Bombay:

> The problem of governing this heterogeneous population was a complex one, which made the imposition of English Law in the island difficult. Aungier solved the problem by granting those ethnic communities [i.e., religious, linguistic, caste] the traditional Indian form of government, called the Panchayat system, whereby the elders of each community settled internal matters, and kept order among the members of the community. While this kind of autonomy ensured the much desired non-interference in the religious and legal affairs of the resident communities of the island, it also led to the perpetuation of largely self-sufficient and insular communities. (Kosambi 1986, 41)

In the case of the twin cities of Bengaluru/Bangalore, the west and east, the indigenous and the civil and military station, these caste orders were refashioned and "municipalized" instead of being "decisively broken" as Narender Pani et al. (1985, 17) have claimed in their brief economic history of the indigenous city. Local power networks were extended and buttressed, and rules continually bent to accommodate them even within the new institutional spaces such as municipalities.[14] The same historical moment saw the 'creative destruction' of metropolitan capitals such as London and Paris under new and eventually binding laws governing urban planning, and the invasive demolition measures that were foisted on rebellious Indian cities such as Delhi and Lucknow after 1857. In other words, there were times and locations where the exercise of state power in the city was unified and singularly successful. However, heterogeneously constituted power networks were the *preferred modes of city governance* in India through most of the colonial period.

What were the prospects of "law becom[ing] a guarantee of the legal status of a person no longer defined by estate and birth" (and one might add caste) in the colonial city (Bhattacharya 2005, 131)? Neeladri Bhattacharya's insightful comment on the lineaments of a 'public sphere' in the colonial setting is invaluable in making sense of the ambiguous promise of the law. The idea of law as functioning within a publicly coded, universally known and categorically stated rights and powers was compromised from the start, with a more complex interplay emerging between the "language of law and discourse of tradition" (ibid., 138). While inner community battles become public battles, the colonized subjects were also able to assert "the reasonableness of encoded law" against the "unreasonableness of autocratic [colonial] power" (ibid., 139). Indeed, the Indian 'public' that was constituted was deeply segmented. While it engaged simultaneously with languages of 'reason,' it arrived at no consensus and blurred the distinctions between public good and community interest. What emerged were spaces of struggle, and equally spaces of control.

In her discussion of changes in Lucknow after the tumultuous events of 1856–1857, Veena Oldenburg writes,

> . . . the vacuum created by the deposition of the king and the dispersal of his court was filled by the municipal committee to serve as the font (albeit with a budget a fraction of the king's) of all jobs and business contracts in the city and the *mufussil* (countryside); to have access in Lucknow was especially prized since a word from the chief commissioner or his secretary could fill a vacancy or secure a contract in any distant corner of Oudh. (Oldenburg 1984, 84)

The new municipalities often allowed for earlier forms of urban leadership to be converted into the emerging system of representative politics.

The incoherence of the 'indigenous city' (as opposed to the clarity and order of the European parts of most cities, particularly the civil and military stations), which was produced and sustained by British policies, endured in the post-independence setting as a distinction between castes/classes. Yet the law emerges as a constitutive and productive process, rather than as a field of defined borders, a process that has been variously described as plural or porous legality.

Back to the Future

The brief turn to the past may bring home some uncomfortable truths about the ways in which privilege has operated, and therefore been challenged, in contemporary India. In the postcolonial city, there has been a continued consolidation of local social powers over, and sometimes against, the power of global capital. Caste has itself become a form of capital within the sphere of representational politics, feeding into larger networks of the party system (see John 2007; Nair 2008b). To these networks of power, the world of corporate capital appears opposed, straining to assert its authority in ever-widening circuits of power, hoping to mop up the surpluses of the city, and to produce the space of a bourgeois citizenship that has long been thwarted. In recent scholarship, the concept of citizenship has been freighted with a plethora of adjectives to capture the ambiguities posed by the law and planning apparatuses for a majority of urban dwellers: citizenship could be "insurgent" (Holston 2008), "flexible" (Ong 1999), and even "democratic" (Weinstein 2012), or it could manifest itself in the everyday. Indeed, in her analyses of the claims of the urban poor to housing, Veena Das points out that "the legal notion that you either have rights or you do not, would make no sense within these strategies of creating rights" (Das 2010, 14). She suggests that the "credentials for rights are built incrementally" (ibid.) around a series of objects that are critical to everyday life in the *jhuggi jopdi* (slum area), such as ration cards, water, and electricity. In such a scenario of 'everyday democracy,' what are the resources for imagining alternative futures, and what are the institutional spaces, other than those of either the state or the market, that might actually be used in fashioning a new urban order? What hope do these 'alternative' power centers and strategies offer to the urban poor for a determined and irreversible change in the conditions of their existence?

Arjun Appadurai has recently used the category of "redundancy" to describe this "multiplicity of claims in the idiom of power: over particular spaces, particular resources, particular relations" (Appadurai 2003). He writes, "You have social forces, social movements, non-governmental movements, popular movements, municipal movements, city governments, state governments, federal governments, all exercising very complex power claims over groups and bodies, locations, resources, etc." (ibid.). The recognition of the multiplicity of claims does not prevent the attempt to schematize them in specific, non-binary ways.

What we are witnessing in Bengaluru today is in fact the recognition that this field of forces is sharply divided, though mutually constituted and even interdependent, and the interdependence is unlikely to disappear in the foreseeable future. We may even detect some blurring of the styles and modalities of each of these spheres (and therefore between what we might agree is the distinction between direct and representative democracy). I illustrate this with an example: the necessity of tapping into (direct) localized forms of power was recognized by an embattled but ambitious corporate head in Bengaluru. Faced with the wrath of not just the local agricultural population, whose lands were being appropriated for the controversial Nandi

Infrastructure Corridor between Bengaluru and Mysore, but also besieged by the torrent of public interest litigations, and the whimsicality of successive avaricious state governments, Ashok Kheny, the managing director of Nandi Infrastructure Enterprise, has enthusiastically embraced the world of local politics. A number of active 'fans associations' have mushroomed all along the Mysore Road, and in areas that are affected by the NICE Nandi Infrastructure Corridor Enterprises project, to honor someone who has played only minor roles in Kannada Films, as a defiant claim to a form of local power that implicitly threatens to disrupt public order (since Fans' Associations otherwise have been at the forefront of, for instance, violent protests relating to language water and job reservations (see Nair 2005). In addition, Kheny routinely appears on platforms with religious leaders and celluloid heroes in order to buttress his claims to forms of non-state power. The simultaneous occupation of legal and non-legal, or even illegal, spheres of political engagement is striking.

My second example comes from the increasing tendency of RWAs to enter, rather than shun, modes of representative democracy, recognizing electoral politics as the only way by which their dreams of order can be realized. Despite the relative lack of success in penetrating this sphere so far, this is a new stage in contemporary politics (Lama-Rewal 2007, 59; Zerah 2007, 61–68). Elected representatives meanwhile recognize the importance of keeping alive the ideologies of planning law, as in the periodic appointment of task forces and commissions which chant the slogan of more comprehensive, better implemented planning.

So is there an Indian urbanism? Would its roots lie in some irreducible civilizational essence, as many colonial and even postcolonial commentators and scholars would have us believe, or are we to seek the roots in a more recent modern past and its experiments in dividing cities and municipalities? Does this legacy urge urban dwellers, and particularly the poorer ones, to seek their own ways of negotiating with the post-independence state, ways that are not always discouraged by the state itself? Far from abdicating its role in post-liberalization India, as contemporary common sense would have us believe, there is clearly a new role for state agencies within an institutional arrangement that seeks to reconcile the *economic* demands of global finance capital (the economy) with the compulsions of the *political*, rooted in local power structures. There is reluctant but tacit acceptance of the local in determining some aspects of land use, despite the continuous effort to bring larger areas of the city under the scrutiny of capital and its apparatuses, including public planning. Ironically, there is widespread recognition among a range of groups that "the management of public affairs is too important to be left to the government" *alone* (see Azevedo 1998, 261). Does this provide grounds for the hope of greater justice and equity, or is it yet another sign of the bourgeoisie's insatiable appetite for a stronger connection between economic and political power, so that a new legal order may be established, and greater incorporation into the circuits of global capital enabled? Alternatively, should we cheer the persistence of political 'interference' on behalf of a wide range of illegalities as a sign of 'resistance' to the unfettered rule of capital? Or do we recognize the structured dependence of the state and capital on such flourishing contempt for planning law?

In his article "The Right to the City," David Harvey provides a somewhat pessimistic view of the processes of urbanization that are underway in many parts of the world (Harvey 2008). Speaking of the necessity of launching "a global struggle, predominantly with finance capital, for that is the scale at which urbanization processes now work," he argues that "the right to the city, as it is now constituted, is too narrowly confined, restricted in most cases to a small political and economic elite who are in a position to shape cities more and more after their own desires" (ibid., 38). I believe that such a vision is unlikely to be realized wholly, not because of some civilizational essence that will constitute the source of resistance to the global modern, but since the coalition of interests that now prevails is one that serves capital well enough while maintaining a tight rein on more explosive reconstitutions of the urban fabric. True, the vision of Haussmann without his despotic powers, namely the phantasmagoric vision of complete juridical control by the bourgeoisie, continues to haunt the imaginations of the middle class: this alone explains the continuous return to the fantasy of totalized planning, to the control of the city. These controls are in fact linked to the expanding circles of finance capital, a new internationalization to which many 'pragmatists' are willing to adapt. To cite the words of the 2008 Kasturirangan Report:

> . . . metropolitan systems are much more networked with the outside world than smaller cities. While this is generally a positive attribute, it does make metropolitan cities vulnerable to external risks. Hence, metro-politan governance cannot be solely internally focused and must respond to major shifts in economic and political practice at both the national and global level. The need for a metropolitan governance structure that

> builds on and leverages Bangalore's cosmopolitan resources is essential
> to develop a global vision of the city. (Report of the Expert Committee
> on Governance, Para 4.16)

The Committee proposes a 63-member body which will consist of 42 elected and 21 nominated members: as many as ten of these are captains of the new economy.

Such unifying efforts at new forms of control of the city appear to feed off a simultaneous vision of neighborhood area committees functioning as the real space of democracy as watchdogs against the venalities to which electoral bodies are prone (see Coelho and Venkat 2009). Indeed, the hope which continues to haunt every civil society plan and agenda is fanned by proliferating RWAs, which have worked out ways of securing their entitlements (to power or water, for instance) from a state increasingly inclined to make citizens pay for an infrastructure which has not yet yielded a service (see Ranganathan 2011; Ranganathan et al. 2009). Do we see in the workings of the RWAs an attempt to produce a consensual, Habermasian 'public sphere' that has been otherwise historically thwarted? Is there a hope that RWAs will meaningfully challenge the elected bodies in their quest for the unified and consensual space of governance? Some scholars have identified these emerging institutions as sites of "counter democracy" (Lama-Rewal 2007) or as important signs of a "deep democracy" which reworks urban governmentalities (Appadurai 2002). There is also the recognition that the market, rather than the state, could be a force for limited democratic change: in this volume Nikhil Anand and Anne Rademacher discuss a market-driven solution to housing needs, which, while it might uphold a democratic process, does not resolve all issues of inequality.

The prospects for the proliferation of such initiatives as an alternative to an exaggerated reliance on the state appear limited in the immediate future. The contests between forms of direct and representative democracy may also continue for the foreseeable future. Languages of citizenship that are being forged in the Indian city, as Veena Das, among many others, has shown, display the signs of this ambiguity: they have absorbed the legal (often combined with the ritual) aspects of planning law and clearly reveal a wide range of engagements with the state and its promises. There is, in other words, no absolute abdication of, or the search for alternatives to, the 'rule of law' and to entitlements and rights bestowed by the state on the urban poor. It is another matter that justice and equality remain distant goals. Unlike those who see the power of capital as pitted against more localized forms of power, which are fostered and rewarded by the electoral process—in short, as mutually incompatible forms of power—it is their very interdependence and systematic nature that must be recognized before a larger politics of hope can be outlined.

Notes

1. Weber elaborated a radical distinction between the occidental and the oriental cities in which the emergence and exercise of a specifically urban law, which protects the privileges of the urban dweller, was a distinguishing mark. While western European cities were founded on the fortress and market, a city commune which developed a court of law, an associational structure, and political forms of partial autonomy and autocephaly (governance in which burghers could participate), in India, caste barriers prevented inter-caste fraternization, with the merchant guilds of Gujarat being the only exception. But in effect, cities in their real form emerge only in the west. In relation to India and China, Weber wrote, "In China, the magical closure of the clans, in India the closure of castes, eliminated the possibility of civic confederations" (Weber 1958, 119).

2. "In addition to the formation of a 'Karnataka Vision Group', eleven Missions and Task Forces such as the Agricultural Mission, Karnataka Education Mission, ABIDe (Agenda for Bengaluru Infrastructure Task Force) have been formed to oversee the development of the State. However, most of these are not representative of various groups (such as Dalits, agriculturists, religious minorities et al.), are largely dominated by corporate interests and those close to the BJP and its affiliated groups, and the functioning of most of these groups is irregular. In addition, there are at least two one-man committees that have been established" (Daksh 2009, 9).

3. The failures of the BATF in the city of Bengaluru did not prevent the prime movers from claiming wider policy and institutional transformation—as Nilekani later claimed, "Many of our inputs went into the National Urban Renewal Mission [of 2005], which is trying to create an institutional framework for participation and accountability" ("Customers Want Us to Shape Their Business"). Interview with Nandan Nilekani, Co-Chairman, Infosys by Sebastian PT and Nandita Datta *Outlook Business Magazine* 2007, http://business.outlookindia.com/print.aspx? articleid=108&editionid=11&catgid=11&subcatgid=9, June 5, 2007, accessed January 18, 2012.

4. Sakrama Scheme Finally Gets the Nod. *Deccan Herald News Service*, December 3, 2009.

5.   Guv Checks Sakrama Bid. *Deccan Herald News Service*, January 10, 2010; Governor Urged to Promulgate Sakrama Ordinance, *Deccan Herald News Service*, January 13, 2010.

6.   The penalties have been categorized in terms of percentages of violation and are different for residential and non-residential structures. For violations in a residential structure there are two slabs: up to 25 percent and from 25 to 50 percent violation. The penalties for these are 10 percent and 25 percent respectively of the market value of the construction which is in violation of the rules and as determined by the Karnataka Stamp Act (Samuel Jacob, "Sakrama Throws Up More Questions than Answers," *Citizen Matters*, December 10, 2007, http://bangalore.citizenmatters.in/articles/view/48-civic-rwa-government-sakrama-throws-up-more-questions-than-answers-legalising-the-illegal).

7.   A. Yasmeen, Sakrama, Touts out to Make Money from Violations. *The Hindu*, November 13, 2007.

8.   "Customers Want Us to Shape Their Business." Interview with Nandan Nilekani, Co-Chairman, Infosys by Sebastian PT and Nandita Datta, *Outlook Business Magazine*, June 5, 2007, accessed January 18, 2010. Emphasis added.

9.   Benjamin is among the most consistent and rigorous of those who argue for the possibilities that have been generated by the loopholes of the law and by the regenerative qualities of local economies (see Benjamin 2000). For an extended argument on accumulation in the urban setting among the poor, see Benjamin and Bhuvaneswari (2001). On the damaging effects of large-scale land acquisitions enabled by planning on the prospects of the urban poor, see Ghosh (2006).

10. Even a book of insightful essays on the limits of the law focuses exclusively on the illegalities of the urban poor, thus the opening statement of the editors: "In the cities of Asia, Africa and Latin America the urban poor often have to step outside the law in order to gain access to land and housing" (Fernandes and Varley 1998, 1).

11. Indeed, reflecting on the periodic and frequent violence that broke out in the cities of Bengaluru and Mumbai, I had suggested that the terms 'law' and 'order' be delinked (see Nair 2008).

12. H. V. Lanchester noted a particularly "Indian way of being," which had aided, as much as it was aided by, the "lapse of effective local government during several centuries" which reduced "the larger towns to disorderly aggregations of dwellings, with inadequate communications and serious congestion in many quarters." He surmised,

> The segregation of caste groups and the tendency of families to remain together through several generations are two important factors conducive to this state of affairs . . . A shop or house throws out a verandah in front then closes it in, and later perhaps puts up another in front of that, besides filling up internal court-yards; and other forms of overbuilding. Only when the street was so narrowed that a single bullock cart began to knock corners off the houses did the process of reducing the highways to a minimum come to an end. (Lanchester 2007, 17–18)

13. Instead of acknowledging the deep-seated horror of activities associated with cleaning that have long been fostered by caste, and the ambiguous possibility of the emergence of civic sense, the Indian 'addiction' to dirt has been biologized. The newspaper item entitled "Do we have the Dirt Gene?" (*Times of India* 2009) was a response to the announcement by the environment minister Jairam Ramesh that India would win the Nobel Prize for filth: "Our cities are the dirtiest in the world." For those who have analyzed Indian proclivities in public spaces as rooted in a radically different cultural understanding of public/private, or indeed of the meaning of garbage (implying therefore the seeds of subaltern resistance as well), see especially Chakrabarty (1991); also Kaviraj (1997).

14. Narayani Gupta discusses the decision of authorities in post-mutiny Delhi to reduce the proposed defensive glacis around the Red Fort from a width of 500 yards to 450 yards, to exempt most of the Dariba where most of the 'loyal' Hindu merchants had their shops (Gupta 1991, 28). Similarly, Oldenberg (1984) shows us that despite attempts to centralize and segregate control of burial practices among Muslims at the Aishbag Cemetery in Lucknow, through which new standards of hygiene were introduced, after the rebellion of 1857, the upper classes were exempted from constraint. Mariam Dossal (1997, 49) remarks on the extraordinary tolerance of Parsi entrepreneur Jamsetjee Jeejeebhoy's illegalities since he had "contributed so largely to every object of public utility and charity" despite objections from colonial officials such as Henry Conybeare and Goldsmid. Such examples abound in studies of the colonial period.

References

ABIDe Governance. 2009. http://abidebengaluru.in/attachments/5/original/Govern _Bengaluru.pdf ABIDe Task Force Agenda. 2008. http://abidebengaluru.in/ attachments/1/original/plan_bengaluru_2020_agenda.pdf, accessed February 19, 2010.

Anand, N. 2011. Leaky States: The Politechnics of Water Supply in Mumbai. In *Urban Navigations: Politics, Space and the City in South Asia*, ed. J. Anjaria and C. McFarlane. 191–212. New Delhi: Routledge.

Appadurai, A. 2002. Deep Democracy: Urban Governmentality and the Horizon of Politics. *Public Culture*, 14 (1): 21–47.

———. 2003. Illusion of Permanence: Interview with Arjun Appadurai. *Perspecta*, 34: 44–52.

Azevedo, S. de.1998. Law and the Future of Urban Management in the Third World Metropolis. In *Illegal Cities: Law and Urban Change in Developing Countries*, ed. E. Fernandes and A. Varley. 258–73. London: Zed Books.

Balachandran, A. 2008. Of Corporations and Caste Heads: Urban Rule in Company Madras, 1640–1720. *Journal of Colonialism and Colonial History*, 9 (2):1–9.

Baviskar, A. 2003. Between Violence and Desire: Space, Power, and Identity in the Making of Metropolitan Delhi. *International Social Science Journal*, 55 (175): 89–98.

Benjamin, S. 2000. Governance, Economic Settings, and Poverty in Bangalore. *Environment and Urbanisation*, 12 (1): 35–56.

Benjamin, S., and R. Bhuvaneswari. 2001. Democracy, Inclusive Governance and Poverty in Bangalore. Urban Governance, Partnership and Poverty, Working Paper 26. International Development Department, University of Birmingham.

Bhattacharya, N. 2005. Notes Towards a Conception of the Colonial Public. In *Civil Society, Public Sphere and Citizenship: Dialogues and Perceptions*, ed. R. Bhargava and H. Reifeld. 130–148. Delhi: Sage Publications.

Chakrabarty, D. 1991. Open Space/Public Place: Garbage, Modernity and India. *South Asia: Journal of South Asian Studies*, 14 (1): 15–31.

Chandavarkar, R. 1994. Girangaon: The Social Organization of the Working-Class Neighbourhoods. In *The Origins of Industrial Capitalism in India: Business Strategies and the Working Classes in Bombay, 1900–1940*. 168–238. Cambridge: Cambridge University Press.

———. 1998. Workers' Politics and the Mill Districts in Bombay between the Wars. In *Imperial Power and Popular Politics: Class, Resistance and the State in India, c. 1850–1940*. 108–117. Cambridge: Cambridge University Press.

———. 2007. Customs of Governance: Colonialism and Democracy in Twentieth Century India. *Modern Asian Studies*, 41 (3): 441–470.

Chatterjee, P. 2001. On Civil and Political Society in Postcolonial Democracies. In *Civil Society: History and Possibilities*, ed. Sudipta Kaviraj and Sunil Khilnani. Cambridge: Cambridge University Press, 2001: 165–178.

———. 2004. Are Indian Cities Becoming Bourgeois at Last? In *Politics of the Governed: Reflections on Popular Politics in Most of the World*. 131–148. Delhi: Permanent Black.

———. 2008. Democracy and Economic Transformation in India. *Economic and Political Weekly*, 43 (16): 53–61.

———. 2009. A Postscript from Kolkata: An Equal Right to the City. In *Comparing Cities*, ed. K. Ali and M. Reiker. 304–324. Karachi: Oxford University Press.

Citizens' Action Forum. 2008. SAKRAMA for a New Equitable Law booklet. http://bangalore.citizenmatters.in/articles/view/64-civic-rwa-urban-planning-government-citizens-verdict-keep-sakrama-in-abeyance-bye-law-violations, accessed January 12, 2010.

Coelho, K., and T. Venkat. 2009. The Politics of Civil Society: Neighbourhood Associationism in Chennai. *Economic and Political Weekly*, 44 (26 and 27): 358–367.

Daksh. 2009. *People. Perceptions. Politics. Summary of the Report on Review of Democracy and Performance of the Government of Karnataka Period: Jun. 2008–Nov. 2009*. Bengaluru. http://www.dakshindia.org/Dec2009/Daksh%202009%20

Summary%2015%20December%202009%20_English_.pdf, accessed January 16, 2010.

Das, V. 2010. Citizenship as a Claim or Stories of Dwelling and Belonging among the Urban Poor. Dr B. R. Ambedkar Memorial Lecture. Delhi: Ambedkar University.

Dossal, M. 1997. *Imperial Designs and Indian Realities: The Planning of Bombay City 1845–1875*. Delhi: Oxford University Press.

Fernandes, E., and A. Varley, eds. 1998. *Illegal Cities: Law and Urban Change in Developing Countries*. London: Zed Books.

Ghosh, A. 2005. Public-Private or a Private Public? Promised Partnership of the Bangalore Agenda Task Force. *Economic and Political Weekly*, 40 (47): 4914–4922.

———. 2006. Banking on the Bangalore Dream. *Economic and Political Weekly*, 41 (8): 689–692.

Gooptu, N. 2001.*The Politics of the Urban Poor in Early Twentieth Century India*. Cambridge: Cambridge University Press.

Gupta, N. 1981. *Delhi Between the Empires*. New Delhi: Oxford University Press.

Hansen, T. 2002. *Urban Violence in India: Identity Politics, "Mumbai," and the Postcolonial City*. Delhi: Permanent Black.

———. 2005. Sovereigns Beyond the State: On Legality and Public Authority in India. *In Religion, Violence, and Political Mobilization in South Asia*, ed. R. Kaur. 109–144. New Delhi: Sage.

Harvey, D. 2008. The Right to the City. *New Left Review*, 53 (September–October): 23–40.

Heynes, D. E. 1991. *Rhetoric and Ritual in Colonial India: The Shaping of a Public Culture in Surat City, 1852–1928*. Berkeley and Los Angeles, CA: University of California Press.

Holston, J. 2008. *Insurgent Citizenship: Disjunctions of Democracy and Modernity in Brazil*. Princeton, Princeton University Press.

Idiculla, M. P. 2009. *The Delayed BBMP Elections And Governance Reforms in Bangalore*. Bengaluru: Centre for Budget and Policy Studies.

John, M. 2007. Women in Power? Gender, Caste and the Politics of Local Governance. *Economic and Political Weekly*, 42 (39): 3986–3995.

Joshi, C. 2003. *Lost Worlds: Indian Labour and its Forgotten Histories*. Delhi: Permanent Black.

Kaviraj, S. 1997. Filth and the Public Sphere: Concepts and Practices about Space in Calcutta. *Public Culture*, 10 (1): 83–113.

King, A. 1976. *Colonial Urban Development: Culture, Social Power, and Environment*. London; Boston, MA: Routledge and Kegan Paul.

Kosambi, M. 1980. *Bombay and Poona: A Socio-Ecological Study of Two Indian Cities, 1650–1900*. Stockholm: Stockholms Universitet.

Lama-Rewal, S. T. 2007. Neighbourhood Associations and Local Democracy: Delhi Municipal Elections 2007. *Economic and Political Weekly*, 42 (47): 51–60.

Lanchester, H. V. 2007 [1947]. Preface. In *Patrick Geddes in India*, ed. J. Tyrwhitt. Bangalore: Select Books.

Masselos, J. 2007. Power in the Bombay "Mohalla," 1904–1915. In *The City in Action: Bombay Struggles for Power*. 25–49. New Delhi: Oxford University Press.

McAuslan, P. 1998. Urbanisation, Law and Development. In *Illegal Cities: Law and Urban Change in Developing Countries*, ed. E. Fernandes and A. Varley. 18–52. London: Zed Books.

———. 1980. *The Ideology of Planning Law*. London; New York: Pergamon Press.

Mukherjee, S. N. 1970. Caste, Class and Politics in Calcutta, 1815–38. In *Elites in South Asia*, ed. E. Leach and S. N. Mukherjee. 33–78. Cambridge: Cambridge University Press.

Nair, J. 2005. *The Promise of the Metropolis: Bangalore's Twentieth Century*. New Delhi: Oxford University Press.

———. 2008a. Law and Disorder. *Economic and Political Weekly*, 43 (15): 16–17.

———. 2008b. *All In The Family? Gender, Caste and Power in an Indian Metropolis*. Amsterdam: SEPHIS.

———. 2010. Cantonment and Its Imagined Boundaries. Unpublished manuscript.

Nilekani, N. 2005. General K. S. Thimayya Memorial Lecture, December 17. http://www.genthimayya.org/nandantrans.html, accessed January 10, 2010.

Sebastian PT and Nandita Datta Interview with Nandan Nilekani. "Customers Want Us to Shape Their Business." Co-Chairman, Infosys by *Outlook Business Magazine* 2007. http://business.outlookindia.com/print.aspx?articleid=108&editionid=11&catgid=11&subcatgid=9.

Oldenburg, V. T. 1984. *The Making of Colonial Lucknow: 1856–1877*. Princeton, NJ: Princeton University Press.

Ong, A. 1999. *Flexible Citizenship: The Cultural Logics of Transnationality*. Durham and London: Duke University Press.

Pani, N., V. Vyasulu, and Tara Anand, 1985. Impact of Colonialism on the Economic Structure of Indian Cities: Bangalore 1800–1900. In *Essays on Bangalore*, Vol. I, ed. V. Vyasulu and Amulya Reddy. 1–34. Bangalore: Karnataka State Council for Science and Technology.

Ranganathan, M. 2011. Contested Waters: Associational Politics and Market Based Reforms at Bangalore's Periphery. In *Urban Navigations: Politics, Space and the City in South Asia*, ed. J. Anjaria and C. McFarlane. 165–190. Delhi: Routledge.

Ranganathan, M., L. Kamath, and V. Baindur. 2009. Piped Water Supply to Bangalore: Putting the Cart before the Horse? *Economic and Political Weekly*, 44 (33): 53–62.

Rao, P. V. L. S. and V. K. Tewari. 1979. *The Structure of the Indian Metropolis*. Bombay: Allied Publishers.

Ravindra A. et al. 1997. *The Committee on Urban Management of Bangalore City*. Report submitted to the Government of Karnataka.

Report of the Bangalore Development Committee. 1954. Bangalore: Government Press.

Report of the Expert Committee on Governance in the Bangalore Metropolitan Region and Bruhat Bangalore Mahanagara Palike. 2008. http://www.kuidfc.com/website/webpage.nsf/8f50067eff32acf3652574190040e0a2/0214c48af0

6bc65a652574190040ae1a/$FILE/Dr.%20Kasturirangan%20Committee%20
Report%20on%20BBMP.pdf, accessed January 20, 2010.

Roy, A. 2009. Why India Cannot Plan Its Cities. Informality, Insurgency, and the Idiom of Urbanization. *Planning Theory*, 8 (1): 76–87.

Sanyal, K. 2007. *Rethinking Capitalist Development: Primitive Accumulation, Governmentality, and Post-Colonial Capitalism*. Delhi: Routledge.

Sarin, M. 1982. *Urban Planning in the Third World: The Chandigarh Experience*. London: Mansell Publishing Limited.

Tindall, G. 2000. *City of Gold: the Biography of Bombay*. Delhi: Penguin.

Venkatarayappa, K. N. 1957. *Bangalore: A Socio-Ecological Study*. Bombay: University of Bombay.

Weber, M. 1958. *The City*. Ed. and trans. D. Martindale and G. Neuwirth. New York: Free Press.

Zerah, M. H. 2007. Middle Class Neighbourhood Associations as Political Players in Mumbai. *Economic and Political Weekly*, 42 (47): 61–68.

3
One Air, Two Interventions: Delhi in the Age of Environment

Awadhendra Sharan

Introduction

September 2010. Delhi slowly creeps towards hosting the Commonwealth Games in October, which will announce its arrival as a world city. China did it with the Olympics in 2008 and now it is Delhi's turn, albeit on a smaller scale. But not all is well. India's premier newspaper *The Times Of India*, which had once run the famous campaign "From Walled City to World City," has been opposing the Games for some time now, citing various corrupt deals that have led the city to be half-prepared at best. Stadiums with leaky roofs, widespread dengue and other diseases, and inadequately addressed security concerns do not quite make a world-class city. And there is something else worrying the government. A large advertisement in the prominent newspapers of the city seeks to draw the attention of industrial units to something more elusive:

> In order to reduce the air pollution in city of Delhi in view of forthcoming Common Wealth [*sic*] Games, Delhi Pollution Control Committee has decided to strictly regulate the operation of Emission Control System by Air Polluting Units.
>
> All the industrial units operating in conforming Industrial Areas and Notified Areas for Redevelopment as per MPD 2021 are hereby directed to install/operate air pollution control devices/emission control systems with immediate effect and ensure compliance with the standards stipulated under Environmental Acts/Laws. (Delhi Pollution Control Authority (DPCC) Public Notice, *The Indian Express*, September 12, 2010)

Delhi has been an Air Pollution Control Area since 1987. This advertisement, nearly quarter of a century later, must speak rather poorly of the policy measures that have evolved over this period to clean the city's air. But industries are not alone; indeed, they are not even the most significant air polluters, that ignominy being reserved for vehicular pollution, which contributes to nearly two-thirds of the city's pollution. Much has been done in regard to that too, though critics point to the sheer growth in numbers of vehicles on the roads and the persistent use of diesel in private vehicles which have successfully negated any gains (Rajamani 2007). Implementation failures have been the bane of India, argue the planners and, even more significantly, the Supreme Court (hereafter the court), resulting in this sad state of affairs (Rai and Shafi 1975; Verma 2002). Policies, in this view, have been correct but their impact has been distorted by poor executive action. Political economists, by contrast, point to the new wave of environmentalism as being at the expense of the urban poor, the constitutional imperative for clean air being exclusionary in practice rather than an expression of a politics of care. "For the bourgeois environmentalist," Amita Baviskar writes, "the ugliness of production must be removed from the city. Smokestack industries, effluent-producing manufacturing units and other aesthetically unpleasant sites that make the city a place of work for millions, should be discreetly tucked away out of sight, polluting some remote rural wasteland. So must workers who labour in these industries be banished out of sight" (Baviskar 2002, 41). Ghertner (this volume) draws attention to cultural politics and aesthetics in the making of the contemporary urban in which the evaluation of a desirable urban environment is framed within a 'world class city' fantasy. Gururani (also in this volume) points to the 'flexible' regime of planning which makes possible the simultaneous articulation of Delhi's suburban zone as a frontier zone of neoliberal capitalism and a classic example of 'problem' urbanization, that is, low on public infrastructure, high on crime. This is a city, in other words, being made by the middle class in its own image or in the image of a 'shining' other—London, New York, Paris, or (increasingly) Shanghai—in which the worlds of the poor have little legal recognition. Rene Vernon (2006), writing specifically about vehicular pollution, echoes their views. Delhi's vehicular air pollution measures, he suggests, may not have led to human displacements but have certainly led to the displacement of pollution, as those vehicles considered unsuitable for the country's capital increasingly find their place in the smaller cities. India's professional middle class, which is engaged in environmental and judicial activism, he suggests, have successfully pressured an oftentimes sluggish state to adopt and implement more rigorous urban environmental and planning policies, most of which reflect their class bias.

This chapter suggests a different reading of the contemporary city, one in which 'environment' has emerged as the new constitutive element of urban modernity, much as 'society' once was. Indeed there may be little exaggeration in suggesting that environmental safety is to the twenty-first-century city what welfare was to the twentieth. How do we understand this transformation, in which earlier concerns of waste and externalities (pollution) are conjoined with the challenges of global warming and climate change? How do we trace the pathways that will lead to a 'desirable' state of the environment? The 'walled city to world-class city' framing is one way of setting out to answer these questions. And yet, this may not entirely suffice for apprehending the risks and uncertainties that inform contemporary urbanism and anticipate its future. Much that we took for granted over two centuries of modernist rule—science, safety, justice—has come unstuck and offers little consolation in imagining the creation of more livable cities. We need a new vocabulary to describe and address both the risks and desires through which we seek to fashion the contemporary urban, one that permits the coming together of the social and the epistemological.

The cleaning of Delhi's air, I suggest, is a good instance of the unfolding of this new vocabulary, suggestive of two entirely different strategies for the production of the contemporary urban, one addressed to law (and illegality) and the other oriented towards precaution (and risk mitigation). Together, these strategies address the same problem, through the same court and through similar civic groups, but they do so in ways that suggest divergent paths for Delhi's urban and environmental future. Studying them is to underline not only the social relations of power in the city but also the epistemic frameworks that permit the articulation of notions of environmental risk and danger, safety and precaution, in the present and the near future.

Zoning and Expulsion

> Only those industrial processes which are almost non-polluting should
> be reserved for the small-scale sector or which have very cheap pollution
> control technologies available. The existing polluting units will just have
> to close down . . . Take all polluting processes to the large-scale sector,

which are relatively easier to control, and let them wipe out the polluting small-scale sector. The faster we do this, the less blood will be spilled later. (Agarwal 2007, 68)

In the mid-1980s, the lawyer-activist M. C. Mehta filed several petitions before the Supreme Court of India arguing that local authorities had failed to take necessary steps to protect the residents of the city from the harmful effects of pollution.[1] The dimensions of the problem were large and the language suitably apocalyptic—"the people living in Delhi were sitting on a volcano without knowing when it would erupt," Mehta petitioned.[2] The remedies sought were immediate and encompassing; the court was petitioned to pass necessary orders to ensure that hazardous units were shifted away from the city and that air pollution from stone crushing was stopped.

The history of hazardous/polluting industries and their location within and outside the city dates from the 1960s, when the first master plan of the city was drawn up. The key challenge facing the planners of Delhi was of urban chaos and haphazard developments in the wake of partition and the flow of refugees from across the newly minted borders of Pakistan and India (Datta 1986). Accordingly, the opening declaration of the Master Plan defined its purpose as "[t]o check the haphazard and unplanned growth of Delhi . . ." (DDA 1962a; DDA 1962b Vol. i, 1). Industry, characterized by fragmentation and dispersal, presented an equally chaotic picture. Many establishments, having rapidly grown over the course of just one decade, operated under conditions of overcrowding; several industries "though not excessively insanitary or unsafe" were not considered suitable for "well-rationalized and modern manufacturing activity" (DDA 1962a; DDA 1962b Vol. ii, 138). The problem, as the planners posed it to themselves, was to gather up the various industries, which varied in size from the huge Delhi Cloth Mills to the individual potter, and put them somewhere where they could function more efficiently while being less of a nuisance to the commercial and domestic life around them.[3]

The key to achieving this was the idea of zoning and a presumed distinction between noxious and non-noxious industries and conforming/non-conforming ones. Approximately 500 firms employing roughly 45,000 people were surveyed. Of the total land under small-scale industries, about 40 percent was reported to produce nuisance; the comparative figures for medium size and large-scale industry were 52 percent and 63 percent respectively.[4] Based on these figures, it was decided that certain industries—namely those associated with stench, smoke, fumes, etc., and posing hazards to those residing in their neighborhoods—were to be totally prohibited within the city (DDA1962a, 85). Large industries and those designated as rural were also considered to be best located outside the city (DDA1962a, 75, 83; DDA1962b Vol. i,188). For those left behind, proper zoning was recommended. Tempered by the economic realities of Delhi, the locations being recommended were of an intermediate type, breaking substantially with existing mixed land-uses and sub-standard factory conditions without resulting in the relocation of all factory establishments to areas distant from the central city (DDA 1962a, 44). Several different types of industrial establishments were proposed. First among these were flatted factories, multistoried buildings with high-density employment which could house many of the small industries that operated in commercial areas. These were to be located in the central area of Delhi. Corresponding to these, but located in the outlying areas and with lesser intensity of use, was a proposal for industrial-cum-work centers (DDA 1962a, 17–18). No nuisance industries were to be allowed in these zones, and each industry to be permitted was to be subject to performance requirements concerning noise, vibration, smoke, dust, odor, effluent, and general nuisance (DDA 1962a, 76). By contrast, some exceptions were to be made in areas earmarked for extensive industrial development, where all the noxious industries that had been located in the residential areas were to be relocated, even if they were small, so long as they met performance standards to keep disruption to a minimum (DDA 1962a, 20–21). Those that conformed to these location policies were also to be distinguished from the non-conforming industries, the latter being defined as those in contravention of the proposed regulations in a particular use zone, i.e. those that would not be permitted in the particular location after the Plan had come into effect. Once again there was an exception—uses of lands and buildings that were lawfully established prior to the enactment of the zoning regulations but which were 'non-conforming' would not be prohibited outright. In the absence of strong incentives to move out and adequate provision of new space, the Plan proposed, "the vigorous enforcement of regulations alone would have large adverse effects in curtailing industrial employment" (DDA 1962a; DDA 1962b Vol. ii, 138).

In sum, non-conforming industries, with the possible exception of some industries listed under the extensive industrial zone, could not be conflated with noxious industries. Nuisance implied expulsion from the city;

non-confirmation implied their gradual move towards appropriate location within the city through fiscal and other incentives, guided by the need to retain significant industrial employment in the city (DDA 1962a, 44). The key in Delhi, as had happened elsewhere, would be to distinguish between traditional industries (dyeing, dairy, etc.) that could be more easily expelled, and modern industry, for which the bar of being a nuisance was raised much higher and therefore the possibility of remaining within the city was much higher![5]

The city, however, refused to yield to this fiction of an absolute distinction between non-conforming and noxious industries. Syed Shafi (1965), writing soon after the Plan came into effect, upheld the basic principle of land-use planning, but then went on to point out that according to a survey of noxious industries carried out by the Delhi Development Authority (DDA), it was found that out of the 9,860 licensed firms, 5,345 or 54.2 percent were non-noxious or non-nuisance types. Moreover, a large number of the noxious industries were in fact so-called 'industrial shops,' and could not be considered, given their small size and the service nature of their operation, to be manufacturing units. Many of them also had very small turnovers and in most cases their workers lived in the immediate vicinity. In most cases, the 'industrial shops' were also located within the housing premises of the owners, sourcing raw materials locally and also selling their products in nearby wholesale markets. For all these reasons, until a satisfactory solution was devised for these units, it "would be virtually impossible to clear the blighted areas" (Shafi 1965, 144).

The mid-term review of the plan, conducted roughly a decade later, observed that though the situation was better than in the pre-plan period, significant difficulties still remained. Shifting of non-conforming industries or trades had not made much headway nor had a single flatted factory been built, leading to a further deterioration of conditions in living areas. The most debilitating fate was that of the old city where there continued to be "the percolation of all kinds of noxious activities and trades in areas once meant for noble and graceful living" (Government of India (GoI), Town and Country Planning Organisation (TCPO) 1973/1995, 9). Even more radically, the review suggested that some of the assumptions of the plan were out of sync with the realities of the city, suggesting that a substantial proportion of economic activities in the city were in the unorganized sector and were being carried out in a manner that was not amenable to the typically Western planning approach based on complete functional segregation. It would be long before this segment of the economy was completely eliminated, if at all, and it was only reasonable, the review suggested, that appropriate adjustments in land uses be made, consistent with felt needs (GoI, TCPO 1973/1995, 33–34).

Master Plans, however, are not necessarily the most reflexive documents. The next plan for the city, notified in 1990, made appropriate noises about taking into consideration just such an altered reality, pointing to the massive growth of the industrial sector since 1975, especially in electrical goods and electronics, and in rubber, plastic, and petroleum products (DDA 1990/96, 9). It recognized too that according to existing regulations, "a large number of existing industrial units would be non-conforming" (DDA 1990/96, 9). But none of this stood in the way of its replication of the recommendations of the previous plan. Expulsion of the especially noxious industries as well as some measures for the containment of pollution in the industrial units left behind in the city once again formed the backbone of the twin strategy. Hazardous and noxious industries, together with heavy and large industries were not to be permitted in the city. Extensive industries were to be permitted only in already identified industrial areas, with existing non-conforming industries to be relocated to these within three years. Light and service industries were also to be permitted, with the non-conforming industries of this type being relocated to appropriate industrial zones within three to five years. Household industries could only comprise non-polluting industries (DDA 1990/96, 9–11).

The plan was not intended to be a document about how pollution, inside or outside the city, was to actually be curbed, nor did it suggest anything beyond appropriate location policies. There was one exception though. There were reportedly eighty-two water polluting industrial units in Delhi, about which the plan recommended that "these units should make individual/ joint arrangements for treatment of the effluent. About 30 percent of these units which are located in other than industrial areas should be immediately shifted to the industrial areas" (DDA 1990, 16). For official planners, and indeed for some independent observers, it was not the plan that was in error, but those who sought exception from it (Verma 2002). In its response to Mehta's petition, the court made reference to these planning guidelines. In March 1995 it directed the Central Pollution Control Committee to issue individual notices to 8,378 industries indicating that they were "polluting

industries and . . . operating in non-conforming areas in violation of the
Delhi Master Plan."[6] To this, more were added bringing the number to 9,164.
In August, an affidavit filed by the government of India stated that out of
these industries, 1,557 were operating in non-conforming use zones, out
of which 170 industries were in category H (highly polluting) and needed
to be relocated out of Delhi, while 1,387 belonged to groups which required
relocation within the city, in conforming use zones. In September that same
year the justices granted six weeks to the Delhi Pollution Control Committee
(DPCC) to "adopt any method to complete the necessary survey and place
before this Court a complete list of hazardous industries."[7] The DPCC duly
filed the list of H (a) and H (b) industries in November, which was subject to
instant dispute by the units concerned. In the meantime, the immediate list
of H-category industries was arrived at, numbering 168, which were directed
to stop functioning and operating in Delhi with effect from November 30,
1996 and were to relocate themselves to any other industrial estate in the
National Capital Region (NCR).

These were not the only numbers in play, a survey conducted by the Delhi
government stating that there were 93,000 industries operating in non-
conforming use zones, located in unauthorized colonies, urban villages,
resettlement colonies, the walled city, and other residential pockets (GoI,
Ministry of Environment and Forests [MoEF] 1997, Ch. 6).[8] In December
1995 a note prepared by the National Capital Regional Planning Board
was placed before the court making a clear distinction between hazardous/
polluting and non-confirming industries and their spatial relocation:

(i) If the industries were non-polluting, they would be accommodated in
the regular planned industrial areas/estates/zones already developed
or under development in the NCR by the concerned authorities of the
respective state.

(ii) In case of industries currently listed as polluting/hazardous:
When these industries are set up at their new location and they
improve their technology and if they no longer remain polluting
or hazardous, they can be located in regular planned areas. If such
industries continue to remain polluting special industries zones
could be created so that they do not adversely affect the living environment in the vicinity and such industrial zones to have special
infrastructure facilities to take care of the pollutants and provide
protective belts around them to mitigate the effect of polluting effluents, smoke, gases, noises etc.; and any accidental release thereof.
(WP 4677, August 7, 1996)

More followed over the next few months and years. In September 1996 the court ordered the closing down of 513 industries and their relocation outside Delhi by January 31, 1997 (Lok Sabha 1996). The next month it ordered the closure of forty-six hot-mix plants. A month later brick kilns were added to the list of H-category industries (SCI WP 4677, November 26, 1996). Things were in a lull for a while thereafter, before the court intervened again, citing the tardy implementation of its orders on the part of the local administration. In September 1999, it ordered that if industries in residential areas could not be shifted or relocated for any reason by December of that year, then these must cease to function (SCI WP 4677, May 7, 2004). The state government asked for an extension of the deadline on the plea that a large number of industrial units, and with them the workers and their families, stood to be affected (SCI WP 4677, May 7, 2004).[9] However, this was declined. Twenty-seven polluting industries that included those listed in category F—acids and chemicals, dyeing and bleaching, electroplating, etc.— were asked to stop operations by January 4, 2001, while December 31, 2001 was fixed as the date by which all non-conforming industries would have to cease operations in the city.[10] However, the numbers were yet uncertain, the court itself observing, in the context of the demand for *in situ* regularization (below):

> . . . regarding the total number of industrial units functioning in residential/ non-conforming areas, different surveys have given different figures . . . the nature of survey that had been conducted resulting in the proposal of INSITU regularization . . . is neither scientific nor precise nor reliable. It does not even contain detailed particulars of industries— whether they are polluting or non-polluting, licensed or unlicensed. (SCI WP 4677, May 7, 2004)

The closure of industries, it followed, was also the cause of insecurity for workers. The political significance of this was not lost on the major political parties. The opposition party accused the Delhi government of having failed to develop the necessary infrastructure and, more critically, of having misrepresented the court's order and created panic by confusing polluting industries with non-conforming ones. Both the local ruling and opposition party took issue with the attitude of the urban development minister of the central government who believed that acting in a manner which ran contrary to the Master Plan was a recipe for disaster.[11] For both, the political strategy behind simultaneously obeying the court's orders and ensuring that industry did not suffer was to make a case for redesignating those residential units which had 70 percent or more housing industrial units as industrial areas.[12] The court worried about the 32,000 industries which would not be covered by *in situ* regularization, not to mention the 30 percent of residents who were legal and would suffer for no fault of their own (SCI WP 4677, May 7, 2004).[13] In a famous echo of the judgment which had ruled that giving land to squatters was like rewarding pickpockets, the case of non-conforming industries also drew the court's ire: "The changes in the Master Plan or its norms to accommodate illegal activities not only amount to giving reward for illegal activities but also results in punishing the law abiding citizens" (SCI WP 4677, May 7, 2004).

Mehta, the original petitioner, returned to defend his case in public. Environmental security, he argued, was not the cause of economic and livelihood insecurity; on the other hand to permit the functioning of polluting and non-conforming industries was a call to lawlessness, in no less a place than the nation's capital (*Rashtriya Sahara* 2000).[14] And on the all-important question of pollution and new health burdens elsewhere, he argued that "indeed there will be dangers there too [in Bawana, Narela, and other areas where industries were to be relocated]. Therefore while relocating these industries adequate means to tackle the pollution caused by them should be developed" (*Rashtriya Sahara* 2000). The government periodically responded by pointing to the facilities at the new industrial estates to tackle pollution, industrialists periodically bemoaned the absence of adequate facilities, and critics raised serious doubts as to whether common effluent treatment plants and other such measures had the necessary technical and regulatory capacities to tackle pollution from mixed wastes flowing from multiple sources.

Taming Pollution

> At least theoretically, controlling pollution from industry is easier. There are numerous technologies . . . that can help reduce factory pollution . . . If that is not possible, pollution controllers can simply insist on relocating the plant . . . *But a city is stuck with its vehicles. They stay with the city and the city lives with them. Thus, they have to be tamed to cut down on the pollution.* (CSE 1996, 8, emphasis in original)

In addition to the failure of the government to regulate hazardous and noxious industries, Mehta's petitions had also mentioned the problems associated with vehicular pollution. There were reportedly 800,000 motor vehicles operating in the city, with a further 80,000 new ones being registered each year. More than 70,000 vehicles entered the capital every day from the neighboring state. Additionally, there were over 1 million bicycles, 60,000 cycle rickshaws, and 4,000 handcarts that plied in the city, all of which contaminated the air. Consequently permissible limits were exceeded for carbon monoxide, hydro-carbons, nitrogen oxide, sulfur dioxide, and suspended particulate matter, which were often toxic in character and carried the possibility of causing brain diseases and respiratory ailments. Almost all diesel power trucks and tempos were reported to have smoke densities far above the permissible limit. In light of this, the petitioner prayed that the Delhi Administration and the Delhi Transport Corporation (DTC) be directed to take action against owners of vehicles that emitted noxious gases and smoke.

Things moved rather slowly at first. An Air (Prevention and Pollution) Act had been legislated in 1981 that defined an air pollutant as "any solid, liquid or gaseous substance present in the atmosphere in such concentration as may be or tend to be injurious to human beings or other living creatures or plants or property or environment" (GoI MoEF 1981). The authorisation for dealing with such pollution was also clearly laid out, with the Central Pollution Control Board (CPCB) being asked to advise, plan, and help execute plans for the prevention and control of air pollution. For this purpose, the CPCB was to collect, compile, and publish data relating to air pollution and the measures devised for its effective prevention; prepare manuals, codes or guides for the same; and lay down standards for the quality of air. The CPCB responded with a National Ambient Air Quality Monitoring (NAAQM) Network, to measure pollutants such as suspended particulate matter (SPM), respirable suspended particulate matter (RSPM), sulfur dioxide (SO2), nitrogen oxide (NOx), and carbon monoxide (CO). Such "measuring and understanding air pollution provid[ing]," in its own words, "a sound scientific basis for its management and control" (CPCB 2009).

In 1987, the Air Act was amended, strengthening the enforcement machinery, imposing stiffer fines on violators and introducing a citizen's initiative provision (Divan 2000). Around the same time, the Delhi administration began an education drive to encourage owners to have their vehicles voluntarily checked for emissions. There were also major crackdowns on vehicles emitting excessive exhaust.[15] Ambient air quality standards for Delhi were introduced, even as the World Health Organization declared Delhi to be the fourth most polluted city in the world in terms of SPM. Soon thereafter, a monitoring committee on ambient and automotive emission levels was set up to examine the impact of surface transport on the state of air in Delhi (SCI WP 13029, March 14, 1991). The court also set up a special committee under the chairmanship of retired Justice Saikia to examine the issue in detail. Among the recommendations of the Saikia Committee was the use of compressed natural gas (CNG) as an alternative fuel, on the grounds that it polluted less, cost less, and was more widely available in the country than petrol or diesel.

Once again, there was a lull until the Supreme Court directed the central government to set up a new statutory committee to be called the Environment Pollution (Prevention and Control) Authority (EPCA) under the provisions of the Environment Protection Act, 1986. The committee was duly established in April 1998 and tasked with monitoring the progress of the *White Paper on Pollution in Delhi*, that dealt with environmental issues pertaining to the NCR, and also to serve as a fact-finding body for the court. Specifically with respect to vehicular pollution the government mandated that the EPCA would "take all necessary steps to ensure compliance of specified emission standards by vehicles including proper calibration of the equipment for testing of vehicular pollution, ensuring compliance of fuel quality standards, monitoring and coordinating action for traffic management and planning" (GoI, MoEF 1998). In its very first progress report, the EPCA suggested additional pollution policies for Delhi that built on the action plans of the Delhi administration and the central government, but were possibly bolder and more specific (Bell et al. 2004). Whereas the other plans had talked about encouraging the use of clean fuels in public transportation, the EPCA proposed switching all taxis and autorickshaws to a clean fuel, banning all eight-year-old buses except those on clean fuel, and gradually moving the entire bus fleet to a single clean fuel—CNG. Its recommendations gained immediate legal backing with the court ruling on July 28, 1998 that no bus more than eight years old could operate in the city except on CNG or other clean fuels after April 1, 2000, and that the entire fleet of city buses, public and private, be converted to single fuel mode on CNG by March 31, 2001.[16]

The court's order elicited some compliance and much foot dragging. The transport minister of Delhi reportedly assured the residents of the city that all buses would soon operate on either CNG or propane.[17] On the other hand, the chief minister, while flagging the first 'non-polluting' CNG bus on June 24, 1999, also expressed some reservations about the possibility of meeting the court's imposed deadline.[18] And as the deadline of March 31, 2001 drew nearer, the protests of those who stood to be affected grew sharper. Once again Delhi faced the prospect of chaos and violence (Rajalakshmi 2001). But the court was not in the mood to oblige or condone. All the reasons placed before it seeking further postponement, it reasoned, were mere excuses designed to frustrate its efforts with no satisfactory explanation offered by either the administration or the private transporters as to why they had not pointed to their difficulties earlier. Not surprisingly, the court refused to give a blanket extension, though it did hold out some exceptions for those who had made demonstrable efforts to convert (SCI WP 13029, March 26, 2001). Those in favor of diesel, however, continued to make pleas before the court and outside it. In a bid to bring a closure to this simmering dispute, the court, in its order dated March 26, 2001, issued the following directions to the Bhure Lal Committee:

> During the course of the argument, it was contended before us that low sulphur diesel should be regarded as a clean fuel and buses be permitted to run on that. It was submitted that in some other countries ultra low sulphur diesel which has sulphur content of not more than 0.001 per cent is now available. We direct the Bhure Lal Committee to examine this question . . . The Committee may submit a report to this Court in that behalf as also indicate as to which fuel can be regarded as "clean fuel", which does not cause pollution or is otherwise injurious to health. (SCI WP 13029, March 26, 2001)

Several parties presented their views before the Bhure Lal Committee, almost unanimously in favor of low sulfur diesel and against the adoption of a single fuel (EPCA 2001, 26–37). Specters of high costs, unreliable and insecure supply, and technology lock-in were raised. Simultaneously, positive improvements in the quality of diesel and petrol since the original order of July 1998 were pointed to, within an overall argument that advocated mixed fleets and the setting up of emission standards based on available or anticipated technologies, rather than the use of specific fuels. The committee rebutted each of these, once again making a strong case for CNG, as part of a fifteen-point integrated approach for tackling vehicular pollution in the city.[19] The most critical factor, it argued, was the public health burden on account of air pollution in Delhi, especially the presence of RSPM that was less than 10 micron in size in the ambient air. Any cost-benefit analysis, in its view, had to take into account not only the future costs of CNG but also the countervailing health costs of air pollution, for which unfortunately no estimates were yet available.[20] The committee also felt that there were no major problems regarding CNG distribution infrastructure or the security of CNG supply that could not be speedily redressed. And on the specific issue of the relative merits of petrol, diesel, CNG, and other fuels, the report suggested that the definition of "clean fuel" needed to be addressed in the context of the quality of fuels available, availability of emission control technologies, prevailing environmental considerations, and existing knowledge of health pollutants. Taking these into account, it observed that "among the hydrocarbon fuels, which were commonly used for automobiles, it was not possible to specify a 'clean fuel' which did not cause pollution or was not otherwise injurious to health . . . [though] fuels like CNG, LPG and propane . . . were less polluting" (EPCA 2001, 10–13). In the process, the committee also changed the terminology from 'clean fuel' to 'environmentally acceptable fuel,' which itself became an issue of debate. More critically, the single fuel approach was opposed at other levels.

In September 2001 the government of India constituted a committee of experts of national repute headed by R. A. Mashelkar, director general of the Council of Scientific and Industrial Research (CSIR) to:

> Recommend an Auto Fuel Policy for major cities and rest of the country, to devise a roadmap for its implementation, and recommend suitable auto fuels, automobile technologies and fiscal measures for ensuring minimization of the social cost of meeting environmental quality and institutional mechanisms for certification of vehicles, fuels as also monitoring and enforcement measures. (GoI MoEF 2001, 1)

The committee's guiding principles were not very different from those of the ECPA, with public health being cited as a prime concern at the very outset. Air quality, the Mashelkar Committee opined, again perhaps not very differently from the ECPA, depended upon several factors, of which vehicular pollution was one important component. Vehicular pollution, in turn, depended upon several factors, of which the specific choice of fuels was one. From here however, the paths diverged significantly, with the Mashelkar Committee suggesting that "evidence based analysis backed up by scientifically backed data, especially under Indian conditions, ought to be the cornerstone of any sound policy" and went on to add that "rather than a rigid and prescriptive policy, a flexible policy, which allows a multi-fuel and multi-technology option for reaching prescribed emission norms, was considered desirable" (GoI MoEF 2001, 2). In the absence of adequate data related to emission source apportionment, emission inventory etc., the committee suggested it was not possible to set vehicular emission norms based on air quality targets alone (GoI MoEF 2001, 4). And with regard to auto fuels, it was of the view that tailpipe emissions, and not the fuel per se, affected the ambient air quality. Therefore any combination of engine technology and fuel that gave the prescribed vehicular emission norms needed to be considered acceptable from the environmental angle (GoI MoEF 2001, 5). In a clear difference from the ECPA's recommendations, the interim report concluded:

> In the developed world and elsewhere, vehicular emission standards and auto fuel quality necessary to meet the standards alone are prescribed, giving choice to the public, manufacturers, owners and operators of motor vehicles to choose the vehicle type and the fuel. The Committee recommends that the same policy be adopted for India. (GoI MoEF 2001, 11)

The CNG saga had begun in the fond hope of an eventual consensus, with the court's request to the counsels being to look at the problem "not as an adversarial litigation but to come forward with useful deliberations so that something concrete could finally emerge for easing the situation" (SCI WP 13029, March 14, 1991). But by the next decade, it was quite evident that policy on the basis of scientific consensus was near impossible to achieve. The Mashelkar report was immediately accepted by the government but drew quick criticisms too.[21] The court too was far from being satisfied. It not only suspected the motives for setting up this committee but also observed, notwithstanding the long list of experts, "the composition of the Mashelkar Committee was such that none of its members was either a doctor, or an expert, in public health. The said committee submitted its report which does not show any serious concern with the health of the people" (SCI WP 13029, April 5, 2002). Disputations no longer remained confined to courtrooms either, with scientific experts and non-specialists alike engaging in intense media debates on the nature of evidence in favor of one or the other technology, economic costs and practical futures, technological capacities, patterns of mobility, funding and interests and challenges of public health, all of which made evident the many-fold nature of the differences that underpinned this debate.[22] Disputes in print and on television were not enough either, the very bodies of the buses becoming a medium for defining a "clean fuel" with the adjective "pollution free" painted before CNG on the new bus fleet of the capital being wiped out, on the argument that no fuel was 100 per cent pollution free![23]

'Thin,' uncertain data, as evident in the contending viewpoints, eventually led the court to the articulation of a different mode of reasoning, marshaling health-based evidence of the perils of pollution while simultaneously taking recourse in the 'precautionary principle.' As explained by the court, the 'precautionary' and 'polluter pays' principles were both necessary components of ecologically sustainable development and within the ambit of Indian laws. What this implied was that the government and the statutory authorities must anticipate, prevent, and attack the causes of environmental degradation and where there were threats of serious and irreversible damage, lack of scientific certainty should not be used as a reason for postponing measures to prevent environmental degradation. In the specific case of automobiles, where environmental implications were bound to be present in any auto policy, it was even more imperative that even in the absence of adequate information, they lean in favor of cleaner technologies and refuse rather than permit activities likely to be detrimental to human health. Emission norms had been in place for a very long time without any appreciable record of compliance. Under the circumstances, for the Mashelkar Committee and those inclined to its point of view, to recommend that the role of the government be limited to specifying norms was naïve at best and a "clear abdication of the constitutional and statutory duty cast upon the Government to protect and preserve the environment," at worst (SCI WP 13029, April 5, 2002). So far as the court was concerned "it is clear that the alternative fuel of CNG, LPG and electricity is a preferred technology which critically polluted cities like Delhi need as a leapfrogging technological option" (SCI WP 13029, April 5, 2002). It therefore had no hesitation in reconfirming that "our order dated 28.7.1998 with regard to conversion of entire city bus fleet (DTC and private) to single fuel mode of CNG does not require any modification or change. That direction stands" (SCI WP 13029, April 5, 2002).

This was a fairly new line of approach, drawing upon international customary law. As a guide to policy and action, it offered a different orientation to the more familiar assimilative capacity approach that had guided development for much of the twentieth century. Simply stated, the assimilative capacity approach assumed that science could accurately predict threats to the environment; it could provide technical solutions to mitigate such threats once they had been accurately predicted, and there would be sufficient time to act while making the most efficient utilization of scarce financial resources (McIntyre and Mosedale 1997, 222). Failures of this approach, with conclusive scientific proof of the detrimental effects of activities or substances coming too late, the argument runs, have led, on a sector by sector basis, to the adoption of a precautionary approach, a bias in favor of safety and caution. The 1992 Rio Declaration on Environment and Development, among other international conventions, formalized the principle. "In order to protect the environment, the precautionary approach shall be widely applied by States according to their capabilities. Where there are threats of serious or irreversible damage, lack of full scientific certainty shall not be used as a reason for postponing cost-effective measures to prevent environmental degradation."[24] The adoption of the precautionary principle, however, was not the abandonment of credible information or scientific data, with every major statement on it continuing to argue that states must continue to cooperate in research and act in a manner so as to obtain and share the best possible scientific evidence available, thereby leading to better decision-making (McIntyre and Mosedale 1997, 239–241). More science, John Adams (1997) writes, would not harm. However, and this is what a precautionary approach brought in its wake, far more important were the inferences based on what we do know. And it is in drawing our attention towards this perspective—being biased in favor of health impacts, even if greater harms from particular substances (diesel) could not be fully established vis-à-vis others (CNG), rather than sound policy backed by credible evidence, as suggested by the Mashelkar Committee—that the court offered a new and innovative mechanism for taming air pollution in Delhi.

Conclusion

Exile and taming, I have argued, have been two different modalities of dealing with air pollution. In the case of industrial pollution, the court has favored the former, while drawing a distinction between non-conforming and polluting units, and within these, between 'rural' and 'modern' industries. This strategy, I suggest, is addressed more to law than to environment and the confusion of the two categories, non-conforming/polluting, I have argued, has led to enormous socio-political conflict without necessarily yielding a cleaner or safer environment. Developing detailed strategies of pollution control was neither the purpose of the plan nor does it seem to be the most useful in this regard. And even if the plan were to be followed in letter and spirit, I argue, it remains to be asked whether it is still desirable to manage work and life in our cities through zoning (and exile), given the additional energy burdens it entails, while serving no greater purpose than to merely redistribute locally sourced risks of industrial production (Gleeson 2000).

In the instance of vehicular pollution, the question is configured differently. It is one of our relationships with an expert-led science-for-society mode of thinking, in times of radical uncertainty: the "skilled scientific distillation" of environmental problems, such as impacts of air pollution on health, "for non-specialist users, such as policy makers and public audience" to act upon (Scott and Barnett 2009). This is not simply to rehearse the old question of the relationship between technical experts and political/bureaucratic power (MacLeod 1988). Rather, it is to ask new questions about the manner in which we make democratic choices in an increasingly complex and conflicted technological world, one in which the scientific disputes are not easily contained/resolved within committee rooms and court chambers but are possibly magnified even further through mediatization and articulation in the public domain (Leiss 2001). Many commentators, who have otherwise differed on their assessments of CNG and diesel as the preferred fuel, have echoed each other in upholding the banner of science. However, what the court's intervention has suggested is not the certainty and prestige of science but the articulation of another principle—the precautionary principle—through which we may anticipate and prevent irreversible damage and thereby hope to create a safer and more sustainable future.

Notes

1.   On the career of public interest litigation in India, see Sathe (2002).

2. M. C. Mehta V. Government of India and Others, Writ Petition (Civil) 4677, Supreme Court of India, 1985.

3. A. Aptay and Jhabvala, Why a Master Plan for Delhi. *Hindustan Times*, August 21, 1960.

4. Weekly Report, Sept. 30–Oct. 12, 1957, Albert Mayer (AM) Papers, Box 23, Folder 11, University of Chicago, Special Collections.

5. On this distinction between modern and traditional industries when considered as nuisance, see Christine Rosen (2003).

6. Supreme Court of India (SCI). Writ Petition (Civil) (WP) 4677, August 7, 1996.

7. SCI. Writ Petition (Civil) (WP) 4677, August 7, 1996.

8. There is some inconsistency in the official numbers, as reported from time to time. The court's judgment of May 2004 mentions that the survey conducted by the DPCC in 1995–96 showed that there were approximately 126,000 industrial units in Delhi, of which 101,000 were in non-conforming areas. Supreme Court of India (SCI). Writ Petition (Civil) (WP) 4677, May 7, 2004.

9. The argument offered by the government was that close to 700,000 workers stood to be affected if these industries were closed. SCI WP 4677, May 7, 2004.

10. A monitoring committee was appointed to oversee that these orders were executed and that illegal industrial activity in Delhi was stopped.

11. Factories Near Homes to go by Dec 31. *Hindustan Times*, December 4, 2002.

12. DDA Decides Not to Close Industries. *Hindustan Times*, December 21, 2002; Small Units to Stay in Colonies. *Hindustan Times*, January 29, 2003; Panel to Study Change of Land Use in 24 Areas. *Times of India*, February 4, 2003.

13. The court also drew attention to the fact that the plea for *in situ* regularization did not even exclude industries such as electroplating, dyeing, pickling, anodizing, forging, and casting that were polluting in nature. SCI WP 4677, May 7, 2004.

14. *Mauzuda Sthiti ke Liye Prashashan va Sarkar Doshi* [Government and Administration Responsible for Current Situation]. *Rashtriya Sahara*, November 28, 2000.

15. SCI. Writ Petition (Civil) (WP) 13029, November 14, 1990.

16. There were several other recommendations which did not witness as much controversy. See, SCI WP 13029, order dated July 28, 1998.

17. *Parivahan mantri ne kaha, dilli mein propane busein chaliyi jayengi* [Transport minister says that Delhi will introduce propane run buses].

18. *Pradushan mukt bus ka chalna shuru* [Pollution free buses start plying]. *Hindustan Times*, June 25, 1999.

19. For the comprehensive list of suggestions, see *Report on Clean Fuels* (EPCA 2001, 9–10).

20. The only available estimation was one arrived at by the World Bank in 1991–92 that estimated it to be to the tune of Rs. 10 billion per annum for Delhi. See *Report on Clean Fuels* (EPCA 2001, 5).

21. Mashelkar Report Accepted by the Ministry, Says Ram Naik. *Asian Age*, January 7, 2002; More Flak for Mashelkar, Report Goes to Cabinet. *Times of India*, January 8, 2002.
22. Acrimonious debates among scientific experts, Anthony Giddens and others have argued, are a major reason for the distrust of official scientific institutions in contemporary Western societies. The view is contested by Brian Wynne who argues instead that even in the earlier stage of "simple modernity" there was a culture of distrust and alienation with respect to scientific and technological interventions. See Wynne (2004).
23. CNG and "Pollution Free" Can't Go Hand-in-Hand. *The Statesman*, September 5, 2001.
24. Rio Declaration, cited in Lesley McAllister (2005, 154).

References

Adams, J. 1997. *Risk*. London: Routledge.
Agarwal, A. 2007. Delhi's Latest Environmental Fix. In *Anil Agarwal Reader 03*. 67–68. Delhi: Centre for Science and Environment.
Baviskar, A. 2002. The Politics of the City. *Seminar*, 516: 40–42.
Bell, R. G., K. Mathur, U. Narain, and D. Simpson. 2004. Clearing the Air: How Delhi Broke the Logjam on Air Quality Reforms. *Environment*, 46 (3): 22–39.
Central Pollution Control Board (CPCB). 2009. *National Ambient Air Quality Status 2008*.
Centre for Science and Environment (CSE). 1996. *Slow Murder. The Deadly Story of Vehicular Pollution in India*. Delhi: CSE.
Datta, V. N. 1986. Punjabi Refugees and Greater Delhi. In *Delhi Through the Ages. Essays in Urban History, Culture and Society*, ed. R. E. Frykenberg. 442–462. Delhi: Oxford University Press.
Delhi Development Authority (DDA). 1962a. *Master Plan of Delhi*. Delhi: DDA
———. 1962b. Master Plan of Delhi 1962. *Work Studies*, Vol. i and ii. Delhi: DDA.
———. 1990 (Reprint 1996). *Master Plan of Delhi*, 2001. Delhi: DDA.
Delhi Pollution Control Authority (DPCC). Public Notice. *The Indian Express*, September 12, 2010.
Divan, S. 2000. Legislative Framework and Judicial Craftsmanship, *Seminar* 492: 67–74.
Environment Pollution (Prevention and Control) Authority for the National Capital Region (EPCA). 2001. *Report on Clean Fuels*. http://cpcb.nic.in/divisionsofhead-office/pci3/02_Clean_fuels_report.pdf, accessed January 24, 2012.
Gleeson, B. 2000. Reflexive Modernization. The Re-Enlightenment of Planning? *International Planning Studies*, 5 (1): 117–135.

Government of India (GoI), Town and Country Planning Organisation (TCPO). 1973/1995. *Review of the Master Plan of Delhi*, Delhi: TCPO.

Government of India (GoI), Ministry of Environment and Forests (MoEF). 1997. *White Paper on Pollution in Delhi with an Action Plan*. Delhi: GoI. http://moef.nic. in/divisions/cpoll/delpolln.html, accessed January 24, 2012.

———. 1998. *Constitution of the Environment Pollution (Prevention and Control) Authority for the Ncr*. Delhi: GoI. http://envfor.nic.in/legis/ncr/ncrauthority.pdf, accessed January 24, 2012.

———. 2001. *Interim Report of the Expert Committee on Auto Fuel Policy*. Delhi: GoI

Leiss, W. 2001. *In the Chamber of Risks: Understanding Risk Controversies*. Montreal, QC: McGill-Queen's University Press.

Lok Sabha. 1996. *Lok Sabha Debates*, November 28.

MacLeod, R. 1988. Introduction. In *Government and Expertise: Specialists, Administrators and Professionals*, 1860–1919, ed. R. MacLeod. 1–24. Cambridge: Cambridge University Press.

McAllister, L. 2005. Judging GMOs: Judicial Application of the Precautionary Principle in Brazil. *Ecology Law Quarterly*, 32: 149–174.

McIntyre, O. and T. Mosedale. 1997. The Precautionary Principle as a Norm of Customary International Law. *Journal of Environmental Law*, 9 (2): 221–241.

Rai, P. B. D., and S. S. Shafi. 1977. The Planned Development of Delhi. Innovations and Action. In *City Development Plans and their Implementation*. 142–156. Delhi: Centre for Urban Studies, Indian Institute for Planning and Administration.

Rajalakshmi, T. K. 2001. The CNG Conundrum, *Frontline*, 18 (18): 1–14.

Rajamani, L. 2007. Public Interest Environmental Litigation in India: Exploring Issues of Access, Participation, Equity, Effectiveness and Sustainability. *Journal of Environmental Law*, 19 (3): 293–321.

Rosen, C. 2003. "Knowing" Industrial Pollution: Nuisance Law and the Power of Tradition in a Time of Rapid Economic Change, 1840–1864. *Environmental History*, 8 (4): 565–597.

Sathe, S. P. 2002. *Judicial Activism in India: Transgressing Borders and Enforcing Limits*. New Delhi: Oxford University Press.

Scott, D. S., and C. Barnett. 2009. Something in the Air. Civic Science and Contentious Environmental Politics in Post-Apartheid South Africa. *Geoforum*, 40: 373–382.

Shafi, S. S. 1965. Non-Conforming Industrial Uses and the Role of "Flatted Factories" in Urban Renewal. *Journal of the Institute of Town Planners of India*, 42 & 43 (March–June): 140–144.

Verma, G. D. 2002. *Slumming India: A Chronicle of Slums and Their Saviours*. Delhi: Penguin.

Vernon, R. 2006. Remaking Urban Environments. The Political Ecology of Air Pollution in Delhi. *Environment and Planning A*, 38: 2093–2109.

Wynne, B. 2004. May the Sheep Safely Graze? A Reflexive View of the Expert–Lay Knowledge Divide. In *Risk, Environment and Modernity: Towards a New Ecology*, ed. S. Lash, B. Szerszynski, and B. Wynne. 45–80. Newbury Park: Sage.

4
The Troubled Passage from 'Village Communities' to Planned New Town Developments in Mid-Twentieth-Century South Asia

William J. Glover

This chapter* posits an intellectual genealogy for understanding how comprehensively-planned new towns became a focus of planning attention in twentieth-century India. Though comprehensively-planned new towns were built in small numbers in India beginning in the nineteenth century (and earlier if we consider examples from the pre-British period such as Jaipur, for instance), the largest number were built following independence in 1947. According to Robert Home, "India accommodated some five million people in 118 new towns built between independence in 194[7] and 1981, in what has been probably the largest new town programme in the world" (1996, 206). If we add the several new towns built prior to independence and the many that have been constructed since 1981 then we would find the numbers—in terms of both towns and population—to be considerably higher than that. Indeed, new town developments are enjoying a resurgence in popularity across South Asia today though it is perhaps too soon to say whether the genealogy traced here remains as relevant as it once was: as contributions by Nair and Gururani (this volume) make clear, the physical and social landscapes imagined at mid-century in India now filter through

* An earlier version of this chapter was published as William J. Glover (2012), The Troubled Passage from "Village Communities" to Planned New Town Developments in Mid-Twentieth-Century South Asia, *Urban History*, 39 (1): 106–120. Reprinted with permission from Cambridge University Press.

disparate legal and legislative sieves whose overlaps and discontinuities have secreted new opportunities for, and obstacles to, what can be imagined for the future.[1]

There were a number of factors that made new town development plausible and desirable. These include economic imperatives that grew out of post-independence industrial policy, when both state-run and private industries secured efficient ways to combine industrial capital with locally available resources and labor. Most of the new towns built in India housed managers, workers, and support personnel for steel, fertilizer, oil refining, and other industrial concerns, though towns planned for administrative and other purposes shared both conceptual and spatial principles in common with them. Demographic forces also played a crucial role in the history of India's planned new towns, including crises resulting from periodic famines and the influx of political refugees into cities at India's partition. In this regard, new towns were seen by many as a way to insure the even distribution of population between larger and smaller cities. Finally, in a variety of ways only hinted at here, both of the last century's two world wars indelibly shaped the rationale (and designs) for new towns in India, not least by mobilizing an international coterie of new town proponents to place their planning agenda on firmer institutional footings. While these larger events and processes directly shaped the intellectual genealogy I consider here, and I will address each of these issues schematically, many features of that genealogy predate these processes or cannot causally be derived from them.

The Village and the City

My first argument may seem paradoxical: new town discourse depended importantly on changes in the way rural society was conceptualized in relation to urban society in India. If colonial suburbs emerged partly in response to overcrowding in India's densest cities, then planned new cities gained conceptual force in the context of rapid rural to urban in-migration during the middle decades of the twentieth century. The latter kind of urbanization forced important changes to an older set of assumptions about what differentiated rural from urban society. To put it schematically, whereas in an earlier period the world of the village dweller was seen as radically separate from that of the urban dweller, rapid urbanization forced theorists to entertain the implications of there being a kind of 'sliding scale' between the two. The new town concept became relevant, in part, because of its seeming potential to shape and nurture a rapidly proliferating new kind of subject—the villager in the city. While this sociological concept informed numerous mid-twentieth-century studies of existing Indian cities, it played a more determinate role as *a priori* grounds for new town aesthetics than it did for any other urban setting. As I hope to demonstrate, despite often being seen as an emblem of modernity—and one thinks here of places like Jamshedpur, Chandigarh, or Islamabad[2]—the new town idea was actually socially conservative in that new towns were seen as being promising precisely for their ability to nurture "inherited tendencies and habits" in their residents rather than fostering wholly urbane subjectivities (Mukerjee 1940, 224–225). Like a number of other 'modern' forms in twentieth-century India, the new town was designed in part to invoke the Indian village, or at least much of its social framework.

The Indian village played a more abstract role in establishing a second relevant context for this history. This was the role India played in the development of the concept of the 'village community,' a staple of late nineteenth-century Anglo-European social and political science. Though earlier formulations exist, Henry Sumner Maine's elaboration of the concept beginning in 1861 (which he subsequently refined) was certainly the most influential. Most authors point to the formative role Maine's experience as legal member of Council in India played in the development of his magnum opus, *Ancient Law*, a work Maine characterized as a study of "the earliest ideas of mankind, as they are reflected in Ancient Law, and . . . the relation of these ideas to modern thought" (1888, v). Maine's research focused on the history of society as evidenced in the evolution of its juridical forms; the 'village community' emerged in his work as one such ancient form established on the basis of collective (as opposed to individual) proprietorship over land. The society bound by the village community form was characterized by its perduring conservatism, and by its hierarchical organization based on the family or clan as the fundamental unit.

For some nineteenth-century theorists, the village community compared positively with the degenerated society industrialism drew in its wake; for others, the village community was a negative check on progress that stood for cultural stagnation and social inequality (Dewey 1972; Dumont 1965). Whichever view one held, however, consensus prevailed that actual village communities were all but extinct in modern industrial society, even if traces of their existence could be found in contemporary land usage and nomenclature applied to agrarian tracts in England, Scandinavia, Russia, and elsewhere. In India, however, Maine surmised that village communities continued to flourish intact well into the present.

John Stuart Mill, writing in 1871, commented on Maine's discovery: "Mr. Maine found that the state of things in regard to landed property which exists in India wherever it has not been disturbed by British legislation, is strikingly in accordance with that which recent historical investigations prove to have once existed in what are now the most advanced communities" (1871, 61–62). What made Maine's work all the more valuable, according to Mill, was that his discovery came not from ancient books or treatises but from "the 'large and miscellaneous official literature' in the records of the Indian Government, and from 'the oral conversation of experienced observers who have passed their maturity in administrative office'" (1871, 61–62). The existence of the ancient village community in India was confirmed, in other words, in the handwritten notes filed by colonial officers in the field. As Clive Dewey put it, "in England, save for a handful of 'survivals,' the village community was a purely historical phenomenon, studied by historians; but in India it was an omnipresent reality, utilized by revenue officials in assessing and collecting the land revenue" (1972, 291).

The same empirical studies of India's villages, supplemented in later decades by ethnographic accounts, became the bedrock of another core concept in nineteenth-century evolutionary social science, and in later modernization theories. In its most general form, this was the idea that primitive and modern societies occupy dichotomous social worlds that are linked, one to the other, through some manner of evolutionary process. The first mode of society is said to be held together by group or associational ties (for which the 'family' forms the ideal case) rather than individual autonomy and self-interest. Determinate dimensions of social life are constituted *in situ* through the sedimentation of customs, shared beliefs, and mores. Social interaction is characterized by regular face-to-face contact between people who know one another and share collective interests in common. The second mode of society, in contrast, is based on relations that "arise from the free agreement of Individuals," rather than from larger associational forms such as kin groups, family, or co-religionists (Maine 1888, 169). Individuals uphold obligations in this second mode on the basis of contractual agreements, rather than through the protocols that bound collectivities together.

The empirically observable features used to classify societies of the first type are historical and particularistic, and include such things as religious belief, consanguinity, and in the Indian context, importantly, caste. The features for classifying the second type of society are universal rather than particularistic, and apply to any and all of its members. These include such things as aggregate age profiles, income, health, and education levels. Note that the latter are all measurable qualities, and thus capable of being compared against statistically derived norms. If in the first type of society—let us call this Social 1—the key goal of change over time is 'improvement,' then in the second type of society—let us call this Social 2—the key goal of change over time is 'development.'[3] Improvement is addressed to communities tied together through bonds of kinship, culture and shared history in a particular place; development, conversely, is concerned with the proper distribution of "beings [and activities] on a territory" in accord with normative standards and goals (Rabinow 1992, 56).

Versions of this sociological model can be traced through several intellectual genealogies, including Maine's depiction of societal development as moving from social ties based on *status* to ones based on *contract*, Ferdinand Tonnies' late nineteenth-century distinction between societies organized according to *gemeinschaft* or *gesellschaft* (the first term often translated as 'community' and the second term as 'society'), Emile Durkheim's distinction between "mechanical" and "organic" solidarities, and so forth. What makes this relevant to the present discussion is how the transition from Social 1 to Social 2 in India was mapped onto the transition from rural to urban life. Put somewhat differently, if for industrialized Western societies the transition was seen as largely historical, in India the movement from one to the other was simultaneously historical and spatial.[4] Indian sociologist Radhakamal Mukerjee, who we will encounter more fully below, stated this principle succinctly and often. Here is an example from an article he wrote in 1943:

> In most rural communities [Social 1] the bulk of social action is based on primary, face-to-face, integral, intimate relations as discernible in the family, the clan, the caste and neighbourhood groups. The norm of social action is derived from the familial and cultural types of grouping, characterized by mutual sharing of resources, risks and rewards, and this regulates and "humanises" fractional, rational, contractual phases of behaviour and relations [Social 2] associated with ecologic, economic or mechanical types of grouping. (Mukerjee 1943, 646)

The rest of this chapter will trace how a small interdisciplinary group of planners, sociologists, economists, geographers, and reformers of various stripes asserted their prescriptions for urban development in India as they conceptualized society moving from one state to the other. Their work underscores how much a developmentalist, modernizing, postcolonial state—with its five-year plans, massive bureaucracies, and statistically derived policy goals—may have at one time owed to a culturalist strain of social theory for crafting a vision of India's urban future. As I hope to suggest in the closing passage, that theoretical strain may well be partially responsible for structurally embedding a pernicious form of conservative xenophobia at the very core of Indian planning orthodoxy.

'Soft' Materialist Determinism

As a set of sociological and morphological propositions about what form social life in India's cities should take, twentieth-century planning discourse shared an earlier nineteenth-century materialist conviction that living arrangements and the physical conditions of social life directly molded the moral character of both individuals and societies in predictable and determinate ways (see Baucom 1999; Comaroff and Comaroff 1997; Glover 2005; Scott 1995; Srivastava 1998). This idea was as relevant to nineteenth-century British efforts to establish 'islands of Englishness' to help shore up their ethnic identity (including such things as racially exclusive clubs, 'hill stations,' and suburban residential districts) as it was to mid-twentieth-century Indian urban planners who sought to ameliorate the social disjunctions of urban in-migration in their designs for new industrial towns. A number of scholars have now studied the development of colonial-era suburbs in this light, paying particular attention to how space and built form were designed to address Anglo-European anxieties over racial difference and an (unrealized) desire for social and racial segregation, and to support evolving middle-class ideals of gentility, domesticity, and conjugal sexuality as these changed in subtle ways across the long nineteenth century (see Archer 1997; Blunt 1999; Chattopadhyay 2000; Chopra 2011; Cohn 1962; Glover 2008; Hosagrahar 2005; King 1976). These predominantly residential enclaves of White colonial residents and their Indian servants stood out physically from other 'native' suburbs in Indian cities by virtue of their exorbitant use of space, by privileging the isolated single-family house as a building typology, and by expressing greater adherence to the concepts and norms of sanitary science than the latter settlements did. Colonial suburbs inhabited by the White colonial community in India also enjoyed the lion's share of municipal investment in such things as water supply, carpeted roads, sewage, and police protection.

This type of suburb was constructed beginning in the late eighteenth century in India, and remained present despite alterations throughout the period of British rule. The importance of this kind of residential arrangement for structuring domestic experience among the British expatriate population in particular was significant, something underscored by how often suburbs form privileged topoi in the fiction of Kipling, Forster, and Orwell, among others. As literary critic Todd Kuchta has observed, regardless of the details of their actual settings, colonial society in these authors' works was almost always *suburban* society. And it was suburban society of a certain sort: one shot through with anxiety, ennui, and a peculiarly colonial sense of the 'uncanny.' This literature also reminds us that by the early decades of the twentieth century suburban settings were seen by many as "pretentious and second-rate" (Kuchta 2003, 307), condemned for their "appalling monotony, ugliness and dullness" (*The Times* [London] 1904, n.p. cited in Hardy 1991, 10) and declared bereft of the vibrancy and cultural opportunities available to the city dweller. Whatever the content of these colonial narratives, whatever the tribulations of the White expatriate characters who inhabited them, and whatever departures from Anglo-American histories of suburbia the colonial suburb may demand, these settings held in focus a sense of the 'social' that privileged historical, cultural categories—including race, ethnicity, the nature of the family, and a sense of shared culture—in crafting a physical milieu capable of upholding culturally distinct values. This is what I have called Social 1.

From Isolation to Congestion

By the turn of the twentieth century, this type of (largely expatriate) colonial suburb had become largely irrelevant as an urban problem-space. By that time, industrialization, in-migration from the countryside (often on the heels of plague or famine), and natural population growth in cities brought new issues to the fore. Historical data on growth rates for India's cities are not fully reliable but what evidence we do have suggests that urban growth was rapid in many regions by the turn of the twentieth century, particularly in larger cities. In many older cities, the physically constrained and densely crowded inner districts reached full capacity by the last decades of the nineteenth century, something that generated a brisk demand in many cities for unoccupied land on the periphery (Bulsara 1964; Rao 1965).[5]

Early legislation targeting the amelioration of urban congestion in India included the 1898 Bombay Improvement Trust Act, which formalized procedures for acquiring land, laying down infrastructure (roads, sewers, water pipes), and preparing plots for development. A number of other municipalities established improvement trusts in subsequent decades, and in 1915 Bombay (again ahead of other cities but soon to be imitated) passed its first town planning act, based largely on the British Town Planning Act of 1909 (Home 1996, 81–83). The creation of improvement trusts and the passage of town planning acts broadened the range of options available to planners for channeling urban growth, including the option of constructing newly-planned towns. As Nandini Gooptu has noted, the post-First World War period saw the emergence of an "urban-based 'constructive' civic nationalist vision," among the growing middle classes in India, who "increasingly saw civic institutions, town governance and urban development as the motors of modernization, progress and national efficiency" (2001, 79).

Ebenezer Howard's promotion of the 'garden city' new town development model in England at the turn of the twentieth century exerted an important influence on this group. Howard's goal was to replace the noxious quarters of the inner city and the stultifying boredom of the countryside with a decentralized, socially-integrated, medium-sized town that combined the best qualities of rural and urban life (see Fishman 1982; Hall and Ward 1998). In its own way, Howard's model valorized the positive social features associated with the idealized 'village community,' particularly in the work of architects Raymond Unwin and Barry Parker who actualized Howard's plans (see Meller 1990, 234; Buder 1969). It also presents an early but significant example of planning thought that drew city and countryside together in a single frame, something I will develop further in a moment. Through Howard's advocacy, and through that of the international coterie of promoters, planners, and reformers that formed around him, the garden city presented an alternative to progressive reformers in India who decried the political effects of improvement trust urbanization—which in most cases entailed slum clearance, displacing the urban poor, and the erection of middle-class housing schemes on recently-cleared parcels (see Gooptu 2001; Hazareesingh 2001).

Scottish town planner, biologist, and environmental sociologist Patrick Geddes was the most significant figure promoting Howard's ideas in India, though Geddes's intellectual significance to this history far exceeds his connection to Howard. Geddes held a number of official and unofficial positions in India between 1914 and 1919, including professor of civics and sociology at the University of Bombay, and planning consultant to numerous municipalities and princely states. In the latter capacity, Geddes wrote some fifty town planning reports on nearly as many Indian cities. His reports have usually been read as revealing a sympathetic approach to the indigenous quarters of Indian cities, arguing for their conservation and improvement through "conservative surgery," rather than wholesale demolition or slum clearance (something which often put Geddes at odds with colonial officials in the towns that he visited). I want to suggest instead that we look at the role Geddes played in enabling the change from Social 1 to Social 2 to emerge conceptually as a *transition*, rather than as an abrupt change, since while the impact of Geddes' physical plans for Indian cities was relatively minimal, Geddes' writing and other activities had a disproportionate impact on the way planners, economists, and sociologists conceptualized, studied, and proposed plans for Indian cities.

In large part that influence came about through Geddes' insistence on the interconnectedness of cities and their hinterlands in a regional context.[6] By emphasizing the synthesis of woodland, field, and city as integrated parts of a 'regional' whole (which was the rhetorical purpose behind his famous "valley section" diagram), Geddes's work established a generative departure from previous thinking on the Indian city, since colonial officials and Indian nationalists alike continued to see the Indian village as a more or less isolated phenomenon well into the early twentieth century.

This was in sharp contrast to the situation in England. By the last quarter of the nineteenth century, the very real problems of poverty, poor health, and environmental degradation in England's agricultural villages was becoming increasingly visible. George Godwin, editor of *The Builder* magazine and a tireless advocate of housing reform in mid-nineteenth-century England, drew attention to the insanitary state of English villages as early as 1859, the same year the Royal Commission reported on the health of the Indian Army (Godwin 1972[1859]). Thirty years later, journalist George Millen traveled throughout southern England to document the state of the rural poor, publishing his findings in a regular column in the London *Daily News*. Millen challenged the stereotypical rural image of "prosperous villages and charming little homes, embowered in orchards and flower gardens, and tenanted by a comfortable and contented peasantry, healthy, thriving, happy, and beyond all comparison better off than the corresponding class in our great towns." Instead, his columns described a rural landscape of "sordid" poverty, "tumbledown ramshackle, damp and draughty" houses, and intractable zones of disease (1999 [1891], 20–24).

Works like these and others during the late nineteenth century served to link the English village to the industrial city conceptually, since problems of poverty, child labor, poor housing, and rampant disease were seen to be shared by both. Modernization and its deadly discomforts affected the village and the metropolis together in real time, in other words, just as solutions to those shared problems were seen to necessitate simultaneous reforms in both the countryside and the city. The same connections took much longer to be drawn in India, however, and Geddes's emphasis on the 'region' as the proper unit of analysis for understanding the Indian city initiated an approach that necessitated the simultaneous consideration of conditions in the countryside as well.

Geddes's town planning reports and sociological publications undertaken while he was in India mark the intrusion into Indian sociology of organicism as an epistemological frame for understanding the relationship between human society and its physical milieus. While there is no space here to treat Geddes' planning work in India with any detail, his repeated emphasis was on the interdependence of physical, natural, and indeed psychic phenomena in the constitution of the city and its regional setting, his call for "selective surgery" was a mode of intervention into the city fabric designed not to disrupt the organic whole. As architectural historian Arindam Dutta writes, "Geddes's surgical metaphors construed the ideal urban intervention into the geocultural environment as if [it were] a graft onto a living corpus, where change is already at work. The new intervention, at once historical and architectural, must mitigate its foreignness, its exceptionality, so that the 'improved' elements are indistinguishable from the ongoing life of the ever-evolving whole of the existing environment" (2005, 427). Geddes's call to resolve the transcendent (culture in evolution) with the empirical (life in its many varieties on the ground) as a working methodology depended on establishing a multidisciplinary basis of knowledge—drawing on, among others, sociology, biology, economics, psychology, anthropology, geography, history, aesthetics, physiology, chemistry, and botany—whose findings would be exhaustively annotated—"not only logical but graphic in presentment, as far as may be" (Geddes 1920, 3)—to provide a framework for intervention.

With his emphasis on the exhaustive cataloging of physical and social features present on site, and on the multidisciplinary field of knowledge this annotation required, Geddes helped push the fledgling new discipline of town planning in India towards the systematic, scientific, and empirically-based methods that characterized the academic social sciences more generally at the time. As I suggested earlier, these are the kinds of methods whose metrics presupposed—and indeed helped produce—the theoretical validity of society organized according to the principles of Social 2. Geddes's well-publicized 1916 report on Lucknow, for example, written in collaboration with architect and town planner H. V. Lanchester, claimed that "every section" was based on detailed "study upon the ground," and that all of the proposed plans had been "tested to scale, criticized . . . from many points of view," and submitted to re-evaluation before the "final preparation of sketches for the draftsman in the office" (1916, 1).[7] In an exhibition that accompanied his report, detailed survey maps of the city were presented with overlays indicating population densities, occupational groupings, the distribution of religious groups, and statistics on epidemic disease. While Geddes had little to do with actual implementation of the work, many of his plans for Lucknow were eventually carried out by L. M. Jopling, chairman of the Lucknow Improvement Trust, and J. Linton Bogle, chief engineer of the city (Jopling 1923).

The improvement of Lucknow was well publicized, and Bogle went on to write a popular planning manual in 1929, entitled *Town Planning in India*. In this work Bogle, a mechanical engineer by training, replaced Geddes' emphasis on close survey and observation (and neglected to credit Geddes in the book) with a set of universally applicable "rules" regardless of time or place (Bogle 1929). These included rules governing minimum amounts of open space in newly-developed settlements; the distribution of schools, parks, and shops; the width of roads; the height of houses; residential densities per acre, and so forth. While Bogle's book was addressed primarily to municipal groups eager to improve the dilapidated areas of existing cities (which was also the major focus of Geddes' earlier efforts), he made positive mention of the garden city movement in England at the time, the emergence of model factory towns to house industrial workers in Europe, and the development of Model Town on the outskirts of Lahore, a garden city built by Indian residents that was remarkably faithful to Ebenezer Howard's prescriptions (Glover 2008, 151–157). For reasons I will discuss in a moment, the latter kind of planned new town environment increasingly became the favored frame of reference in urbanization discourse.

Peasants into Indians

The First World War also played a role in preparing the ground for some of these transitions. In his book, *From Garden Cities to New Towns* (1991), historian Dennis Hardy emphasized the importance of the war in prompting "a high degree of millennial expectation" among advocates of the town planning movement in England more generally, and in prompting a return to basic principles among advocates of the garden city movement in particular. A small "breakaway" group from the mainstream movement in England— which by that time had grown content to see the spread of bedroom-community "garden suburbs" instead of the more holistically conceived "garden cities" championed by Howard—argued strenuously for government sponsorship of new town construction to facilitate post-war reconstruction (1991, 127–134). F. J. Osborn's 1918 book, *New Towns After the War* (written under the pseudonym "The Townsmen") helped publicize this view and insure its continued prominence. A revised version of this book became a central intellectual piece of England's post-Second World War 'new town' movement.

It was during the First World War that Geddes collaborated with Radhakamal Mukerjee (1889–1968) in India, a sociologist who helped establish the theoretical foundations for an 'urban ecology'-based planning discourse in India over the course of his long and varied career. In an article published in *The American Journal of Sociology* in 1932, Mukerjee underscored the region as the prime unit of social ecological study in a formulation that characteristically effaced Geddes's influence: "The cultural order is woven within the skeleton of the ecological order, and it is the intermeshing of the two orders, organic and spiritual, which sets before us the complex web of the whole life-community in its completeness" (1932, 350). The basis for sustaining the "community in its completeness" was establishing a harmonic balance between economic development and ecological forces, something that required the expansion of ecological knowledge and "a re-orientation of the results of field-workers as well as systematizers in such diverse specialized branches of learning as economics, agriculture, entomology, bio-chemistry, and epidemiology" (1932, 353).

For Mukerjee (like Geddes), village and city could not be rigidly separated, either as analytical categories or as empirical domains: "The metropolis, the city, the country-town and the village are all links in an ecological process," he wrote, "which interpenetrates and over-reaches them all . . . Urbanism, if it be not segregative and pathological, normally rests on a balanced development of cities, country towns and villages" (1932, 161). At the same time, however, Mukerjee warned that the increasing integration of rural and urban society was accompanied by "a chaos and confusion of the relations between cities, country towns, and villages" with occasionally disastrous defects (1932, 12).

In a series of lectures delivered at the University of Lucknow in the 1930s and later published under the title *Man and his Habitation* (1940), Mukerjee described this confusion in the form of a protracted crisis. For him, the most legible evidence of crisis was found in the "hybrid industrial centres" growing uncontrollably on the periphery of larger cities—something Mukerjee described as the "liminal towns of the new East." These settlements, Mukerjee argued, were "for the most part [geared for] the single man, who moves from one hut to another with an unusual frequency, uprooting him from all objects, habits, and attitudes, which formerly rooted him to the soil, home, and community in his traditional cultural milieu" (1940, 13). The arboreal metaphor of "rooting" and "uprooting" in this and other passages highlights the privileged role natural and material environments played for him as agents of social determination.

Mukerjee intersected directly with most of the figures discussed thus far. Geddes' famous "Place–Work–Folk" schema (adapted from Le Play's "*Lieu–Travail–Famille*") was most fully worked out in a series of articles published in the *Indian Journal of Economics* (in 1920 and 1922) during the time he worked with Mukerjee. That journal was co-founded in Allahabad by economist H. Stanley Jevons (son of the more famous economist William Stanley Jevons), who wrote a planning report for the city of Allahabad in 1919 (Geddes 1920). Mukerjee, Jevons, Bogle, and Lanchester, from the fields of sociology, economics, engineering, and town planning, respectively, helped durably install Geddesian ideas at the center of a new, multidisciplinary approach to planning the Indian city (see Mukerjee 1930).

By the 1920s, other developments, other forms of research, and other sociological theories had helped unravel confidence in the putative isolation of India's villages. By the early decades of the twentieth century villages had become the focus of nationalist political mobilization and also of more paternalistic anti-nationalist government 'village uplift' campaigns, which entailed among other things the introduction of village sanitation schemes, competitive games, scientific farming methods, improved grain seeds and livestock, medical relief, and, briefly, village radio broadcasts or 'community listening' schemes (e.g., Brayne 1928; Jodhka 2002; Zivin 1998). Scholars from the incipient field of rural sociology began theorizing the effects of modernization on rural communities beginning in the 1920s, and by the 1930s the term "rurbanization" was used analytically by American and British sociologists to describe "the interpenetration of urban and rural life, particularly the penetration of the countryside by influences emanating from the city" (Carpenter 1932, 39).[8] While ethnographic and sociological research on Indian villages proliferated only after independence, by the early 1950s researchers had already catalogued a long list of such influences, including the following list compiled by prominent anthropologist M. N. Srinivas:

> . . . formal partition of the joint family (though sentimental ties are still strong), recourse to law courts to settle family disputes, diversification and specialization of occupations, black marketing, prostitution, the appearance of community leaders and "incipient capitalists with one leg in Villages and another in City," factionalism created by the leading political parties a network of good roads, [the] popularization of buses and motor-cycles, cash wages, bonuses and cost-of-living allowances, coffee-and-tea-houses, cinemas and shopping centres, welfare services, luxury goods, cosmetics, laundry services, measures of famine control and public health, involvement in a monetized national and interna-tional economy, payment of taxes in cash, growing cash crops, using mill and factory made goods, accepting improved agricultural practices, higher education, etc. The changes have also brought unemployment, population and immigration increases, the spread of allopathic practi-tioners, ration shops, and the like. (cited in Trivedi 1976, 18)

One major effect of the numerous sociological and ethnographic studies carried out on Indian villages during the 1950s and 1960s was thus to demonstrate how intricately connected most villages were to urban economies and processes. In a 1958 article, Srinivas argued that this had been the case for a long time: "the typical Indian village was not self-sufficient even in the days of primitive communications, and it is absurd to talk of 'reviving' something that never existed" (1958, 80). Yet despite presenting ample evidence of social transformation, few of these studies went so far as to describe village and urban communities as functionally identical.

In 1947, the year of India's independence, University of Chicago anthropologist Robert Redfield published an influential article on what he called the "folk–urban" continuum, a concept that would form the framework for multiple urban and rural ethnographies in subsequent years in India. While Redfield developed the concept based on his ethnographic work in the Yucatan during the 1920s and 1930s, the concept was easily extended to other geographical settings. Redfield's basic argument was that "folk societies" shared a number of features in common wherever they happened to be, and that these were in more or less polar contrast to "the society of the modern city" (Redfield 1947, 293). The folk society of Redfield's description was an ideal, rather than actually existing type, another feature which made the concept transportable beyond its original setting. Explicitly linking his model to earlier concepts developed by Maine, Durkheim, and Tonnies, Redfield's description of the folk society maps neatly onto our earlier definition of Social 1, given above:

> Such a society is small, isolated, non-literate, and homogeneous, with a strong sense of group solidarity . . . Behavior is traditional, spontaneous, uncritical, and personal; there is no legislation or habit of experiment and reflection for intellectual ends. Kinship, its relationships and institutions, are the type categories of experience and the familial group is the unit of action. (1947, 293)

As an ideal type, no actually existing society fully attained all of the qualities Redfield described. At the same time, every existing "folk society" had some combination of these qualities, and could be characterized according to how far it was from or close it came to the ideal. This is what made the "folk–urban" model a *continuum*, and Redfield included urbanizing societies within the model through the intermediate category of "peasant" society:

> The vast, complicated, and rapidly changing world in which the urbanite and even the urbanized country-dweller live today is enormously different from the small, inward-facing folk society, with its well-integrated and little-changing moral and religious conceptions . . . Where cities have arisen, the country people dependent on those cities have developed

economic and political relationships, as well as relationships of status, with the city people, and so have become that special kind of rural folk we call peasantry . . . many a village or small town has, perhaps, as many points of resemblance with the folk society as with urban life. (1947, 306)

Despite being subjected to considerable criticism—for being overly simplistic, for deriving from too narrow an empirical basis, and for failing to develop the 'urban' end of the continuum sufficiently, for example—Redfield's model remained influential throughout the 1950s and 1960s in India, a period of time that witnessed unprecedented rapid urbanization alongside massive, state-planned technological change. Chicago anthropologist Milton Singer, who often collaborated with Redfield, helped extend the latter's framework to the Indian setting where it formed a central paradigm in numerous village ethnographies and studies of peripheral urbanism.[9] While most of these studies documented departures from the folk ideal in the actually existing communities being studied—sometimes in exhaustive detail—the fundamental difference between 'rural' and 'urban' values continued to hold analytical purchase. Morris Opler, another American anthropologist trained at Chicago, reflected a common opinion in an article published in 1956: "The involvement of [villages] with organizations, places, and events outside of the village is considerable and it seems that this has been the case for a very long time. Yet it has not interfered with the separate identity and cohesiveness of the community, which in some respects is more marked than before" (1956, 10).[10]

Recapitulating the Indian Village in Planned New Towns

In the remaining section of this essay I want to highlight the ways in which the intellectual genealogy I have been tracing thus far began to affect the more projective discourses and practices of urban planning. While the sociological ideas I have been tracing organized a wealth of mid-century (and later) studies of existing large cities, they played a more determinate role as *a priori* grounds for new town organization and aesthetics than they did for perhaps any other urban setting.

One of the earliest people to identify the potential benefits of planning entirely new cities in India—rather than modifying older ones—was Radhakamal Mukerjee, as briefly noted above. For Mukerjee, newly planned towns held out the promise of completely avoiding the prior mistakes and problems that beset existing cities, including uncontrolled growth, caste-segregated neighborhoods, and various sorts of demographic imbalances (including an excess of single men, low birth rates, high mortality, and so forth). With proper planning, the material environment could produce more felicitous conditions for balanced society than was possible in the overgrown and socially deleterious city. "Only a restoration of immediacy of relationships and of communal life through neighbourhood . . . occupational, or cultural groups can bring about balance and normality in urban culture," Mukerjee wrote, and immediacy was for him both a social and a spatial quality. He argued that new town designs should support "face-to-face relationships" and communal activities—both of which were features that characterized village society—and provide "facilities for dramatizing . . . communal life and expressing baulked or sublimated social affections" (Mukerjee 1940, 226).

For Mukerjee and others, the development of new towns entailed an effort to effect a certain concatenation of disparate social worlds—Social 1 and Social 2, if you will—into a synthetic whole, one that necessitated a distinctive spatial armature. Looking at the plans of new towns that were actually built during the immediate post-independence period in India, one sees the physical trace of these ideas most clearly in the towns' formal geometries—in their emphasis on a central space or building, or in the aggregation of 'neighborhood units,' each individually focused on a school, temple, or community hall at the center. Otto Koenigsberger, who was responsible for planning several new towns in post-1947 India as director of housing for the Ministry of Health (from 1948 to 1951), described the "neighborhood unit plan"—a design promoted by American planner Clarence Perry in the 1920s—as "the best possible link with the type of community [known from villages]," arguing that "a village-like neighborhood makes it easier for [new residents] to understand their *civic responsibilities* than [they could in] a large, amorphous city" (1952, 105; emphasis added).[11] Though the translation of 'civic' virtues from a non-urban milieu may seem paradoxical here, and indeed may point to the extreme pliability the term 'village' had acquired by that time, the small-scale 'village-like' urban neighborhood became an overwhelming focus of design and community development efforts in mid-twentieth-century planning discourse (see Clinard 1966). This is one of the most enduring physical artifacts of the period, and it corresponds to a much more widely diffuse political project by the Indian state "to give the empirical form of a population group the moral attributes of a community" (Chatterjee 2004, 57).[12] As Shubhra Gururani points out (in this volume), current reworkings of this social/physical emblem lie at the core of current 'flexible' planning initiatives in rapidly growing satellite cities like Gurgaon today.

In the way these designs emphasize the importance of close proximity— through the provision of 'gathering' places, through structuring opportunities for frequent 'face-to-face' contact, and by placing community buildings in the middle of neighborhoods and commerce only at the edges—an aesthetics emerges in the new town that marks a rupture with what existed at the time (and here I am thinking both of informal squatter settlements and state-provided residential 'lines' of the sort emblematized by Bombay's *chawls*), but also an effort to recuperate key features of an older, imagined, village milieu. The fact that the new town with its neighborhood unit looks almost nothing like the village it seeks to recapitulate marks the rupture. At the same time, the new town attempts to recuperate something older: that is, a kind of society putatively based on the collective rather than the individual, on people's organic habits and psychological needs rather than on independent will and the restless search for the 'new.' It is in this sense that I suggest we see new town development as a socially 'conservative' project. Here is Mukerjee once again:

> . . . social planning implies a correct understanding of the settled social attitudes, habits or institutions, which the city-dweller still cherishes, and their conscious nurture and adaptation to [a] new milieu . . . it is through the inherited tendencies and habits rather than will that man achieves progress. (1940, 224–225)

The reformatting of village and urban worlds that the new town represents thus necessarily engages deeper social processes and more longstanding concerns in South Asia than either its earlier promoters (who saw them as emblems of progressive change), or those who today might dismiss it (as a regrettable by-product of Westernization) have usually recognized. Ashis Nandy has argued that certain "core concerns and anxieties of Indian civilization have come to be reflected in the [literal and metaphoric] journey from the village to the city," evidence for which is provided by how central that journey has been thematically in modern Indian cinema, literature, and politics (2001, 24). We can place new town developments in the mid-twentieth century somewhere in this frame to ask, along with Nandy, whether that journey has finally been exhausted as a figure through which Indian modernity is imagined as a condition of urban life.

Nandy argued that:

> . . . the village is no longer a living presence in mainstream Indian intellectual life. In the various visions of the future floating around in the region there is much that is worthwhile, but not the vivacity of an imagined village. The village is quickly becoming a place where strangers live, where *sati* and untouchability are practiced, where ethnic and religious riots have been taking place for centuries, and where, unless the civilized intervene, the inhabitants continue to pursue the sports of homicide and robbery. (2001, 23)

And if the role played by the village in constituting an urban imagination has changed, so too has the nature of the city being conjured undergone considerable change.

India's largest cities, the so-called 'metros,' are notable as sites for a new configuration of middle-class activism, effected through new configurations of 'community,' and directed towards holding municipalities accountable for insuring property values, privacy, security, and a healthy urban environment. Despite the putatively liberal values these initiatives hold in focus, asserting the rights to a 'bourgeois city' on behalf of a subculture of elites not infrequently entails an illiberal campaign of squatter evictions, anti-encroachment campaigns, and gentrification projects that regularly drive poor and disenfranchised communities out of older areas while keeping them away from new ones (e.g., Baviskar 2003; Chatterjee 2004). Given the importance Indian planning discourse has given to establishing the conditions for 'community' to flourish based on spatial proximity and shared cultural affinities and habits—we might say, thus, on the principles of Social 1—the post-liberalization Indian metro seems destined to intensify class, religious, and ethnic exclusivity as the basis for neighborhood formation (see Nair, this volume). The question is how the urban armatures the historical protagonists I have discussed above produced (and indeed that are continuing to be produced) need to be rethought in light of these trends, and in light of the genealogies that brought them into play.

Notes

1. New town developments that run the gamut from gated communities to 'integrated townships' have proliferated in recent years in both India and Pakistan. While little scholarship has been published on this phenomenon thus far, it has been the subject of scores of newspaper articles. For examples, see A. Gentleman, Real India Seeps into Gated Villas: Professionals Protest as Their Luxury Community Fails to Keep out Dust, Heat, and Squalor. *The Observer*, August 26, 2007; S. Gupta, Inside Gate, India's Good Life; Outside, the Servants' Slums. *New York Times*, June 9, 2008. More scholarly works include Brosius (2009); Schindler (2007).

2. Jamshedpur is a planned industrial city in the Indian state of Jharkand built by the Tata Steel Company beginning in 1907. Chandigarh was built under Jawaharlal Nehru's guidance as the capital of independent India's newly configured Punjab province beginning in 1956; among other prominent mid-century modernist architects, Le Corbusier played an important role in its design. Islamabad is the capital city of Pakistan planned by Constantinos Doxiades beginning in 1958. Of these three, only Chandigarh has received ample attention by urban historians. On Jamshedpur, see Dutta (1977). On Islamabad, see Nilsson (1973); Yakas (2001). Ravi Kalia has written three monographs on newly planned capital cities in India that foreground their progressiveness, including one on Chandigarh. See Kalia (1994; 1999; 2004). The literature on Chandigarh is extensive. Interested readers might compare Vikramaditya Prakash's recent monograph on the city (2002) with Norma Evenson's book (1966). Prakash foregrounds the city he grew up in during the 1970s and 80s, while Evenson wrote about the city one decade earlier.

3. My use of the '1' and '2' terminology is inspired by an essay Dipesh Chakrabarty wrote some years ago. What makes this heuristic strategy useful for my purposes—even at the cost of being unoriginal—is that while there are more well-established labels available to characterize these basic differences (see below), choosing one over another would mask how broad the spectrum of scholarship organized around these distinctions in some form or another really is. The differences between particular genealogies of theory seems less critically important, therefore, than what they shared in common. That sharing helped facilitate the transfer and appropriation of statements, images, and concepts across well-defined disciplinary boundaries, something I see as an important aspect of the history of discourse on the city in South Asia. See Chakrabarty (2000, 47–71).

4. Ferdinand Tonnies' elaboration of *Gemeinschaft* and *Gessellschaft* appears first in an 1887 work by that title. See Tonnies (1957). Maine's theory on the transition from 'status' to 'contract' appears in Maine (1888). Political theorist Karuna Mantena reassesses Maine's contributions to colonial constructions of traditional society in Mantena (2010).

5. According to deci-annual census data, in 1901–11 rural population grew much faster than urban population; in 1911–21 there was an overall decrease in the rural, and a modest increase in the urban population; from 1921–31 urban growth increased nearly 20 percent; in 1931–41 the urban growth rate was 32 percent. The highest urban growth rate was during the period 1941–51, which is recorded at 41.4 percent. The Second World War and partition are usually seen as the twin causes of such a high growth rate during that census period.

6. Geddes was part of a larger 'regional survey' movement whose proponents saw geographical knowledge as an almost quasi-mystical attainment of the fully developed 'citizen.' Geographer David Matless notes that this movement marked "a more general conscious reflection on the part of . . . geographers regarding the ways in which they figured the world," (1992, 476) including, I argue here, the way rural and urban societies were imagined in relation to one another.

7. Whether Geddes actually carried out detailed surveys himself is open to question, however. See Hall (2002, 268–270); Dutta (2005).

8. The term 'rurban' was reputedly first coined by rural sociologist C. J. Galpin in his book, *Rural Life* (1923).

9. Redfield planned to do fieldwork in Orissa in the late 1950s but fell sick on his arrival in India and returned to the US. Redfield and Singer's development of the concept of Great and Little tradition(s) to explain the role cities played in cultural change is laid out in their 1954 article. On the continuing influence of Redfield's framework in South Asian anthropology (and in Buddhist studies in particular), see Wilcox (2004).

10. See also Dumont and Pocock (1957).

11. Perry's scheme is described succinctly in Perry (1929). For the application of Perry's scheme in India, see Vidyarthi (2010). The 'neighborhood unit' continues to have its supporters today, including among proponents of the New Urbanism movement in the US, see Lawhon (2009).

12. Chatterjee described how disenfranchised groups of city dwellers have to negotiate a relationship with the welfare state by asserting forms of community based on locale as being formally akin to those recognized as belonging to enfranchised, civil society. My inversion of Chatterjee's subject and object here is meant to suggest that states, too, are sometimes involved in the same project.

References

Archer, J. 1997. Colonial Suburbs in South Asia, 1700–1850. In *Visions of Suburbia*, ed. Roger Silverstone. 26–54. London: Routledge.

Baucom, I. 1999. *Out of Place: Englishness, Empire, and the Locations of Identity*. Princeton, NJ: Princeton University Press.

Baviskar, A. 2003. Between Violence and Desire: Space, Power, and Identity in the Making of Metropolitan Delhi. *International Social Science Journal*, 175: 89–98.

Blunt, A. 1999. Imperial Geographies of Home: British Domesticity in India, 1886–1925. *Transactions of the Institute of British Geographers* (new series), 24 (4): 421–440.

Bogle, J. M. L. 1929. *Town Planning in India*. Bombay: Oxford University Press.

Brayne, F. L. 1928. *The Gurgaon Experiment*. London: Miller and Sons.

Brosius, C. 2009. *India Shining: Consuming Pleasures of India's New Middle Classes*. New Delhi: Routledge.

Buder, S. E. H. 1969. The Genesis of a Town Planning Movement. *Journal of the American Institute of Planners*, 35 (November): 390–398.

Bulsara, J. F. 1964. *Problems of Rapid Urbanization in India*. Bombay: Popular Prakashan.

Carpenter, N. 1932. Courtship Practices and Contemporary Social Change in America. *Annals of the American Academy of Political and Social Science*, 160 (March): 38–44.

Chakrabarty, D. 2000. The Two Histories of Capital. In *Provincializing Europe: Postcolonial Thought and Historical Difference*. Chapter 2, 47–71. Princeton, NJ: Princeton University Press.

Chatterjee, P. 2004. *The Politics of the Governed: Reflections on Popular Politics in Most of the World*. Delhi: Permanent Black.

Chattopadhyay, S. 2000. Blurring Boundaries: The Limits of "White Town" in Colonial Calcutta. *Journal of the Society of Architectural Historians*, 59 (2): 154–179.

———. 2002. "Goods, Chattels, and Sundry Items": Constructing 19th Century Anglo Indian Domestic Life. *Journal of Material Culture*, 7 (3): 243–271.

Chopra, P. 2011. *A Joint Enterprise: The Making of Colonial Bombay, 1854–1918*. Minneapolis, MN: University of Minnesota Press.

Clinard, M. 1966. *Slums and Community Development: Experiments in Self-Help*. New York: Free Press.

Cohn, B. 1962. The British in Benares: A Nineteenth Century Colonial Society. *Comparative Studies in Society and History*, 4 (2): 169–199.

Comaroff, J., and J. Comaroff. 1997. *Of Revelation and Revolution: The Dialectics of Modernity on a South African Frontier*. Chicago: University of Chicago Press.

Dewey, C. 1972. Images of the Village Community: A Study in Anglo-Indian Ideology. *Modern Asian Studies*, 6 (3): 291–328.

Dumont, L. 1965. The "Village Community" from Munro to Maine. *Contributions to Indian Sociology*, 9 (December): 67–89.

Dumont, L., and D. Pocock. 1957. For a Sociology of India. *Contributions to Indian Sociology*, 1 (1): 7–22.

Dutta, A. 2005. Organicism: Interdisciplinarity and Para-Architectures. *Journal of the Society of Architectural Historians*, 64 (4): 427–430.

Dutta, M. 1977. *Jamshedpur: The Growth of the City and its Regions*. Calcutta: Asiatic Society.

Evenson, N. 1966. *Chandigarh*. Berkeley, CA: University of California Press.

Fishman, R. 1982. *Urban Utopias in the Twentieth Century: Ebenezer Howard, Frank Lloyd Wright, Le Corbusier.* Cambridge, MA: MIT Press.

Galpin, C. J. 1923. *Rural Life.* New York: The Century Company.

Geddes, P. 1916. *Town Planning in Lucknow: A Report to the Municipal Council by Professor Geddes.* Lucknow, Uttar Pradesh: Murray's London Printing Press.

———. 1920. Essentials of Sociology in Relation to Economics. *Indian Journal of Economics,* 3 (1): 1–56; 257–305.

Godwin, G. *Town Swamps and Social Bridges.* Intro. Anthony D. King. 1859. Leicester: Leicester University Press, 1972.

Glover, W. J. 2005. Objects, Models, and Exemplary Works: Educating Sentiment in Colonial Punjab. *Journal of Asian Studies,* 64 (3): 539–566.

———. 2008. *Making Lahore Modern: Constructing and Imagining a Colonial City.* Minneapolis, MN: University of Minnesota Press.

Gooptu, N. 2001. *The Politics of the Urban Poor in Early Twentieth Century India.* Cambridge: Cambridge University Press.

Hall, P. 2002. *Cities of Tomorrow: An Intellectual History of Urban Planning and Urban Design in the Twentieth Century.* 3rd ed. London: Blackwell Publishing.

Hall, P., and C. Ward. 1998. *Sociable Cities: The Legacy of Ebenezer Howard.* Chichester: John Wiley and Sons.

Hardy, D. 1991. *From Garden Cities to New Towns: Campaigning for Town and Country Planning, 1899–1946.* London: E & FN Spon.

Hazareesingh, S. 2001. Colonial Modernism and the Flawed Paradigms of Urban Renewal: The Uneven Development of Bombay City, 1900–1925. *Urban History,* 28 (2): 235–255.

Home, R. 1996. *Of Planting and Planning: The Making of British Colonial Cities.* London: Taylor and Francis.

Hosagrahar, J. 2005. *Indigenous Modernities: Negotiating Architecture and Urbanism.* London: Routledge.

Jodhka, S. 2002. Nation and Village: Images of Rural India in Gandhi, Nehru, and Ambedkar. *Economic and Political Weekly,* 37 (32): 3334–3353.

Jopling, L. M. 1923. Town Planning in Lucknow. *The Town Planning Review,* 101 (January): 25–36.

Kalia, R. 1994. *Bhubaneswar: From a Temple Town to a Capital City.* Carbondale, IL: Southern Illinois University Press.

———. 1999. *Chandigarh: The Making of an Indian City.* New Delhi: Oxford University Press.

———. 2004. *Gandhinagar: Building National Identity in Postcolonial India.* Columbia, SC: University of South Carolina Press.

King, A. 1976. *Colonial Urban Development: Culture, Social Power, and Environment.* London: Routledge and Kegan Paul.

Koenigsberger, O. H. 1952. New Towns in India. *Town Planning Review,* 23 (2): 95–132.

Kuchta, T. 2003. Suburbia, *Ressentiment,* and the End of Empire in *A Passage To India. Novel: A Forum On Fiction* (Summer): 307–329.

Lawhon, L. L. 2009. The Neighborhood Unit: Physical Design or Physical Determinism? *Journal of Planning History*, 8 (2): 111–132.

Maine, H. S. 1888 [1861]. *Ancient Law: Its Connection with the Early History of Society, and its Relation to Modern Ideas*. 5th ed. New York: Henry Holt and Company.

Mantena, K. 2010. *Alibis of Empire: Henry Maine and the Ends of Liberal Empire*. Princeton, NJ: Princeton University Press.

Matless, D. 1992. Regional Surveys and Local Knowledges: The Geographical Imagination in Britain, 1918–39. *Transactions of the Institute of British Geographers* (new series), 17 (4): 464–480.

Meller, H. 1990. Robert Beevers, *The Garden City Utopia: A Critical Biography of Ebenezer Howard* [book review]. *Journal of Historical Geography*, 16 (2): 251–252.

Mill, J. S. 1871. Maine on Village Communities, 1871. In *The Collected Works of John Stuart Mill, XXX—Writings on India*, ed. J. M. Robson, M. Moir, and S. Moir. 215–228. Toronto, ON: University of Toronto Press.

Millen, G. 1999 [1891]. *Life in the Victorian Village: The Daily News Survey of 1891, Vol. 1*, ed. L. Bellamy and T. Williamson. London: Caliban Books.

Mukerjee, R. 1930. The Regional Balance of Man. *The American Journal of Sociology*, 36 (3): 455–460.

———. 1932. The Ecological Outlook in Sociology. *The American Journal of Sociology*, 38 (3): 349–355.

———. 1940. *Man and His Habitation: A Study in Social Ecology*. London: Longmans, Green, and Company.

———. 1943. Ecological and Cultural Patterns of Social Organization. *American Sociological Review*, 8 (6): 643–649.

Nandy, A. 2001. *An Ambiguous Journey to the City: The Village and Other Odd Ruins of the Self in the Indian Imagination*. London: Oxford University Press.

Nilsson, S. 1973. *The New Capitals of India, Pakistan, and Bangladesh*, trans. E. Andréasson. Lund: Studentlitteratur.

Opler, M. 1956. The Extensions of an Indian Village. *The Journal of Asian Studies*, 16 (1): 5–10.

Osborn, F. J. 1918 [1943]. *New Towns After the War*. Revised and reissued. London: J. M. Dent and Sons.

Perry, C. 1929. City Planning for Neighborhood Life. *Social Forces*, 8 (1): 98–100.

Prakash, V. 2002. *Chandigarh's Le Corbusier: The Struggle for Modernity in Postcolonial India*. Seattle, WA: University of Washington Press.

Rabinow, P. 1992. France in Morocco: Techno-Cosmopolitanism and Middling Modernism. *Assemblage*, 17 (April): 52–57.

Rao, M. S. A. 1965. Six Decades of Urbanization in India, 1901–1961. *The Indian Economic and Social History Review*, 2 (1): 23–41.

Redfield, R. 1947. The Folk Society. *The American Journal of Sociology*, 52 (4): 293–308.

Redfield, R., and M. B. Singer. 1954. The Cultural Role of Cities. *Economic Development and Cultural Change*, 3 (1): 53–73.

Schindler, S. 2007. A 21st-Century Urban Landscape: The Emergence of New Social-Spatial Formations in Gurgaon. In *Sarai Reader 07: Frontiers*, ed. M. Narula, S. Sengupta, J. Bagchi, and R. Sundaram. 499–508. Delhi: Sarai Programme, Center for the Study of Developing Societies.

Scott, D. 1995. Colonial Governmentality. *Social Text*, 43: 191–220.

Srinivas, M. N. 1958. The Industrialization and Urbanization of Rural Areas. *Sociological Bulletin*, 5 (2): 79–88.

Srivastava, S. 1998. *Constructing Post-Colonial India: National Character and the Doon School*. London: Routledge.

Tonnies, F. 1957 [1887]. *Community and Society (Gemeinschaft Und Gesellschaft)*, trans. C. P. Loomis. East Lansing, MI: Michigan State University Press.

Trivedi, H. R. 1976. *Urbanism: A New Outlook*. Delhi: Atma Ram and Sons.

Vidyarthi, S. 2010. Reimagining the American Neighborhood Unit for India. In *Crossing Borders: International Exchange and Planning Practices*, ed. P. Healey and R. Upton. 73–94. Abingdon, UK: Routledge.

Wilcox, C. 2004. *Robert Redfield and the Development of American Anthropology*. Langham, MD: Lexington Books.

Yakas, O. 2001. *Islamabad: The Birth of a Capital*. Karachi: Oxford University Press.

Zivin, J. 1998. The Imagined Reign of the Iron Lecturer: Village Broadcasting in Colonial India. *Modern Asian Studies*, 32 (3): 717–738.

5
Flexible Planning: The Making of India's 'Millennium City,' Gurgaon

Shubhra Gururani

Introduction

Located roughly 30 kilometers south of the national capital of India, the city of Gurgaon,[1] in the district of the same name, is a rapidly changing urban frontier. At once remarkable and revolting, the landscape of Gurgaon is an odd mixture. Alongside countless glossy towers, shopping malls, and posh condominiums, there are equally large numbers of buildings under construction with construction workers perched at giddying heights above a sea of rubble, rocks, cement, donkeys, fellow migrants, and imported machinery including trucks and tankers. The entire city of Gurgaon is materially and symbolically under construction, waiting to be developed, mapped, and unmapped. As anyone will tell you, Gurgaon has been noticeably under construction for almost three decades now.

Until recently, apart from Japan's Suzuki Motors, which set up a car manufacturing plant in collaboration with Maruti Udyog Limited in the 1970s, Gurgaon was a sleepy little township primarily associated with everything agrarian and rustic. Today, the story of Gurgaon is anything but rural. Gurgaon was incorporated in the Delhi Metropolitan Region in Delhi's first Master Plan in 1962, but after a twenty-year period of 'neglect,' since the late 1980s when the Indian economy was liberalized, Gurgaon, in the words of a senior town planner, has witnessed a "miraculous and meteoric rise" (fieldwork interview, May 10, 2009). Indeed, with the advent of the housing and IT boom, and heavy influx of foreign investments, present-day Gurgaon, with glitzy towers, corporate head-offices, gigantic malls, and state-of-the-art residential housing enclaves, stands as India's poster child for neoliberal success. Its population has trebled since 1981 as large numbers of middle-class families and migrant workers from all over India have come to live and work in Gurgaon.[2] At this juncture, Gurgaon has come to stand as a 'key articulator' in a new and changing regional geography of mobility, networks, and connectivity that increasingly exceed the limits of the nation, and even the continent.[3] It represents, in Anna Tsing's words, a frontier, "an edge of space and time: a zone of not yet—not yet mapped, not yet regulated. It is a zone of unmapping: even in its planning. It is being imagined as it is being planned and unplanned" (2005, 28). Gurgaon is a frontier of liberal capitalism.

However, in this vista of rapid social and spatial transformation, amidst an unmistakable sense of hope, exhilaration, and opportunity, Gurgaon stands as a paradox. On the one hand, it embodies the narrative of India's arrival on the stage of global finance capitalism, a success story, in which a former village and rural area stand reformed and transformed in the service of technology and capital. On the other hand, Gurgaon is a city of urban malaise, of 'problems'—with water, transportation, electricity, sanitation, and so on—many of which have resulted in several public interest litigations and protests by citizen groups such as resident welfare associations. Even though Gurgaon is besieged by problems and meager infrastructure, land prices continue to rise and a growing number of middle-and upper-class residents continue to populate the gated housing enclaves. They do so because they are able to access a range of privatized services through multiple arrangements, while the large numbers of migrant workers live in crammed housing, with minimal if any access to basic amenities like water, transport, electricity, and health services, and make do in a socially, politically, and visually divided and unequal city, which is blatantly comfortable with its unevenness.

In light of these contradictions and in thinking of how we might account for a city which, despite its glitter and gloss, is fraught with so many 'problems,' in this chapter I will focus on the discourse and practice of urban planning. I find plans and planning provide a productive point of entry through which to analyze the process of urbanization in India as they render the national, regional, and sub-regional politics of government and governance, negotiation, and resistance explicable and offer the prospect of teasing out the shifting priorities and the ambivalences of state power. But, while plans represent a complex, multilayered, and multivocal ensemble of codes and meanings, as 'optical artifacts' they stand as a formal expression of a connected system that endeavors to establish a 'proper' relationship between people and things. Planning, on the other hand, is a practice. It doesn't unravel in neat and predictable ways, but is open to messy and multiple manipulations, coercions, and unintended outcomes. It is a governmental techno-politics par excellence involving human and more-than-human players, an instrument of modern statecraft that simultaneously sets boundaries and secures consent for its exclusions (Roy 2003). Planning, in short, is a live and lively process and a contested domain that generates unexpected collaborations and conflicts that can make the plan possible, or not, as the case of Gurgaon amply demonstrates.

In presenting an account of its regional production and planning, I wish to argue first, that Gurgaon is neither an artifact of neoliberal Indian economic success, a spectacle that was produced by ingenious and innovative strategies of private capital, as is commonly assumed, nor is it a malaise that has resulted overnight from unregulated or unsystematic planning, an example of what a land developer described as "successful accident" (fieldwork interview, May 13, 2009). Instead, as I will show below, the story of Gurgaon is squarely embedded in its planning endeavors, and dates back to the period when the cartographies of Gurgaon and the National Capital Region, New Delhi, were simultaneously being etched. I step back to the period of the 1960s and 1970s, when the practices of urban planning, master plans, and national capital regions were taking shape in post-independent India, and show that the making of Gurgaon is ensconced in a history of contradictory planning imperatives and ambiguous political goals of sovereignty that paved the way for the unequal and deeply divided city we see today.

Second, by tracking the discourse and practice of planning and describing how plans have been redefined, manipulated, and relaxed, I argue that this divided and seemingly dysfunctional city is not a product of flawed planning or Third World ineptitude. Gurgaon manifests a different sort of planning that incorporates flexibility and systematically accommodates the desires and demands of the wealthy and political elites. This flexibility, commonly referred to by planners, is what I am interested in exploring here. I label this exercise of accommodation and concession 'flexible planning.' As I see it, flexible planning encompasses a range of political techniques through which exemptions are routinely made, plans redrawn, compromises made, and brute force executed. It is not a random act, but has a cultural logic that offers access to material and discursive maneuvers of state power, legal and extra-legal networks, and relations of influence. It is a critical component of urban governmentality and is readily deployed to inscribe the social geographies of cities like Delhi and Gurgaon, and most likely in other places as well.

In the growing scholarship on urban governmentality in cities of the global South, there are many powerful accounts of slum evictions, illegal settlements, and resettlements that have drawn our attention to the arbitrary and contradictory nature of urban planning and described the multiple ways in which urban plans disenfranchise the urban poor.[4] Indeed, urban planning is fraught with arbitrariness, where infractions are tolerated, negotiations enacted, and allowances offered. But the exploration of flexible planning describes that it is not just the slum dwellers and the urban poor who devise strategies to deal with the state apparatus; the elite and wealthy are equally, if not more, deft at dodging and crafting alliances to secure their positions of power. The case of Gurgaon, as I will describe in a moment, offers an interesting scenario in which there are no enclaves of slum dwellers and illegality. The entire city is flexibly planned through the complex maneuvering of power by local politicians or powerful elites and relies on a system of exemptions and exceptions. Gurgaon as a whole, from the perspective of the 'plan' is an illegal settlement. It is not an illegal settlement that is surreptitiously occupied by the urban poor, but on the contrary, it is an illegal settlement that is boldly secured through class power, political allegiances, and, more recently, global capital. Ironically, the rationale and technologies of flexible planning are so powerful that even though most of Gurgaon's urban forms are unauthorized and illegal, they are not questioned, challenged, or demolished as some slums in Delhi are. Instead, glossy buildings, shopping malls, and special economic zones are glorified and even sanctified as they stand in the popular imagination as emblems of modernity.

If entire cities like Gurgaon are planned flexibly through sanctioned illegality, it then becomes important to sketch its contours, if we can, and examine the implications of flexibility on the neat distinctions between legal and illegal, sanctioned and unsanctioned that have informed urban planning in terms of how it is performed, and through whose authority. Concomitantly, we have to ask what the contours of the legal would look like if illegality in places like Gurgaon were to become the norm. It is in the blurring of these boundaries between legal and illegal and in the practices of flexibility that I hope the story of Gurgaon offers a point of departure from standard urban theory and urges us to rethink the categories and terminologies that have so far guided the liberal tenets of urban planning.

In the following section, I discuss the contours and practice of flexible planning, and then turn to the specific case of Gurgaon. The final section argues for a rethinking and revising of the conventional conceptual tools that have so far guided urban theory, as urban sites like Gurgaon offer us an opportunity to craft a new framework that exceeds the bounds of Euro-American categories of the urban.

Planning: A Rule of Experts

In *Rule of Experts* (2002), Timothy Mitchell shows how the idea of the economy came to be constituted in the middle of the twentieth century and draws our attention to the complex techno-politics[5] of social calculation and calculability that contributed to the making of expertise. In similar ways, planning—which appeared as a technical and bureaucratic domain in which state policy in post-independence India could be determined—came to be considered a field of expertise (Chatterjee 1993). Armed with its own logic and practices of mapping, charting, exempting, vesting, and authorizing the contents and configurations of land and resources, urban planning in India took shape in the crucible of transnational expertise in the 1950s and 1960s.[6] But, in the process of transfer and translation, it established its particular techno-politics of boundaries, exemptions, exclusions, and, as I argue, flexibility.

As I pursued the question of Gurgaon's planning and development and posed the delicate questions of how the exercise of planning took shape, how land was acquired for development, and how Gurgaon was planned, a retired planner told me,[7]

> Land was acquired in all possible ways. Nobody really knows exactly how, it is a business here—grab, bribe, control, freeze, whatever . . . We made integrated plans, but then there is plan and there is politics. One politician came and wanted things one way, and then there was another politician . . . Small and big politicians, local *sarpanchs* [village heads], businessmen, all wanted a say, the politics took over and I quit. *We have the plans but they don't matter, it is all politics.* (fieldwork interview, June 5, 2009, emphasis added)

In every conversation, the planners in the Urban Development and Town and Country Planning Office, expressed their frustration with the limitations they faced, and referenced 'politics' as the problem. The details of what constituted politics were never really clarified but there pervaded a commonsense understanding of what was meant by the term. It seemed to imply a range of actors including party politicians, business elites, government officials, caste and community leaders, and powerful other 'personalities' who constituted a network of influence, pressure, and threat and regularly intervened in matters of town planning and land acquisition. On this topic, the chief town planner of Gurgaon said,

> Planning has to be regimented and we try to stop chaotic development but we also have to take into account other issues into consideration [sic]. We have to consider the conditions [halat], the politics, and do the planning. Sometimes we have to talk, explain [baat-cheet kar ke, samajha ke], sometimes compromise [aage-peechhe kar ke], sometimes we have to use force [jabarjasti] to develop the city in a right way. We have to be flexible. This is appropriate planning. (fieldwork interview, May 22, 2009, emphasis in original)

As I interviewed more and more planners at different levels of the bureaucracy, I soon realized that the idea of flexibility is well entrenched in the planning discourse in Gurgaon and, in fact, it very much described the long established practice and 'politics' of planning in Gurgaon. The descriptions of planning were often qualified by terms like 'flexible,' 'appropriate,' 'comprehensive,' and 'integrated,' and as the planners described the city plans or master plans, they consistently acknowledged the limitations of planning posed by poor or non-existent land records, competing claims on land, and the deeply politicized nature of land acquisition that in effect charted the messy contours of planning. Flexibility in planning, according to them, is not only necessary but it is also appropriate. From their perspective, flexible planning appears not as an antithesis of planning, or as bad planning, rather, in Bourdieu's (1977) sense, it represents a "regulated improvisation" of practice. Such planning recognizes and responds to political pressures, shifting alliances, insurgent interventions, and material and ecological restrictions. More recently, in the context of liberalization, it has presented a strategy of accumulation of capital through which cities can become financially competitive.

But, as a planner would say, isn't all planning, in a sense, flexible? Indeed, as an undertaking designed to map objects, landscapes, humans, and non-humans, planning is saturated with material, social, and ecological contingencies, and must adopt a degree of flexibility. Planning takes into account the probable and the improbable; it acknowledges oppositions and impediments. In the context of Gurgaon, however, where land markets are highly distorted, I argue that flexibility connotes more than pragmatism. It is, as the planners repeatedly indicated, a deeply political and politicized enterprise, implicated in the local and multilocal matrix of power, and in the calculus of political patronage and electoral politics. Answers to questions concerning how, exactly, flexible planning takes shape, how it is rendered instrumental, whose land tenure is acknowledged, and who can contest encroachments and acquisitions describe a robust and even violent politics of class, caste, and political allegiances which actively inform the process and practice of urbanization in places like Gurgaon. In other words, flexible planning, as I will show below, is imbricated in social relations of power and actively constitutes the everyday politics of sovereignty and political authority, which are powerfully expressed through emergent and unequal urban formations.

Resonant with Roy's (2004) notion of "informal vesting," or Yiftachel's (2009) conceptualization of "gray cities," flexible planning embodies elements of informality. Roy in her study of Calcutta describes the practices of territorialized flexibility as a "technique of discipline and power" and argues that informal vesting, is "not simply a sphere of unregulated activities, but . . . a realm of regulation where ownership and user rights are established, maintained, and overturned through elaborate 'extra-legal systems'" (2004, 159). From the perspective of Gurgaon planners, such planning through improvisation is not a case of exceptionality but is routinely deployed. In fact, according to them, flexibility is what makes the plan and planning feasible. But the mechanisms of flexibility are neither random nor do they render the plan dysfunctional. Even though the plan may seem to fail to map territories and normalize practice, it serves a purpose. As the case of Gurgaon shows, the plan may fail to map territories or 'normalize' practice but it performs ideological and symbolic work. By bestowing meaning and value on certain forms of capitalist urban development, the plan stands not as a fully-formed mission but as a highly tense space that creates room to stabilize elite hegemony by recognizing some claims, while overlooking and undermining others. Like informal vesting, flexible planning grapples with the very messy and intricate everyday politics of caste, class, and patronage, and accommodates personal and political pressures from local and regional political leaders and elites. In short, flexible planning juggles multiple contradictions and through a range of techniques attempts to not only reconcile the contradictions but importantly also makes an urban landscape of competing wills and vision possible.

The aspects of flexible planning I describe here, partly related to the ethnographic material I have collected so far, focus on the complex machinations of sovereign power through which the state devises a series of exemptions and asserts its authority differentially, or flexibly. As I perused the various urban plans and acts, it struck me that an important element of flexible planning is the designing of exemptions. Exemptions, as sanctified acts that free from burden, duty, or obligation—like tax exemptions—are powerful passages that are written in every plan and make the exercise of flexible planning possible. Through an ensemble of arrangements, ranging from legitimate to illegitimate, the plans create 'zones of exemption,' which are not always external to the domain of law, but are mostly (and not always) sanctified by the logic and practice of lawful planning. In the zones of exemption, the state is able to enter into alliances with different groups or individuals, recognize ownership, or exercise force. Depending on political configurations, the zones of exemption are deployed to opportunistically facilitate or hinder urban development, overlook deviations from plans, create room for concessions, or in critical moments show compassion and allocate subsidies to some and not others. Such careful maneuvers describe how in the heyday of India's development, marked by grand visions of improvement and modernity, the strategic and effective logic and practice of exemptions were put in place. As I show, these have come to not only powerfully pave the way for (neo)liberal exemptions, but also feed into the thorny cultural politics of class and caste. Importantly, in places like Gurgaon that embody the rural–urban continuum and sit awkwardly on the margins of metropolitan centers like New Delhi, I would argue there is even more room for flexibility. In the absence of a 'proper' plan and, as I show, being largely peripheral to the state gaze, the rural–urban interface is considered, in the words of a real estate agent, a "free for all" (fieldwork, June 1, 2009). Significant improvisation, exemptions, and flexibility were allowed for partly by the enduring ambivalence and anxiety about the place of the village vis-à-vis the city, especially in the context of rapid urbanization as Glover (this volume) shows, and partly by the lack of clear zoning codes, plans, or guidelines for such urbanizing spaces.

While the example of flexible planning I present here focuses on state-led endeavors, I would clarify that the way in which I define flexible planning means it is not limited to the spatial practices of the state. Given its focus on the shifting and emerging networks of power, the analysis of flexible planning necessarily exceeds the domain of the state, especially in the evolving neoliberal context. At this conjuncture of inter-urban competition, when cities are striving for world-class status and are creating favorable climates for businesses and foreign investors, flexible planning is an important tool for the state to use in actively partnering with large private developers and international donors to (re)inscribe the conditions that allow "flexible accumulation through urbanization" (Harvey 1987). For instance, setting up Special Economic Zones and launching more and more public and private partnerships are examples of flexible planning through which the state is able to change the rules of land use, land transfers, tenancy, and eventually plan flexibly in the context of the changing political economy of capitalism.[8]

I now turn my attention to Gurgaon and present a schematic overview of the critical urban planning acts and decisions in the city's history. I will show how the practices of flexibility and exemption initially excluded Gurgaon from the gaze of developers, who viewed it as a 'handicapped' place due to ecological and political limits. Flexible planning then shielded Gurgaon from the attention of the legislatures of land, and then, more recently, protected the city from the state authorities through privatization. It is this story of exemptions and flexibility that I wish to emphasize in order to draw attention to the variegated practices of planning not as simply divergences from the normative ideal of liberal regimes of planning, but also in order to consider how these accounts may proffer a vantage point from which to revise and challenge the deeply liberal, modernist, and Eurocentric foundations of urban planning.

Gurgaon: A Zone of Exemption

The Indian course of national development has been characteristically marked by what Tania Li, in another context, has called "contradictory positions" (2007, 31). The Indian state in the 1950s and 1960s pursued "two co-equal, yet often irreconcilable goals: the economic aim of achieving maximum increases in agricultural output; and the social objective of reducing disparities in rural life" (Frankel 1971, 3).[9] Seeking to simultaneously transform the rural sector by enhancing agricultural productivity through science and technology, develop institutional mechanisms to bring about redistribution, and promote economic growth in industry, the Indian government launched a series of governmental schemes. But the fundamental contradictions embedded in these plans enshrined a developmentalist and liberal logic of urban planning that facilitated uneven development which was manifest in master plans and five-year plans.

Amidst heady political turmoil nationally and internationally, the state of Haryana was crafted out of Punjab in 1966. The 1960s were important and a range of developments at the central, state, and municipal levels of government were critical in configuring Gurgaon's contemporary terrain.[10] In particular, two developments at the national level were formative. The first was the idea of a national capital region that was beginning to take root and led to the passing of New Delhi's first Master Plan in 1962. The second was a clear shift in agrarian policy towards one that favored rich farmers and irrigated landscapes. After several failed attempts to introduce land reform or improve agricultural productivity, the two droughts in 1965 and 1966, wars in 1962 and 1965, and the US food diplomacy in the context of the cold war intended to align India's economic and political policy with US interests, the Indian government launched a new agricultural policy that has been euphemistically called the Green Revolution. Highly reliant on irrigation and chemical fertilizers, India's Planning Commission adopted the High Yielding Varieties Program for wheat and paddy. Haryana was one of the five Indian states that was part of the Green Revolution and has been heralded as a success story. While the epitaphs of the Green Revolution are being written and there is widespread acknowledgement of its unevenness and ecological limits, what is notable is that even within 'successful' states like Haryana, while the irrigated parts of the state 'gained' from the Green Revolution, regions like Gurgaon, with no water, were exempted from any of the developmental goods of the revolution.

The far-reaching impacts of the Green Revolution are still unfolding but it can be safely argued that they have been uneven at best. The trajectories of urban development in the two cities of Faridabad and Gurgaon in Haryana can be linked to this developmentalist intervention. Geographically, Faridabad is located between the Aravali Mountains and the Yamuna River, and has richer alluvial soil and a higher water table[11] than Gurgaon, which is cut off from the Yamuna by the Aravalis and as a result has poor drainage and little possibility of irrigation. With the coming of the Green Revolution, Faridabad 'gained' significantly from a system of tubewells and irrigation[12] and was able to further enhance its already high agricultural productivity, while Gurgaon was rendered *unfit* for development. By the 1970s, the significant difference in agricultural productivity between Faridabad and Gurgaon resulted in lower land prices in Gurgaon than Faridabad. And since land in Gurgaon was deemed agriculturally less worthy, the conversion of agricultural land to non-agricultural purposes was relatively easy and was effectively facilitated in the 1970s by the Haryana state government. At the same time, while Faridabad 'benefited' from subsidies from both central and state governments which was advantageous to most farmers, both big and small, in Gurgaon only a few of the larger farmers were able to consolidate their positions and access governmental subsidies and lift-irrigation schemes. Smaller and poorer farmers in Haryana were gradually pushed off their land (Patnaik 1987). In short, the Green Revolution, along with other intensive and selective economic development programs introduced in the height of modernist development, initiated a course of uneven development that not only produced a fragmented landscape but also consolidated the powers of the political elite and secured a caste-class calculus of electoral politics and patronage. The legacy of this still marks Gurgaon.

Simultaneously, while the rural areas were surrendered to the dictates of science and technology, the question of the urban hardly figured on the planning horizon in the first two decades after independence. It was only towards the end of the 1950s and in the early 1960s that the question of the urban began to take root. The Third Five Year Plan (1961–66) took up the issue of urbanization for the first time, and there was a growing consensus on developing an integrated and regional plan to meet the economic needs of the nation state. For instance, following on from the recommendation of the Interim General Plan for Greater Delhi (1956), in 1961 a high-powered board was set up under the union minister for home affairs to give "serious consideration for a planned decentralization to outer areas and even outside the Delhi region" (Government of India 1956, 9), introducing the idea of the capital region for the first time. Not surprisingly though, the goal of urban planning and development was strongly guided by the imperatives of industrialization and influence by the looming specter of Malthus.

Recently there have been several rich accounts that masterfully capture the pulse and everyday politics of Indian urbanisms, but, barring few exceptions, the focus of this scholarship has largely been on cities like New Delhi, Mumbai, and Bangalore. There has been very little attention paid to the rural–urban areas that circle these metropolises and grapple with such 'transitional' or peri-urban frontiers where urban expansion is most noticeable.[13] Glover (this volume) traces the conceptual shifts in urban planning and describes how, at the turn of the twentieth century, planners like Patrick Geddes and sociologist Radhakamal Mukerjee emphasized the need to consider the rural and the urban as integrated domains and promoted the idea of 'regional' planning, though in practice only feeble efforts were made to materialize their recommendations. In the 1960s, when city master plans, like those of Delhi and Bombay, were first drawn, they acknowledged the relationship between the city and the village and the need to develop regional plans,[14] but their reach and implementation was limited and fell far short of being regional. In Delhi, the first Master Plan was passed in 1962 and the Delhi Development Authority (DDA) was set up to implement the plan.

This was a critical moment in the history of urban planning as this master plan was an exercise not in city planning, but in regional planning, and had a direct bearing on the neighboring states of Haryana and Uttar Pradesh. According to Delhi's master plan, "to achieve rational growth of Delhi which has been expanding in a most haphazard way . . . and to plan this whole area as a *composite unit* and have an integrated and balanced overall programme of development," (DDA 1962, 1, emphasis added) an area of about 2,072 square kilometers was designated as the Delhi Metropolitan Area. This was a significant development for two reasons. First, the DDA became the sole agency to implement the master plan and came to control most of the land sale and development in Delhi. In this context, private developers like Delhi Land and Finance (DLF), whose role in Gurgaon I will discuss below, were literally pushed out. Second, as many critics have noted,[15] while the DDA provided housing for the poor it subsidized the middle and upper classes more than the poor. With increased migration from rural areas as the population of Delhi rose, the DDA was unable to keep pace and there was a shortage of housing, necessitating an expansion into the peri-urban areas. The designated metropolitan area covered the entire territory of Delhi as well as the five ring towns in the two neighboring states of Haryana and Uttar Pradesh—Loni and Ghaziabad in Uttar Pradesh and Ballabhgarh, Bahadurgarh, and Gurgaon in Haryana—and one town, Narela, in the Delhi territory (DDA 1962, 1). While it was proposed that two new towns, Ghaziabad and Faridabad, be developed as "industrial towns," with projections of relatively higher proportions of workers engaged in manufacturing (close to 14 percent of the total population in 1981), it is important to note here that in the Delhi Master Plan, 1962 Gurgaon was considered to be a "handicapped" district town "for want of water sources" and hence only modest growth was considered possible (1962, 3). Evidently, even though the DDA was set up to implement the plan regionally, its governance was administratively limited to Delhi and it could only implement the plan in the area that was confined within the union territory of Delhi and not in the belt circling New Delhi. For example, the master plan covered a total area of 2,072 square kilometers under its domain but its legislative power could reach only 1,485 square kilometers, leaving the fate of the ring towns, including Gurgaon, ambivalent and suspended. Since there were no interstate or state-level bodies that were set up to oversee development in the ring towns like Gurgaon, a great deal of confusion prevailed. The neighboring state of Uttar Pradesh prepared a draft plan for Ghaziabad and areas contiguous with it, which was incorporated in the Land Use Plan for Delhi Urban Area (Delhi Development Authority 1962). It established local bodies over time which took the administration of these new urban territories in their hands. In Haryana, then Punjab, these issues were not addressed. Since Haryana was created in 1966, there were no established urban administrative bodies to deal with the newly configured geography of this urban region, creating ample room for negotiation and manipulation of the different components of the plan. Apparently, despite the intent to promote regional development, in practice the implementation of the plan could only be realized partially, creating room for flexible and regionally variegated planning.

In this formative moment, while Gurgaon was deemed to have no prospects and was largely exempted from the planners gaze, the neighboring town of Faridabad was identified as one of the 'new towns' that harbored Nehru's dream of modern, industrial India.[16] Planned with the help of a German architect, Otto Koenigsberger, Faridabad was a bustling 'city' of partition refugees from the North-West Frontier Province. Both the central and state governments were committed to bolstering industrial development and made significant investments in the Faridabad–Ballabhgarh Urban Complex, revived the Badarpur power plant, improved irrigation through the Agra Canal, built roads, and provided subsidies to several industries so they could move from Delhi to Faridabad.[17] In the case of Gurgaon, minimal efforts were made to develop the region, provide agricultural subsidies, or attempt to improve transport, power, or sewerage, thereby producing a highly uneven geography of industrialization. As a result, Faridabad emerged as a thriving industrial town, which L. C. Jain (1998) has described as the "city of hope," while Gurgaon remained a "village" with cheaper land prices. In short, even though Faridabad and Gurgaon were demarcated as part of the Delhi Metropolitan Area, Gurgaon unlike Faridabad was lodged ambivalently in the rural–urban continuum and was repeatedly exempted from the gaze of the planners. But, starting in the 1970s and accelerating in the 1980s, the tide began to shift and the Haryana state government—and in particular the then chief ministers of Haryana—had much to contribute to the making of the spectacle that is Gurgaon today.

In order to describe the techno-politics of flexible planning and show how exemptions were made and for whom, I turn my attention to three acts that were critical in making the uneven geography of Gurgaon. First, the 1963 Punjab Scheduled Roads and Controlled Areas Restriction of Unregulated Development Act, second, the 1972 Haryana Urban Land Ceiling Act, and third, the 1975 Haryana Development and Regulation of Urban Area Act. These acts are important as they were passed right after Delhi's Master Plan was crafted and during the period when the new state of Haryana was taking shape. They help describe the art of flexible planning.

The 1963 act is one of the key urban acts that were passed to "prevent haphazard and substandard development along scheduled roads and in controlled areas in the State of Haryana" (1963, 230). Left untouched for the first few years, it became operative only in the 1970s and in many ways has been instrumental in shaping Haryana's urban geography. The act identified certain areas as "controlled areas" that were to be developed by Haryana Urban Development Authority (HUDA). Even though these zones were intended for 'controlled' and planned urban development, there was nothing controlled about them as their definition and boundaries over time became subject to significant manipulation and redefinition by a range of different actors operating at different levels. With the knowledge of the state administration and often in collaboration with local politicians, large private developers like DLF and Ansals manipulated the definition and boundaries of these so-called controlled areas. They offered very high land prices and acquired land from villagers on which to build private housing (Real Estate Review, *Economic Times*, March 2, 1990). In Gurgaon, the area up to 8 kilometers outside the municipal town limit was initially identified as a "controlled area" in which land use patterns were specified. But, this 8-kilometer belt included around fifty villages and their agricultural land. As private developers came to acquire land in controlled areas, agricultural land that was outside the controlled areas was also acquired through careful coercion and generous compensation. As a result, the boundaries of controlled areas became meaningless and by the mid-1990s the entire district of Gurgaon was identified as one.

The accounts of the manipulation of controlled areas abound. Explaining the highly politicized nature of controlled areas, one of the Town and Country Planning Office (TCPO) officers said, "Controlled areas were redefined several times. The *sarpanch* was involved, lots of money exchanged hands, some tried to resist but the Aheers [Yadavs] are not as organized here. Lots of land was first declared *banjar* [unproductive] and then through the 'power of relaxation,' land was taken and good compensation given" (fieldwork interview, May 15, 2009). Instead of being controlled by the plan, controlled areas were feverishly redrawn by "big developers, land-grabbers, and politicians" (*Economic Times*, March 2, 1990). According to the Punjab Scheduled Road and Controlled Areas Act (1963), "power of relaxation" implies that "the Govt. may in public interest, relax any restriction or conditions in so far as they related to land use prescribed in the controlled area in exceptional circumstances" (263), and the state can accordingly acquire land or even subvert the entire plan. Even though the 'power of relaxation,' is an important aspect of all urban plans, in Gurgaon it emerged as an important technology of flexible planning and was extensively deployed by HUDA. In describing how the controlled areas were changed, a town planner said, "Power of relaxation was used in almost each and every case, mostly due to political pressure, the villagers were compensated but mostly it was the *sarpanch* and his family that benefited the most. He alone claimed compensation for hundreds of acres of land. Now there is a court case over this in every village" (fieldwork, May 25, 2009).

Through a regulated improvisation of plans and planning, acquisition of land was made possible in Gurgaon. In short, the first attempt at 'regulated' urban development and zoning, inadvertently or not, created zones of exemption in which the government could and did deploy flexibility in response to the shifting contours of political and economic alliances and priorities. As the rules were changed, exceptions and exemptions were made and the power of relaxation exercised, and through flexible planning, private developers with the acquiescence of the state came to play a decisive role in Gurgaon's development and infrastructure delivery.[18]

Subsequently, the Haryana Land Ceiling Act 1972, Haryana Housing Board Act 1973, and the 1975 Haryana Development and Regulation of Urban Area Act were passed. The 1975 act was particularly important as it was intended to "regulate the use of land in order to prevent ill-planned and haphazard urbanization in and around towns in the State of Haryana" (415). It was passed under the then chief minister of Haryana, Bansi Lal, who had close ties with the then prime minister, Indira Gandhi, and her younger son Sanjay Gandhi. According to this act, which has since been modified, "any owner desiring to convert his land into a colony shall make an application for it and pay the prescribed fee and conversion charged to the Haryana Urban Development Fund" (1975, 423). As a result, planners and others now acknowledge that the act openly introduced a system of payments and permissions to rework the Master Plan and facilitated the entry of private developers. Again through serious political manipulation, vast tracts of agricultural land were designated for urban development, often with the acquiescence of the villagers. It is through a creative interpretation of this act that Bansi Lal's friend Sanjay Gandhi, son of the then prime minister Indira Gandhi got a 'license' to acquire 1,200 acres of land for the Maruti car plant in Gurgaon. DLF, the largest private developer in India, also got his first license to make housing colonies in 1981.[19]

In Delhi in the late 1960s, with the establishment of the Delhi Development Authority (DDA), Delhi's land and housing came under the DDA. As a result, private land developers like the DLF which had built several private housing colonies since independence were driven out. In desperation, Mr. K. P. Singh, son-in-law of the then CEO of DLF, Chaudhry Raghvendra Singh, tried buying and developing land in Faridabad as it was a rather vibrant urban and industrial center, but he was not in luck. As one DLF staff member said in recounting this period, "Singh Sahab and Faridabad did not get along from the very beginning. He started so many projects there, but was eventually forced to abandon them" (fieldwork interview, May 12, 2009). But, Gurgaon and Mr. Singh certainly did get along. DLF's expulsion in the 1960s from Delhi was a vital moment for Gurgaon. Starting in the late 1970s, but much more actively in early 1980s, in a messy politics of land and caste, DLF deftly manipulated the regulatory laws and with the 'blessings' of several political leaders acquired large tracts of agricultural land, some of which they later sold. The fact that Gurgaon was under a municipal council in 1979, unlike Faridabad which was under a municipal corporation, meant that securing relaxation, negotiating development charges, and changing land use and zoning laws was directly under the chief minister and did not require dealing with the labyrinthine bureaucracy. This in part explains Mr. Singh's luck in Gurgaon.[20] Additionally, the presence of active labor unions in Faridabad was an important element as it deterred easy acquisition and re-classification of land.

Amidst all this, the passing of the Land Ceiling Act was a critical trigger. In 1976, the Urban Land Ceiling and Regulation Act (ULCRA) was passed "with a view to preventing the concentration of urban land in the hands of few persons and speculations and profitability therein and with a view to bringing about an equitable distribution of land in urban agglomeration to subserve the common good"(1). This was an important Act as it seemed there was a lingering consideration of equity implicit in the provision of low-income housing and the curbing of land price increases. A separate department known as the Competent Authority, vested with all the powers of the civil court, was set up to implement the act but very soon it faced several challenges (Acharya 1987). For the purpose of this chapter, it is important to note that even though the act was not just for the city but also for the urban agglomerations, the peculiar configuration of the Delhi metropolitan area—that encompassed five of the six ring towns that were in two different states (Haryana and Uttar Pradesh)—made its implementation administratively difficult. As a result, the 5-kilometer ring outside the Delhi border was excluded from the ULCRA. This exclusion was critical for Gurgaon as large swathes of land exchanged hands at this juncture. Similarly, the ULCRA was applicable to land that was identified as 'vacant' in the master plan of the city but this classification was also systematically reworked and manipulated. Finally, built into the act were a range of exemptions that were given to industrial, educational, health, and other public facility institutions but they were wide open to interpretation. Situated in the thick of electoral politics and elite coalitions, M. N. Buch, the former head of the DDA, argues that almost all exemptions made were in fact deeply political and the decision making was not in the hands of government officers but in the hands of political leaders and elites, who were unmapping the landscape of the ring towns, as it was easier to do so on the periphery than in the center. As a result, under Sections 20 and 21, exemptions were granted to large property owners, bogus cooperative societies, and private developers that ultimately led to large areas of agricultural land in Gurgaon being converted and developed by different private builders, like DLF. So dramatic and contentious was the impact of the ULCRA that a planner in Gurgaon speculated that this was one of the main reasons why the Gurgaon district was divided for administrative purposes into Faridabad and Gurgaon districts in 1979. While Faridabad, with a larger population, was governed by a municipal corporation, the city of Gurgaon, after separating from Faridabad, came to be governed by a municipal council which is directly under the chief minister of Haryana, giving him a direct say in matters of land acquisition.[21] There was so much land sold and cash exchanged that a local level bureaucrat remarked, "Deals were not done in thousands or *lakhs*, or even in bags, but in Maruti cars. Cars full of money used to roll in night after night, the villagers were happy but they spent it all, some were smarter but most are either now gone (passed away), have become addicts, or are behind bars" (fieldwork interview, May 10, 2009).

In this scenario of city-making, it is important to note that the manipulation of urban development acts, the ritual of the power of relaxation, and the craft of careful exemption were all exercised through deeply sedimented relations of caste, patronage, and regional and political affiliations. It is beyond the scope of this chapter to present a detailed exposition here, but in a city that has over fifty 'urban villages,' it was the skillful negotiation and juggling of caste dynamics between the land-owning Jats and the Gujjars and Yadavs that was central to the exercise of flexible planning and urban development. In describing the astuteness of Mr. Singh, one *sarpanch* who had 'helped' him said,

> There are more Gujjar and Yadav villages in Gurgaon, few Jat, but mostly Yadav. Mr. Singh is a Jat. He knows how well this all works. Very shrewdly he worked hard to establish good relations with the Gujjars *and* with the Yadavs. He almost had an army of carefully selected brokers, from different castes who helped him assemble land. He offered very good compensation, made sure everybody was happy. Sometimes he used political pressure, filled the pockets of local and even bigger leaders, and some even claim that he funded electoral campaigns. But, most importantly he was an insider and knew how to work the system, an outsider could not have survived here and built a whole city. He was *samajhadar* [knowledgeable], like a *mai-bap* [mother-father, head of the family]. (fieldwork interview, March 1, 2010)

Even though such mediations and negotiations are invisible and it is hard to track their working, they are not *ad hoc*. They are embedded and are systematized through cultural logic and sedimented practices of power that exceed normative ideas of planning. Such micropractices are what Hansen and Verkaik (2009) are identifying when they describe the politics of infrapower and urban charisma, with which Gurgaon seems to be saturated.

In presenting the shifting contours of urban plans, I have examined some of the elements of flexible planning that are embedded in the logic of planning and are selectively deployed for some in the practice of "purposeful construction and consolidation" through which the state and capital are able to deepen their control (Peck and Tickell 2002). Flexible planning, in this sense, does not represent a politics of neglect or contempt for the poor, but instead it describes a politics of sovereignty that exceeds the state and constitutes a relationship of provisional guarantees that can be selectively deployed, by different governance bodies and its allies, for the accomplishment of rule. Importantly, such political practices are not random or outside the domain of state power and operation, as Roy (2003) has incisively shown. They are an exercise in power, inherent in the state, and are in fact systematized and institutionalized (Roy 2003, 159). It is through the practice of flexible planning that the categories and cartographies of power are spatially manifested. While land is differentially valued, and contests and claims are strategically acknowledged or overlooked, the practice of flexible planning works to inscribe and re-inscribe the uneven urban geography in contemporary India.

Incorporating Flexibility: The Future of Urban Theory

In presenting the details of the urban planning regime, analytically my goals have been twofold. First, as flexibility has come to symbolize a late capitalist ethic of work, labor, mobility, production, and consumption, the genealogy of flexibility in planning demonstrates that the politics and practice of flexibility is laced with historically embedded dynamics of power. These power relations work in the pursuit of political hegemony and respond to the matrix of the dominant caste class. Thus, in charting a history of urban planning and governance in Gurgaon, I have attempted to describe the chaotic and fragmented state of Gurgaon not as a reminder of a lingering Third World lethargy or poor planning, but instead as a highly complex and sedimented urban domain of interactions. In this domain the state (and its complex and heterogeneous allies), embedded in its contradictory positions and under shifting political and corporate ties, has systematically nurtured a politics of 'flexible accumulation', authority, and calibrated resource allocation (see Harvey 1987). Even though I have traced the history of the changing practices of state-centered approaches to urban development, such a focus is not limited to the state and is also particularly instructive for considering exercises of planning that go beyond the state. As is abundantly clear in the context of neoliberal shifts towards urban governance, a whole range of new actors have entered into alliances with the state, and rely heavily, and ever so desperately, on flexible planning.

Second, in presenting a case study of an urban region, it is not my aim to provide yet another entry in the ever-expanding surveys of urbanisms. In the context of globalization, in order to comprehend familiar social processes in diverse sites around the globe, there is a great deal of interest in arriving at overarching frameworks. The structures of social formations such as urban regions in Brazil, China, India, South Africa are then deployed to meticulously showcase the parallels or deviations from the norm as well as demonstrate the transferability and mobility of concepts and theories that are usually generated in the shadow of urbanization in the global north. While seemingly comparative and extensive, this approach to 'other' sites that are off the map is in fact deeply parochial since it continues to be blinkered by the concepts and categories devised in the North (Robinson 2003). The problem with such survey-type comparative analysis is that social formations across the globe, like cities, suburbs, or city-regions, are not only caught up in the exercise of classification but are also assumed to be commensurable units of analysis, overlooking and even undermining the historical realities and relational histories through which cities and urbanization take shape.

I am not making an argument against comparisons here, which I believe are critical, but instead arguing that such comparisons are not comparative enough. Trapped between the persistent binary of theory and data, comparisons tend to be propelled by theory and obfuscate the incommensurable data and divergent histories of places that are off the map. Comparisons inadvertently dissolve into historical generalization and universalizing. Instead of ignoring the anomalies and deviations, for a postcolonial anthropology and geography, it is important to precisely hone our analytical gaze in on them and historicize different forms and practices as they take shape. In other words, the story of flexible planning I present should not be read as a fascinating example of emergent urbanism in the global South, or create a desire for identifying other cases of flexibility. Instead, by presenting an account of meddling, negotiation, concession, and patronage that describes the working of political power and authority, I hope to intervene in the ways in which we think about urban planning and theory. The stories of flexible planning as described in the case of Gurgaon are not deviations from the norm but present an opportunity to rethink the fundamentals of urban planning that are anchored in their places of origin. They must lead us to rethink the frames through which we analyze the urban and contribute to Ananya Roy's call "to produce a new set of concepts in the crucible of a new repertoire of cities" (2009, 820). Towards that goal and to overcome the "asymmetrical ignorance" (Roy 2009, 820) of urban and regional theory, the concept of flexible planning is a step towards "an analysis of heterogeneity and multiplicity of metropolitan modernities" (Roy 2009, 821) that will be productive for all cities, and not just those of the South.

Notes

1. Gurgaon is popularly referred to as India's Millennium City, a nomenclature that was adopted to promote its 'modern' and new urban landscape.
2. Gurgaon covers a relatively small area of 2,753 square kilometers. It population has risen from 57,085 inhabitants in 1971 to 1,146,090 in 1991. The growth rate between 1991 and 2001 was estimated to be 42.85 per cent; the population is expected to be close to 2 million in 2011 (Gupta and Nangia 2005).
3. Mbembe and Nuttall (2004, 360).
4. Partha Chatterjee has noted that, "perhaps the most remarkable development in the governance of Indian cities [was] the emergence of an entire substructure of paralegal arrangement, created or at least recognized by governmental authorities, for the integration of low-wage labouring and service populations into the public life of the city" (2004, 137). See also Appadurai (2000), Baviskar (2003), Benjamin (2000), and Davis (2006).
5. According to Mitchell, "Technopolitics is always a technical body, an alloy that must emerge from a process of manufacture whose ingredients are both human and nonhuman, both intentional and not, and in which the intentional or the human is always somewhat overrun by the unintended" (2002, 43).
6. See Morenas (2010); Sundaram (2009).
7. To protect the identities of all the interviewees, names have been changed and pseudonyms used.

8. The concept of flexible planning is productive in another register as well. The debates that ensued between planners at different levels of bureaucracy and between state and central governments over the last few decades present a fascinating account of how new ideas have been introduced and how new models of urban planning have travelled to India, usually from the United States, but sometimes deflected through other sites. See Glover (this volume) for a rich account of crossbreeding and exchange of planning ideas and practices in town planning through the colonial and post-independence periods in India. In the case of Haryana, while Faridabad was planned as a new town in the 1950s by a German architect, Otto Koenisberger, city planners in the 1960s and 1970s were largely uninterested in Gurgaon. But, since the 1980s, several international donors and large developers like Delhi Land and Finance (DLF) have brought in planners, planning models, and mapping technologies from elsewhere and the examples of Metro Manila, Singapore, and Shanghai have been upheld as they describe how planning theory travels flexibly, although not always predictably. A detailed exposition of this is beyond the scope of this chapter.

9. It is important to note that development policy in India was heavily influenced by the developmentalist vision of the US and the politics of foreign policy as well as aid at the height of the cold war played out on the body politic of newly independent and 'non-aligned' nations like India.

10. The year 1966 serves as an administrative benchmark, although the history of urban planning and governance dates back to the politics of colonial and developmentalist regimes that preceded it. This history is beyond the scope of this chapter.

11. See Debroy and Bhandari (2009).

12. In the Faridabad district the area irrigated by tubewells and canals is 50,000 hectares and 38,000 hectares, respectively (Encyclopaedic District Gazetteers of India, Faridabad 1981, 87), while no irrigation is reported in the Gurgaon district.

13. See Anand and Rademacher, Ghertner, and Gidwani (all in this volume); Baviskar (2003); Weinstein and Ren (2009).

14. Thanks to Leon Morenas for this insight.

15. See Maitra (1991); Mukul (1996); Nath (1970; 1993).

16. India's first prime minister, Jawaharlal Nehru and first president, Rajendra Prasad, were both actively involved in the Faridabad Development Board that was set up at the time of partition (Jain 1998).

17. Faridabad, however, faced its own problems associated with industrial development. It had the most polluting factories, a brutal police force, and a very anti-union political leadership (see http://gurgaonworkersnews.wordpress.com).

18. Similarly, the relaxations for 'agricultural cooperatives' were flexibly negotiated and as a result several rich farmers from Haryana and Delhi's upper classes were able to acquire land and convert agricultural land to 'farm-houses' that now dot the Delhi–Gurgaon Highway.

19. The story of how Mr. K. P. Singh, CEO of DLF, came to acquire his first license is widely circulated and is told with much relish by many smaller developers. As one of the developers, who had worked for over ten years with DLF and is now building his own housing complexes gleefully remarked, "It was a pure accident. One night Rajiv Gandhi's jeep had a flat tire and he was waiting on this very highway. Mr. Singh happened to pass by and stopped to help the stranded driver. As it was to happen, this meeting changed the fate of DLF and with it of Gurgaon. Rajiv Gandhi called the chief minister and this is how Mr. Singh got his license in 1981" (fieldwork interview, June 5, 2009). I subsequently heard others narrate the same episode and I have come across it on the internet too. In his recent autobiography Mr. K. P. Singh unabashedly writes, "Gurgaon would never have happened had it not been for Rajiv" (Singh 2011, 194).

20. Towns with a population less than 2 million are managed by municipal councils, which are directly under the chief minister, unlike municipal corporations, which have a mayor and their own local administration. Even when Gurgaon's population exceeded 2 million, it remained under the chief minister until 2008. It was only in May 2011 that the municipal elections were held and the city's first mayor elected.

21. Wahadan (2010) notes that in 1987, relying on the chief minister's discretionary quota, HUDA parcelled the greenbelt surrounding controlled areas. The 'quotas' were temporarily abolished under Chief Minister Devi Lal but were re-sanctioned in 1989 by Om Prakash Chautala. The discretionary power gave the chief minister the right to acquire land.

References

Acharya, B. P. 1987. The Indian Urban Land Ceiling Act: A Critique of the 1976 Legislation. *Habitat International*, 11 (3): 39–51.

Appadurai, A. 2000. Spectral Housing and Urban Cleansing: Notes on Millennial Mumbai. *Public Culture*, 12(3): 627–651.

Baviskar, A. 2003. Between Violence and Desire: Space, Power, and Identity in the Making of Metropolitan Delhi. *International Social Science Journal*, 55: 89–98.

Benjamin, S. 2000. Governance, Economic Settings and Poverty in Bangalore. *Environment and Urbanization*, 21 (1): 35–56.

———. 2008. Occupancy Urbanism: Radicalizing Politics and Economy beyond Policy and Programs. *International Journal of Urban and Regional Research*, 32 (3): 719–729.

Bourdieu, P. 1977. *The Outline of a Theory of Practice*. Cambridge: Cambridge University Press.

Braun, B., and N. Castree, eds. 1998. *Remaking Reality: Nature at the Millennium*. London: Routledge.

Brenner, N., and N. Theodore. 2002. Cities and Geographies of "Actually Existing Neoliberalism." *Antipode*, 34 (3): 349–379.

Chatterjee, P. 1993. *The Nation and its Fragments: Colonial and Postcolonial Histories*. Princeton, NJ: Princeton University Press.

———. 2004. *The Politics of the Governed: Reflections on Popular Politics in Most of the World*. New York: Columbia University Press.

Davis, M. 2006. *Planet of Slums*. London: Verso.

Debroy, B., and L. Bhandari. 2009. Gurgaon and Faridabad: An Exercise in Contrasts. Working Papers No. 101, Centre on Democracy, Development, and The Rule of Law. Freeman Spogli Institute for International Studies, Stanford, CA.

Delhi Development Authority (DDA). 1962. *Master Plan for Delhi*. Volume 1. Delhi.

Encyclopaedic District Gazetteers of India, Faridabad. 1981.

Frankel, F. 1971. *India's Green Revolution: Economic Gains and Political Costs*. Princeton, NJ: Princeton University Press.

Government of India. 1956. *Interim General Plan for Greater Delhi*. Prepared by Town Planning Office, Ministry of Health, National Capital Region Planning Board.

Gupta, R., and S. Nangia. 2005. Population Explosion and Land Use Changes in Gurgaon City, a Satellite of Delhi. Paper presented at the International Union for the Scientific Study of Population XXV International Population Conference, Paris, France, July 18–23.

Hansen, T. B., and O. Verkaik. 2009. "Introduction": Urban *Charisma*—Everyday Mythologies in the City. *Critique of Anthropology*, 29(1): 5–26.

Harvey, D. 1987. Flexible Accumulation through Urbanization: Reflections on "Post-Modernism" in the American City. *Antipode*, 19 (3): 260–286.

Jain, L. C. 1998. *The City of Hope: The Faridabad Story*. New Delhi: Concept Publishing Company.

Li, T. M. 2007. *The Will to Improve*. Durham, NC: Duke University Press.

Maitra, S. 1991. Housing in Delhi: DDA's Controversial Role. *Economic and Political Weekly*, 26 (7): 344–346.

Mbembe, A., and S. Nuttal. 2004. Writing the World from an African Metropolis. *Public Culture*, 16 (3): 347–372.

Mitchell, T. 2002. *Rule of Experts: Egypt, Technopolitics, Modernity*. Berkeley, CA: University of California Press.

Morenas, L. 2010. Planning the City of Djinns: Exorcizing the Ghosts in Delhi's Post-Colonial Development Machine. PhD diss., Rensselaer Polytechnic Institute.

Mukul. 1996. Building from Above, Displacing from Below: Land Development in Delhi. *Economic and Political Weekly*, 31 (5): 259–261.

Nath, V. 1970. Regional Development in Indian Planning. *Economic and Political Weekly*, 3 (5): 247–260.

———. 1993. Planning for Delhi. *Geojournal*, 29 (2): 171–180.

Patnaik, U. 1987. *Peasant Class Differentiation: A Study in Method with Reference to Haryana*. New Delhi: Oxford University Press.

Peck, J., and A. Tickell. 2002. Neoliberalizing Space. *Antipode*, 34 (3): 380–404.

Prakash, G. 2002. The Urban Turn. In *Sarai Reader 2002: The Cities of Everyday Life*, ed. R. Vasudevan, R. Sundaram, J. Bagchi, M. Narula, G. Lovink, and S. Sengupta. 2–7. Delhi: Sarai, CSDS, and the Society for Old and New Media.

Reddy, K. V. 2005. History Resurrected at Gurgaon. Countercurrents.org, August 18. http://www.countercurrents.org/india-reddy180805.htm, accessed December 2009.

Robinson, J. 2003. Postcolonialising Geography: Tactics and Pitfalls. *Singapore Journal of Tropical Geography*, 23 (3): 273–289.

Roy, A. 2003. *City Requiem, Calcutta: Gender and the Politics of Poverty*. Minneapolis, MN: University of Minnesota Press.

———. 2004. The Gentleman's City. In *Urban Informality: Transnational Perspectives from the Middle East, South Asia, and Latin America*, ed. A. Roy and N. AlSayyad. 147–170. Lanham, MD: Lexington Books.

———. 2009. The 21st Century Metropolis: New Geographies of Theory. *Regional Studies*, 43 (6): 819–830.

Singh, K. P. 2011. *Whatever The Odds: The Incredible Story Behind DLF*. With R. Menon and R. Swamy. New Delhi: HarperCollins.

Smith, N. 2002. New Globalism, New Urbanism: Gentrification as Global Urban Strategy. *Antipode*, 34 (3): 427–450.

Sundaram, R. 2009. *Pirate Modernity: Delhi's Media Urbanism*. New York: Routledge.

Tsing, A. L. 2005. *Friction: An Ethnography of Global Connection*. Durham, NC: Duke University Press.

Wadahan, D. 2010. Integrated Governance and Spatio-Temporal Disparities: A Study of Passenger Transport in Gurgaon, India. Paper presented at the Center for the Study of Law and Governance, Jawaharlal Nehru University, New Delhi, May 15.

Yiftachel, O. 2009. Theoretical Notes On "Gray Cities": The Coming of Urban Apartheid? *Planning Theory*, 8 (1): 88–100.

Weinstein, L. and Xuefie Ren. 2009. The Changing Right to the City: Urban Renewal and Housing Rights in Globalizing Shanghai and Mumbai. *City and Community*, 8: 4.

Websites

Gurgaon District Government Website: http://gurgaon.nic.in/f_industry.html, accessed June 2011.

Gurgaon Workers News (GWN): http://gurgaonworkersnews.wordpress.com/, accessed June 2011.

6
From the Frying Pan to the Floodplain: Negotiating Land, Water, and Fire in Chennai's Development

Karen Coelho and Nithya V. Raman

Introduction

From late 2008 to 2009, the Tamil Nadu Public Works Department launched a spate of large-scale slum evictions targeting about 25,000 slum-dwellers in Chennai and its adjoining municipalities. This drive was aimed at clearing encroachments on nineteen water bodies to restore their water-holding and flood-carrying capacities. Ironically, some of the same water bodies had been declared "defunct" by the government's Housing Board in the early 1990s, to defend its construction of a large-scale housing project by land-filling on the lakebeds. Residents of these slums, if they fulfilled certain criteria, were moved to resettlement colonies located 20–40 kilometers outside the city, typically also on floodplains or lakebeds. The slum demolitions were conducted with a conspicuous deployment of police, and the common sequel was long lines of anxious people waiting at local revenue offices for tokens that entitled them to a resettlement site.

Meanwhile, a series of fires broke out in Chennai's slums in the summer of 2009. While this was hardly an unusual occurrence, these fires were of a size, speed, virulence, and timing that raised suspicions of arson. Residents of the fire-affected slums, sited precariously on strips of land near burial grounds or at the edges of waterways, hinted that some slum residents had set these fires themselves to gain access to the resettlement tokens that were now routinely distributed to slum residents following disasters like fires or floods.[1]

These episodes indexed for us the measures of desperation and pragmatism with which the urban poor living in "objectionable" spaces had come to negotiate their shelter options.[2] They appeared to be balancing the state's evidently hardening intent to reclaim waterfront real estate against the emerging possibilities of obtaining "secure" housing allotments in resettlement colonies. These considerations in turn were weighed against the squalor and struggles faced in their current habitats and expected in the resettlement colonies. Chennai's slum residents, then, framed their negotiating strategies from tight spaces, literally with their backs to the river.

This chapter seeks to show how the complex and changing landscapes of urban land and water are closely interwoven with the complex and changing landscapes of eviction and relocation in Chennai. It argues that the rationalities underpinning projects of spatial engineering in the city have shifted, reversed, and contradicted themselves over time, revealing the ready plasticity of environmental policymaking in growing cities.[3] On the one hand, this is a story of the making and remaking of the city's physical form through historical processes of land reclamation from water bodies through spontaneous settlement, but also and more importantly as part of the state's urban expansion programs for housing and institutional development. On the other hand, this is simultaneously a story of the constitution of the city's social geography through large-scale relocations of the urban poor to flood-prone marshlands or swamps on the edges of the city, particularly since the 1980s. This was a process through which the boundaries between land and water in urban peripheries were reshaped—sometimes casually blurred and sometimes consciously and irreversibly re-inscribed.

These stories, of the state filling water bodies to house people, then removing people to restore water bodies and relocating them onto other water bodies, speak, at one level, of historical shifts in the political and economic rationalities that connect municipal governance to paradigms of planning and social engineering. Where urban water bodies were once seen as land-in-the-making, to be filled and reclaimed for bus stops, housing projects, dump yards, and resettlement sites, they are now seen as lakes-in-the-making, to be cleared, dredged, desilted, and beautified. These shifting rationalities are underpinned by transformations in conceptions of the urban—from developmentalist visions of cities as sites of social and economic mobility, catalysts of modernity for the region, to neoliberal visions of cities as strategic nodes for the operations of financial globalization.[4] Competitive efforts by municipal and state governments to attract global investment, reliant on instruments like credit ratings by independent agencies, critically alter the meanings and values associated with water in the urban landscape. Water bodies and waterways are now, above all, emblems of the city's aspiration to world-class status. Waterfront development, beautification, and eco-restoration are idioms through which cities position themselves in the global arena as well as direct strategies for capital accumulation through real estate value.

Waterways in Chennai have also become preferred sites for high-value infrastructure projects such as elevated transport corridors. Paradigms of infrastructure development in globalizing cities, however, as Koolhas (1994), Gandy (2004), and Swyngedouw (2004) point out, are no longer even notionally oriented toward the integration of urban space or equitable distribution of urban resources. Rather, where land values and real estate surpluses determine the feasibility of (increasingly privately provided) basic infrastructure schemes such as water supplies and roads (Benjamin 2008; Ranganathan et al. 2009), infrastructure development becomes premised on and contributes to a deep fracturing of the urban social body. Thus, water, fundamental to the siting of cities since the beginning of the urban concept, remains critical in shaping and giving substance to class and caste geographies in new global cities. As Gandy has emphasized, water is a critical dimension not only of the physical but also of the social production of urban space.

Elsewhere, we have described how a high-profile project announced by the Tamil Nadu government in 2009 for the restoration of the Cooum River made its bid for public credibility by focusing efforts on the removal of slums from the riverbanks (Coelho and Raman 2010). Potentially threatening or undercutting this river restoration effort was another project, announced simultaneously by the same government, to construct an elevated expressway along the river and into its bed. The two projects, however, converged in their strongly stated goal of slum eviction. The expressway's non-linear alignment was publicly justified by the "clear advantage" it would offer in bringing about the evacuation of slum areas along the riverbanks (Wilbur Smith Associates 2008, Chapter 2, p. 1). Scapegoating the poor has, over the past two decades, become part of the official discourse of salvaging urban ecologies (see also Doshi, this volume, and Ghertner, this volume).

It is important, however, not to overstate the linear nature of historical shifts in environmental rationalities or of administrative logic in studying their implications for the urban poor. Close examination of the way that "urban nature" has been shaped in Chennai through interactions between planning paradigms, social struggles, and technology reveal a set of anomalies, contradictions, and reversals. These suggest that policy shifts are not always governed by teleological progression but rather by arbitrary and convenient measures glossed into ecological rationales. Or that policymaking is sometimes simply incoherent.

This chapter elaborates its points by exploring two parallel sites of shifting urban natures in Chennai. First, it examines the changing morphologies of water bodies—particularly lakes, swamps, and marshes on urban peripheries—as they have been used to accommodate urban expansion and resettlement projects, and more recently, to rescue top-dollar water bodies in the city's core. As an example, it tracks how the Pallikaranai Marsh in Chennai has been exploited over the years, both for siting various municipal infrastructures and for resettling evicted slum-dwellers, deepening the vulnerability of the marsh ecology as well as the urban poor. Second, it examines an eco-park project on the Adyar River, pointing out the paradoxical partnership of eco-restoration with real estate development and elevated corridors, producing effects of uncertainty for the river's sustenance and insecurity for the poorer residents of the area.

Shifting Morphologies of Land and Water in Chennai

The physical forms of land and water bodies have undergone dramatic shifts over the last four decades of Chennai's history. These changes, as traced below, are closely linked with the histories of shelter policies and the politics of conservation in the city.

Making land from water: Urban expansion in the 1970s and 1980s

Water lines in the city have been written and rewritten by various actors over time, settlers, squatters, and builders,[5] but most heavily by the state in projects of spatial re-engineering. Environmentalists often tell the story of Chennai and its surrounding areas by referring to old *eri* maps, which show that most of the lands in and around the city were once pockmarked with tiny water bodies. Monsoon waters flowed across the region from west to east and drained into the ocean. To capture these waters for agricultural uses, local people built bunds in low-lying areas, forming what are now identified as lakes or *eris*.[6] Along with traditional tanks, temple ponds, and rivers, these *eris* formed part of the region's intricate network of seasonal water bodies and waterways, some of which dried out or disappeared during the summer months. These perennial patterns of disappearance became more permanent as the conversion of water to land became a strategy of urban expansion in Chennai.

Planning documents in the early 1970s began to highlight the need for large-scale land acquisition by the government for public-housing projects, primarily in urban nodes and satellite towns on the peripheries of the city, as areas there would be cheap enough to make such acquisition feasible (Alan Turner Associates 1980, 22).[7] Through the 1970s and 1980s a combination of factors, including pressure to develop infrastructure for a growing population, rising land prices in the core city, and the cumbersome and time-consuming nature of land acquisition, pushed government housing and infrastructure projects on to public land that the government already owned, land that was unsuitable for other residential or commercial construction, or land outside the city's boundaries.

From the mid-1970s onwards, the World Bank began lending to the urban housing sector in Tamil Nadu, and began to steer the policies of the Tamil Nadu Slum Clearance Board (TNSCB) from its rather modest efforts at *in situ* tenement construction toward scaled-up models of sites-and-services schemes that the World Bank was advocating worldwide (Raman 2008). These schemes required large amounts of land. Many of these new housing projects for the poor were located on flood plains or other ecologically fragile lands. The Tamil Nadu Housing Board, also with support from the World Bank, implemented what came to be known as the Eri Scheme which relied on filling "defunct" lakes and water bodies to accommodate large housing projects, many of which ultimately benefited middle-income groups. Explicit policies thus enhanced the supply of urban land for housing through landfilling and construction on vast and "useless" expanses of urban lakes, often at considerable cost. In addition to housing, infrastructure such as sewage treatment plants and dump yards were also sited on water bodies: two of the most important freshwater wetland ecosystems of the region, the Kodungaiyur Marsh in the north of Chennai, parts of which had earlier been known as "the lagoon," and the Pallikaranai Marsh in the south of the city were steadily, over the 1980s and 1990s, turned into garbage dump yards for the city.

The ecological implications of siting projects on low-lying floodplains were already evident by 1980, when planning documents commented on how the government, in its "search for easily acquired land" established tenement communities on the flood plains of the city's rivers; this led to disastrous consequences during floods (Alan Turner Associates 1980).[8]

Reclaiming water bodies: The emergence of "ecological value" in the 1990s

The governance of water in Chennai has proceeded through clear epochs: until the 1990s, as outlined above, water in the landscape was of low value in urbanization schemes and water bodies were seen at best as a potential expanse to fill and develop, and at worst as a hazard susceptible to dumping, pollution, and encroachment. It has only been since the 1990s that the concept of "ecological value" began to figure in official planning documents, and increasingly to overlap with commercial value.[9] The government's compulsion to demonstrate concern for environmental issues resulted partly from its participation in global platforms such as the Sustainable Chennai Project (SCP) (see footnote 10), partly from the amplified voice that local civil society environmental groups had achieved, and partly from the increased severity of droughts interspersed and alternating with floods, which created unprecedented crises in the city. More serious attention to flood alleviation, water harvesting, and conservation of rainwater through water body reclamation and restoration began to be articulated, for instance, in Chennai's Second Master Plan published in 2008 (CMDA 2008), and in the planning documents of Metrowater, Chennai's state-run water utility.

A convergence also began to emerge, both discursively and in funding schemes, between these flood mitigation/water-harvesting programs and the increasingly forcefully articulated visions of a "slum-free Chennai." The Slum Clearance Board from the 1990s began to focus its energies on the construction of large resettlement colonies on the urban peripheries, substantially funded by the central government's flood alleviation program, World Bank-sponsored post-tsunami projects, and the Jawaharlal Nehru National Urban Renewal Mission (JNNURM). The latter also funds projects to restore lakes and tanks in the Chennai Metropolitan Area, including the removal of encroachments and eviction of slum-dwellers.

The profound change in Tamil Nadu's political climate relating to issues of the environment and the poor was clearly evidenced in the Tank Encroachment Act passed in May 2007. This act ignored or reversed long-established policies guiding slum clearance in the state of Tamil Nadu and vested unprecedented powers in the Public Works Department (PWD) and the District Collector's Office to effect evictions, entirely bypassing the Slum Clearance Board.[10] The thrust to revive storage capacity in water bodies received powerful political backing by the state's ministers, legislators, and members of parliament in the late 2000s. Slum eviction drives have thus, since the 1980s, received an impetus as never before by being located in two convergent strands of apparently progressive "salvage" discourses: one of ecological restoration and the other of slum resettlement with promises of secure tenure.[11]

In this teleology of ecological enlightenment in urban governance, the urban poor have been positioned as anachronisms, mistaking water for land or clinging to the amorphous boundaries between land and water. Inevitably, then, they are bound for forceful eviction as urban governance faces up to the ecological imperatives of floods, drainage, and water conservation. What disrupts this scheme is that the state's relocation solutions re-insert them back into their anachronistic spaces on lakes or marshlands. The following section outlines the impacts of these resettlements on local ecologies and on the lives of the resettled.

Engineering Habitat and Development on the Pallikaranai Marsh

The Pallikaranai Marsh is part of the larger southern Chennai floodplain, which once contained marshlands, satellite wetlands, and pasture lands (Vencatesan 2007). Extending over 5,000 hectares until about thirty years ago, the marsh absorbed surplus runoff from the region's lakes and tanks, and also served as the primary source of groundwater recharge for residential suburbs dependent on the southern aquifer (Anuthaman et al. 2008).

Less than 10 percent of the original marsh area remains intact today. (Anuthaman et al. 2008). Although locally known as *kaiveli*, a Tamil word for marsh, the area's official classification as a wasteland left the area open for use, both by the city for siting municipal services, and by private developers. Partly owing to the administrative fragmentation of the marsh area into multiple *panchayats* (local government bodies), and partly due to its physical fragmentation by urban residential, transport, and commercial developments as shown below, the city failed to recognize the extent of the marsh, the unity among its various segments, and the interconnections between the marsh, the larger floodplain, and the drainage channels to the sea.[12]

The marsh and its surrounding areas faced a barrage of municipal infrastructure construction from the early 1970s as the Municipal Corporation of Chennai capitalized on this vast expanse of "wasteland" on the city's peripheries. In 1970, it began dumping garbage from the city on a 19-acre portion of the marsh in Sevaram Village (Anuthaman et al. 2008). Within a decade, it moved the dump to a new section of the marsh in Perungudi without permission from state authorities (Neeraja 2009b). Indiscriminate dumping continued here for decades until the dump yard stretched to an area of 57 hectares (Vencatesan 2007). Despite repeated complaints from residents and court orders, the corporation continued to burn unsegregated waste in the dump yard until as recently as 2009. Similarly, two sewage treatment plants located nearby were found to have been regularly releasing untreated or partially-treated sewage into the marsh water for years (Anuthaman et al. 2009).

The city also actively encouraged the colonization and commercialization of areas around the marsh, starting with the construction of the Velachery–Tambaram Road, which cut the marshland into two, and opened hitherto inaccessible areas to the west of the road for development.[13] The city also developed an information technology (IT) corridor along the eastern side of the marsh, with some 15 million square feet of commercial space and residential areas including luxurious gated communities (Devasahayam 2009). Large sections of these developments cut into the eastern side of the marsh and put further strain on already stressed aquifers. A sprawling station for the Mass Rapid Transit System (MRTS) came up on the northern side (Vydhianathan 2007). Allotments were given to institutions like the National Institute of Ocean Technology and the Center for Wind Energy Technology, projects like the Chennai One Information Technology SEZ, and residential colonies like the upscale Secretariat Colony. This proliferation of buildings on the marsh bed was both a cause and a result of the gradual drying of the wetland since the 2000s.

Environmentalists had been agitating against the dump yard and sewage treatment plants for years, but after severe floods affected residential areas along the marsh in 2002, a widespread citizen movement began actively pressing for better floodplain management through restoration and conservation of the marsh. The Save Pallikaranai Marsh Forum was led by local resident welfare associations and, with the support of a sympathetic media, finally pushed the government to commission a holistic study on marsh preservation (Vencatesan 2007). By then, however, what was arguably the most important ecological feature of the marsh, the water channel known as the *Okkium Madugu*, had already been destroyed (as discussed below), leading to the drying up of vast swathes of marshland above and below it.

Thus, even as the state of Tamil Nadu passed some of the most forward-looking legislation on groundwater management, it not only failed to protect the natural systems that replenished its groundwater sources, but it actively encouraged the construction of large-scale municipal and private developments on reclaimed marshland. The manifest damage to the southern aquifer since the 1990s (Devasahayam 2009), and the sudden and significant increase in flooding problems in neighboring parts of the city since the early 2000s speak of the incoherence of the "environmental planning and management" (EPM) frameworks that had been deployed by Chennai's urban planning establishment since the early 1990s.[14]

Resettlement on the marsh

In the late 1990s, 2,202 families living in slums along the Buckingham Canal in Mylapore were evicted to make way for an MRTS line, and moved into a resettlement colony called Mylai Balaji Nagar built on the Pallikaranai Marsh. A decade later, most of these families had returned to the city because they had not been given ownership over the land as promised, and because the colony remained woefully lacking in basic services. Despite the failure of this relocation effort, the government built another, much larger tenement cluster in the marsh, this one called Kannagi Nagar, near the village of Okkium Thoraipakkam (Manikandan 2008; Lakshmi 2006). Construction began in the year 1989, and by the end of 2009 the settlement comprised 15,000 apartments. The scale and pace of the change that this colony wrought on the local area in terms of population alone was enormous: the 2001 census recorded the population of Okkium Thoraipakkam *panchayat* as 29,000, while Kannagi Nagar's 15,000 homes added nearly 100,000 more people from 2002 on, expanding the *panchayat's* population by about 344 percent in less than a decade (Manikandan 2009).

The environmental transformation wrought by this resettlement colony was equally dramatic. The site of Kannagi Nagar required massive engineering interventions in order to make the marshy land suitable for large-scale tenement construction. According to the Slum Clearance Board's project proposal, "The site chosen for rehabilitation . . . is low-lying and requires filling to an average depth of 2.5 meters to bring it up to the level of the surrounding development and to avoid inundation during monsoon" (TNSCB, undated). Engineers from the TNSCB who worked on Kannagi Nagar evinced strong pride in having overcome the challenges that the site posed for this construction. One engineer described in detail their efforts to reinforce the entire 100 acre site with selected earth from quarries.[15]

Environmentalists point out that these engineering feats have caused profound damage to the marsh. Kannagi Nagar is located next to what experts variously call the "aorta" or the "pulmonary vein" of the marsh, the Okkium Madugu. The Madugu formed the primary channel for the critical interchange of freshwater and saline water needed to sustain Pallikaranai's marsh ecology. To counter charges of blocking the area's drainage by the construction of Kannagi Nagar, the PWD built a canal to directly convey waters from the Madugu to the nearby Buckingham Canal. However, as environmentalists point out, the absorptive and flood-mitigative functions of the Madugu were far from fulfilled by an artificial canal. In 2008, when a resident of Okkium Thoriapakkam filed a case against further construction of slum resettlement colonies on the marsh, an expert committee constituted by the High Court to examine the matter argued that the diversion of the Okkium Madugu had already taken its toll.[16] Aerial photographs of the area over time reveal that the PWD's canal could not prevent the marshy areas surrounding Kannagi Nagar turning from the moist green of the marsh to an arid grey.[17] The committee also suggested that the raising of the plinth level in the slum resettlement site of Kannagi Nagar had probably increased flooding in other areas of the city, and that the greatly enhanced problems of flooding in Chennai since 2002, despite the reduction in the total number of rainy days, was directly attributable to the loss of natural buffers like the marsh and wetlands (Anuthaman et al. 2009a).

In April 2007, as a result of the sustained campaign of the Save Pallikaranai March Forum, a series of court orders and committee reports, the government of Tamil Nadu classified 317 hectares of the marsh as "reserve forest," and handed the land to the Forest Department for protection. In February 2010 another 150 hectares was reclassified as forest. News reports celebrated this victory as a success story of the citizen-led movement.[18] However, the reluctance of the government to act on these orders suggests that this view is too optimistic. The Revenue Department dragged its feet in demarcating the boundaries of the reserve forest area, and garbage dumping and burning in the marsh continued long after its designation as a reserve forest (Oppilli 2007, 2009). The court-appointed committee's report grimly concluded that "the whole site is surrounded by housing colonies, including Kannagi Nagar and Secretariat colony, thus making it very difficult to conserve it as a wetland" (Anuthaman et al. 2009a, 3).

New vulnerabilities of resettlement

By late 2009, the 15,000 apartments built in Kannagi Nagar had been filled, most recently by people evicted from the banks of the Cooum River where river restoration and elevated highway projects had been announced. To a visitor, at first sight, Kannagi Nagar's landscape of solid three-story buildings massed against the skyline suggest a relief from the fragility of thatched huts on the city's riverbanks. Yet, it soon became evident that the intricate engineering interventions into the marsh had not succeeded in protecting the colony's residents from the rigors of being housed in the middle of a floodplain. Even a mild spell of rains caused water to collect in pools and stagnate for days, sometimes weeks, with some areas requiring physical removal of water.

But the urban poor are no strangers to floods, or for that matter to fires, mudslides, or a range of other quotidian hazards which are typically incorporated into their annual cycle of coping. One resident of Kannagi Nagar described how, in her earlier slum settlement of Sathya Nagar in the city, the entire community routinely packed away their belongings and moved out of their homes for several weeks every year during the monsoons, camping wherever they could until the floods subsided.[19] Authors like Davis (2006) and Seabrook (1996) have framed settlements of the poor in terms of bitter trade-offs, where homes poised on riverbanks, volcanic hill slopes, quarry edges, or flood-prone marshlands are tolerated for the livelihoods and opportunities to be gleaned from city living. Such precarious sites are poverty's niche in the ecology of the city.

In Kannagi Nagar the critical levers of this trade-off became clear as the loss of livelihood opportunities entailed by the distance from the city acutely enhanced the overall vulnerability of residents' lives, while their susceptibility to floods and other "natural" events remained more or less the same as in their previous habitats. The resettled slum-dwellers also became subject to a host of new risks, including those induced by the paucity of basic services such as drinking water, electricity, schools, and health care in Kannagi Nagar (Raman 2009). It took more than a decade of struggle by residents, through various means including street demonstrations, postcard campaigns, and media stories, for the provision of basic services to approach some level of adequacy. It is only since 2010 that houses in Kannagi Nagar have obtained legal electricity connections, drinking water is supplied with some regularity (once in two days instead of once in ten), and garbage collection services have been initiated. But the greatest insecurity derived from Kannagi Nagar's location: its distance from work, markets, schools, and health facilities. Over the ten-odd years since their resettlement, impoverishment and indebtedness were the predominant characteristics of life in the colony, according to several residents. Many of the resettled people were casual or daily-wage workers who depended on negligible transport costs and flexibility of movement to make a viable living. Both of these conditions were severely compromised by Kannagi Nagar's location, leading to lost jobs and significantly lower incomes, particularly in the early years. When we asked a resident who had lived there since 2001 to compare life in the old slum with her present home, she declared that the old city slums, despite their squalid and insecure conditions, were decidedly better places to live because "at least there we had Rs.10 in our hands. Here we need some money in hand even to go and find work! All our money goes away for buses and doctors and everybody is deeply in debt."[20] The crises of employment, liquidity and economic security had the expected results: residents and news reports highlighted acute problems of alcoholism, crime and violence against women, and a high incidence of suicides by women, usually resulting from despair over marital discord with unemployed or indebted husbands (Neeraja 2009a). The sense of isolation experienced in the settlement caused some new residents to call it *Kannagi Theevu* or Kannagi Island.[21]

Residents were also aware of the ecological fragility of their new homes, heavily massed on a marshland. One young woman described her fear of the possible consequences:

> It is very wrong, very dangerous, stuffing so many people into one place. Disasters are just waiting to happen, and we live in fear. We are on swampy land, this area used to be full of water. We are all wondering when we will just collapse into the mud. And when that happens, where will we run? Who will run out of their buildings first? It is all so crowded here![22]

It also must be noted that in recent scrambles for urban renewal and a slum-free city, Kannagi Nagar, with its poor services and squalid conditions, has become a high watermark for resettlement. Families evicted from slums outside the city, in financially weaker municipalities and *panchayats*, face even more dismal resettlement conditions. The several thousands of families evicted in the mid to late 2000s for lake restoration projects in the larger metropolitan area of Chennai were simply given a cent each of land in villages like Nallur, Kanadalapalayam, or Koodapakkam, 30–40 kilometers away from their original homes. By 2009, most had not received *pattas* or housing and lived in thatched huts with no water, toilet, or electricity. Most of these resettlement areas are also sited on flood plains or shallow lakes, exposing the residents to hazards from snakes and insects. People resettled in these areas have sometimes been forced to evacuate their allotted plots due to frequent fires, sometimes caused by other local claimants to the open lands.

These scenarios of relocation are being framed by local housing rights movements as part of a 'new urban untouchability,' produced through sequestering ever larger masses of city residents, predominantly of the lowest castes, into ghettos in hazardous and ecologically fragile peripheral areas, thereby reproducing the spatial, ecological, and social geographies of caste discrimination.

A study of livelihoods and work in Kannagi Nagar carried out in 2011–12 (Coelho et al. forthcoming) provides a detailed account of how urban poverty is reproduced in post-resettlement contexts through the mechanism of precarious work. The study shows how, while economic developments along the IT corridor have significantly enlarged work opportunities locally, employment still remains an insecure and unstable condition for residents of Kannagi Nagar, primarily because of the poor working conditions (low wages, long hours, lack of safety, job security or social security) found in the globalized economy of the region. Workers from Kannagi Nagar, even those with secondary or higher levels of education, and particularly women, were inserted into the formal sector establishments of the area (large manufacturing, commercial and IT firms or offices) on very poor terms. This was partly because of the supply of cheap labor assured by the large concentration of workers forcibly settled in the colony.

Meanwhile, the phenomenon of evicted slum-dwellers returning to squat informally in or near their previous homes has been largely blocked by the immediate enclosure or reallocation to other uses of the cleared lands by determined city authorities. But rental and real estate relations have in turn spawned new kinds of traffic, this time of workers between the city and resettlement camps. It is not uncommon for resettled families to rent out their new allotments, and use the funds to subsidize their lease of small quarters near their previous workplaces, especially in cases where the substantial earning potential of city work warrants such economies. Resettlement sites in their turn appear to be rapidly filling the void in low-end rental housing markets for the city's working poor.

Eco-Restoration for the Global City: An Eco-Park on the Adyar River

River restoration as part of an urban renewal paradigm in globalizing cities compresses multiple and mutually reinforcing drives of neoliberal governance into its design, among them the creation of infrastructure assets, enhancement of commercial values, and promotion of real estate investments. Within this closed circuit of *raison d'etat*, beautification, restoration, and development serve as metonyms for slum clearance. The story of the Adyar Poonga, an eco-park, highlights how this state-managed eco-restoration project maintains and reinforces the heavy infrastructure-investment bias of current city governance. The Poonga, through its twenty-year history, exemplifies the processes through which discourses around environmentalism, eco-parks, and conservation have become part of the infrastructure required to become a 'global city,' and have threatened the existence of old settlements of the urban poor and artisanal fisherpeople in its vicinity.

Around the mouth of the Adyar, one part of the river curves back in the shape of a flexed arm, creating a rich estuarine ecosystem bounded by an inlet of water known as the Adyar Creek. The area was a focal point for environmental action in Chennai by civil society groups in the 1990s. This section discusses how the state's response to citizens' demands for preservation of the estuary and creek took the form of high-profile proposals for the construction of an eco-park, coordinated by infrastructure-financing institutions in public–private partnership mode. While most of the ecologically-sensitive lands that the environmental groups sought to protect have since been heavily built over and the natural ecology of the creek more or less destroyed, the institutional mechanism set up to implement the eco-park project, the 'Adyar Poonga Trust' (now renamed the Chennai Rivers Restoration Trust) has diversified its mandate to propose elevated transport corridors and infrastructure developments along the Adyar River. Poor communities that inhabited the area, meanwhile, have either been moved out of the city or remain in constant fear of eviction.

In 1993, a group of local associations including the Citizen and Consumer Action Group (CAG), Exnora, and the Environment Society of Madras filed a case against the government seeking to prevent the construction of a memorial to B. R. Ambedkar on 45 acres of land in the Adyar Creek area. The court ruled that the Ambedkar Memorial should be limited to a 1.5-acre site, and asked that the rest of the creek be restored to its original condition.[23] Meanwhile, a powerful land baron of the area, M. A. M. Ramaswamy, who owned large amounts of land in and around the estuary in a neighborhood called MRC Nagar, began to sell and/or build on this land, large parts of which comprised tracts protected from building by the Coastal Regulation Zone (CRZ) rules. Through the 1990s and the 2000s, several large buildings went up on these delicate estuarine lands, including high-end residential complexes, five-star hotels, and commercial real estate targeted at IT companies. In response to these developments, CAG filed another court case, this time against M. A. M. Ramaswamy, asking that building construction be prohibited in this area in line with CRZ regulations. The court ruled in M. A. M. Ramaswamy's favor,[24] and construction was permitted to continue on the majority of the land. New construction was also permitted in MRC Nagar despite the earlier court ruling that the Adyar Creek should be restored to its original condition.

In 2003, partly in response to public pressure to preserve the Adyar Creek, the state government gave 58 acres of the creek area to the Chennai Corporation, which governs the city, to build an eco-park. The cast of actors chosen to create this eco-park was intriguing: the project was initially headed by the Chennai Corporation and the Tamil Nadu Road Development Corporation (TNRDC), a special purpose vehicle (SPV)[25] that had developed major toll roads like the East Coast Road and the IT Corridor in Chennai, and later by the Tamil Nadu Urban Infrastructure Financial Services Limited (TNUIFSL), an agency created to finance infrastructure and promote economic development in the state. Shortly afterwards, the Adyar Poonga Trust (APT) was created through a government order, and comprised a high-level assemblage of bureaucrats that seemed out of proportion to the scope and finances of the project, perhaps indicating the project's symbolic importance to the government. It was chaired by the chief secretary to the government of Tamil Nadu, and trustees included the principal secretaries in the Finance, Highways, Public Works, and Environment and Forest Departments, and the commissioner of the Corporation of Chennai.[26] Ironically, many of these trustees were defendants in the original case filed by the CAG to protect the creek.[27]

Although the APT hired an environmental consultancy firm from Auroville, the Pitchandikulam Forest Conservancy, to advise and develop the plan for the project, environmental groups, including CAG, doubted the sincerity of the government's efforts at ecological preservation on the Poonga. They were apprehensive about what the 'eco-park' would entail, especially as its coordinating agency, TNUIFSL, had no expertise in ecological conservation.[28] Many civil society groups suspected that the government was using the eco-park as an opportunity to gain control of the entire stretch of land, and to open the area up for private real estate development, especially eying Srinivasapuram, the fishing hamlet and declared slum area located on prime land at the mouth of the river.[29]

Joss Brooks, the head of Pitchandikulam Forest Conservancy, disagreed with CAG and other environmentalists' concerns about the government's motivations in promoting the eco-park; according to him, the impetus came from a new breed of enlightened bureaucrats who genuinely cared about environmental protection. He dismissed CAG's preferences for simple environmental protection in the creek as "putting a fence around the area," and suggested that the eco-park proposal arose from a pragmatic acknowledgement that the creek was in an urban area, and environmental protection needed to be combined with human use.[30] He argued that the eco-park served as a signal that Chennai was becoming part of the class of global cities: "To take business away from Delhi, Hyderabad, Bangalore, the bureaucracy here must also speak the language of the global metropolis."[31] Clearly, according to Brooks and others involved with the Poonga project, this language included the vocabulary of eco-parks and environmental sustainability.

There were two sections of the poor who were affected by the battles over the Poonga. The first comprised residents of Rajah Gramani Thottam, a squatter settlement that lay within the 58 acres of the park. The government dealt with these 'encroachers' summarily—they were cleared and moved to Semmenchery in early 2007 (Ellis 2010, 8–9). The other was the fishing village of Srinivasapuram, located on the thin strip of land which abutted the creek between MRC Nagar and the sea. The village had been shifted here from its original location further up the coast in the 1970s when the government built tenements for the fisherpeople.

Srinivasapuram faced significant losses, including fifty lives, in the tsunami of 2004. After the tsunami, its residents were told that they would all be moved to the resettlement site of Semmencheri, outside the city. For the fisherpeople, Semmencheri's inland location made it an unviable option, and they presented a united and vocal opposition to the relocation proposals. Yet they lived in perpetual fear that their neighbors would not hold out against government threats of eviction, and that resistors would be left with no alternate accommodation. This climate of fear was exacerbated by the upscale developments that had gone up in nearby MRC Nagar. One fisherwoman ruefully looked up at the multistoried buildings under construction across the creek and remarked, "They want us gone from here. We are like mosquitos to them."[32]

The eco-park plans brought further insecurity to Srinivasapuram residents. Although it was widely acknowledged that the primary threats to the sustainability of the Adyar Creek came from sewage outflows, and from large-scale real estate development and land infill that blocked tidal interchange in the estuary, the draft plans for the eco-park insisted that "[e]ncroachments along the housing board colony at Srinivasapuram pose a huge threat to the creek and ecosystem," and suggested a means of dealing with the "practical reality of cleansing and transforming Srinivasapuram."[33]

The master plan finally released by Pitchandikulam Forest Conservancy did include the tenements in Srinivasapuram, but proposed increasing their height to accommodate all the hut dwellers within the concrete buildings.[34] The plan also included extensive measures to "contain" slum dwellers within the tenements in the future, including extending walkways through and around the colony and placing public institutions like the Anna University's proposed marine center at the far end of the colony, in the hopes that "the presence of public institutions and spaces would keep away encroachments" (Adyar Poonga Trust 2007, 4.5.5). Thanks to the unity of the fisherpeople and the strength of their support groups, Srinivasapuram residents managed to preserve their claims to the land, but they confessed that remaining on their land required constant vigilance.

Ironically although the eco-park construction was complete by early 2011, environmentalists argue that efforts to preserve what is left of the creek are moot, as the porosity of land and water within the creek, which gave this estuarine area its ecological character, had been lost to infill for real estate development. The eco-park was inaugurated in January 2011, but remained open to the public for all of 3 days. Abandoning the original vision of the park as a space for human interaction with nature in an urban context, the TNUIFSL decided in February 2011 to close the park to all but groups of schoolchildren accompanied by teachers. This decision was officially justified by reference to the fragile ecology of the creek and the necessity to "minimise human interference" in the area.[35] Meanwhile, the APT, originally created solely to develop the eco-park, was renamed the Chennai Rivers Restoration Trust (CRRT) and began to develop proposals for large-scale transport projects for the city, including high-speed elevated road corridors that would run in part along the banks of the Adyar. This diversification of the trust's role further underlines the connections between the eco-park and high-value transport projects as part of the infrastructures of global cities, and the ultimate ecological incoherence written into these infrastructures.

Conclusion

In 2008, a resident of Okkium Thoraipakkam filed a writ petition against TNSCB's proposed construction of an additional 8,000 resettlement homes on the Pallikaranai Marsh in Kannagi Nagar. Based on the advice of an expert committee appointed by the court, the construction was stayed in 2009. This order pitted the TNSCB against the environmental scientists who comprised or assisted the committee; the latter were accused by officials of the board of being anti-development and anti-poor, and even, in one case, of having "blood on their hands."[36]

This incident highlighted for us the false standoff between environmentalism and the poor that is being framed by urban development authorities. This chapter has argued that ecological and social vulnerabilities are closely interlocked in the urban terrain, and has traced the increasingly precarious conditions that both the urban poor and the urban environment are facing from the projects and proposals of the globalizing city. The convergence of two sets of discourses, of ecological restoration and of slum-free cities, both part of the city's bid for global status and investment, has produced scenarios such as mass tenements on endangered and flood-prone wetlands, eco-park projects on dying estuaries, and heavy engineering on rivers.

Changes in the relative values of urban land and water, as well as the politics of municipal administrative units and finances, have determined the spatial placement of the urban poor in and around the city. These movements have been mediated by historical shifts in shelter policies and politics in Chennai, with decades of Dravidian populism and the legacy of *in situ* rehabilitation redirected by global ideologies and finances toward relocation into peri-urban ghettos.

The relational matrix encompassing water, urban geography, class, and citizenship has moved through different epochs of governance. As water lines and flows follow the logics of financial lines and flows, they create new dispositions of urban bodies, from alienated or unemployed workers, or dislocated and commuting masses, to massed buildings on overstressed marshes. This chapter has argued that the politics of urban eco-restoration can only be understood by attending to historical geographies of land–water morphologies and changing imperatives of urban governance. Seen as a whole, however, the outcomes also suggest a fundamental incoherence in environmental policymaking in globalizing cities.

Notes

1. These observations are based on a series of visits that the two authors made to various slums in Chennai as part of fact-finding missions on slum eviction and slum fires in 2008 and 2009.
2. On strategies through which urban poor negotiate the administrative and political thickets of resettlement, relocation and allotment, see Roy (2003).
3. This argument resonates with Gururani's concept of "flexible planning" (this volume), whereby exemptions, compromises, and inconsistencies are institutionalized as policy maneuvers of sovereign bodies in response to class power, politics, and global capital.
4. Matthew Gandy (2004) tracks a worldwide shift since the 1970s away from the public health concerns that underpinned the "bacteriological city" of the nineteenth and early twentieth centuries. This model produced state-centric investments in water infrastructures that reshaped urban space, reconstituted private and public spheres, and created new modern practices of hygiene, sanitation, and bodily discipline. But technical and fiscal challenges in this model left a legacy of incomplete modernity, dividing citizens from subjects. New rationales of urban governance in globalizing cities, he claims, are oriented toward the needs of capital, involve a panoply of providers, and embody a shift from the ethos of municipal civil engineering toward commercial rationales. This paradigm yields new patterns of social segregation as water infrastructures are converted from public goods into marketable commodities.
5. Histories of Chennai report that early growth and settlement in the city occurred through 'in-filling' in the low-lying pockets between the ridged contours of the landscape and between the major radiating transport corridors that gave the city its shape. See Alan Turner Associates (1980); Badrinath (1970).
6. Interview with Advocate T. K. Ramkumar, January 20, 2010.
7. This imperative was repeatedly highlighted, in the Madras Metropolitan Plan 1971–1991 (1971), the Madras Urban Project (1974), and the Master Plan for the Madras Metropolitan Area (1974).
8. The Alan Turner Associates report also pointed out that until the 1980s development controls and land use regulations served primarily to "preserve residential amenity," i.e., to provide for roads, streets, and other developments in previously non-urbanized sections of the growing metropolitan complex, not to prevent development in unsuitable areas. Even when such controls began to be instituted, through revisions of building rules, they hardly if ever related to issues of drainage, flooding, or environmental preservation, mitigation, or restoration.
9. The Sustainable Chennai Project was part of the Sustainable Cities Project (SCP), launched in 1995 by the United Nations Human Settlements Programme (UN-HABITAT) and the United Nations Environment Programme (UNEP). It was locally coordinated by the Chennai Metropolitan Development Authority (CMDA), and was a prominent example of attempts to mainstream commercial

and financial stakes in the restoration of water bodies. The SCP's aim was to build capacities in urban environmental planning and management (EPM) in various Third World cities including Chennai. High-profile city consultations held in the late 1990s identified waterway cleaning as one of four priority issues for EPM interventions, and the principal stakeholders listed in the Sustainable Chennai Project documents included "chambers of industry and commerce," and "financing institutions for water front development" along with government agencies. Apart from some prominent NGOs, the public was not included in the list (Sustainable Cities Programme 2002).

10. The act also provides for punishments for people obstructing the process of evictions and gives immunity from prosecution or legal proceedings to government officers (and contractors) for "Action taken in good faith in pursuance of the Act" (The Tamil Nadu Protection of Tanks and Eviction of Encroachment Act, 2007).

11. A crucial part of the history of policy change relating to the urban poor, which is beyond the scope of this chapter, is that of state-level electoral and political change. Shifts in the political character of the Dravida Munnetra Kazhagam (DMK) party (long seen as patrons and protectors of Chennai's slum populations), and in the electoral calculus of the late 1980s and 1990s (including the All India Anna Dravida Munnetra Kazhagam [AIADMK's] recent electoral successes in Chennai), along with competitive regime compulsions to demonstrate capacities for a neoliberal transformation of the city, have moved slum clearance policies away from *in situ* upgrading to eviction and relocation. For more on this, see Raman (2008).

12. Interview with Jayashree Vencatesan, February 25, 2010.

13. Interview with T. K. Ramkumar, January 20, 2010.

14. A UN-HABITAT document noted in the mid-1990s that "[a]t present several EPM efforts are under way (in Chennai)" and counted among them the Madras Vision 2000 and the Environmental Sanitation Project (ESP) funded by the World Bank. See K. Allaudin and N. Sundararajan: Madras/Chennai*-SCP, http://ww2.unhabitat.org/programmes/uef/cities/summary/chennai1.htm. Accessed on April 3, 2012.

15. Interview with S. Sundaramurthy, Assistant Executive Engineer, Tsunami Planning Coordination and Monitoring Cell, August 9, 2007.

16. Interview with Advocate T. K. Ramkumar, January 20, 2009.

17. The committee's report notes sadly that the "present site, after filling up, may not look much like a marsh. However, the flora on location stand as mute witnesses to the land having been part of a Marsh" (Anuthaman et al. 2009a, 3).

18. According to a *Times of India* article on February 5, 2010, "People's participation, sustained media support, and a responsive government has been the hallmark of the save Pallikaranai campaign, a rare success story in protecting an ecologically sensitive environment despite urban pressures." See, More Area of Pallikaranai Marsh to be Protected, *Times of India*, February 5, 2010.

19. Interview with Manimekhala, January 22, 2010.

20. Interview with Manimekhala, January 22, 2010.
21. Interview with evicted and relocated residents of Pudupet, Langs Garden Road, Chennai, May 25, 2009.
22. Interview with Lata, Resident of Kannagi Nagar, January 22, 2010.
23. Conversation with CAG director Bharath Jairaj, July 5, 2007.
24. The case centered on whether a road separating this neighborhood from the river had existed before 1991, since CRZ regulations permitted development behind existing roads. Despite being presented with satellite photo evidence that the road did not exist before 1991, the court denied the petition (conversation with Bharath Jairaj, July 5, 2007).
25. The TNRDC was formed through a public–private partnership between the Tamil Nadu government and IL&FS (Infrastructure Leasing and Financial Services), a private infrastructure development company.
26. The eco-park seemed to hold strong political cachet. It was promoted heavily and publicly, first by the AIADMK chief minister Jayalalithaa who proposed the park during her regime (see K. Subramanian, Eco Park at Adyar Creek, The Hindu, November 12, 2005), and later by the DMK chief minister Karunanidhi who personally inaugurated the first phase of the eco-park in 2007.
27. Turbulence Ahead—In the Murky Waters of the Adyar Creek? Madras Musings, July 16–31, 2007.
28. Turbulence Ahead.
29. Conversation with Bharath Jairaj, July 5, 2007. These suspicions were deepened when the government requested the court committee appointed to monitor the restoration of the creek in the Ambedkar Memorial case to permit it to "reconstruct" without restrictions any existing buildings within the creek and estuary (cf. Turbulence Ahead, see footnote 44).
30. Conversation with Joss Brooks, August 7, 2007.
31. Conversation with Joss Brooks, August 7, 2007.
32. Interview with Venilla, resident of Srinivasapuram, August 2007.
33. Adyar Poonga Trust (2007, 2.3.6).
34. Srinivasapuram comprised tenements blocks surrounded by hutments largely built by tenement residents to house their expanding families.
35. Times News Network, Eco-sensitive Adyar Poonga open only for school children; Decision On Allowing in Public Later, The Times Of India, Chennai, February 13, 2011. http://epaper.timesofindia.com/Repository/ml.asp?Ref=VE9JQ0gvMjAx MS8wMi8xMyNBcjAwMjAy, accessed on August 22, 2012.
36. Interview on February 15, 2010 with an environmental scientist in Chennai, who wishes to remain anonymous.

References

Adyar Poonga Trust. 2007. *Ecological Master Plan for the Adyar Creek and Estuary Interim Report*, Chennai.

Alan Turner Associates. 1980. Structure Plan for Madras Metropolitan Area, Commissioned by Madras Metropolitan Development Authority.

Anuthaman S. S., and S. Ismail. 2008. Second Interim Report Submitted by the Committee of Experts Constituted by the Honorable High Court in W. P. No. 18888/1997 and W. P. No.13105/2008. October 19, 2008, 9.

———. 2009a. Report Submitted by the Committee of Experts Constituted by the Honorable High Court in W. P. No. 30725 of 2008. May 29, 2009, 3.

———. 2009b. Third Report Submitted by the Committee of Experts Constituted by the Honorable High Court in W. P. No. 18888 of 1997 and W. P. No. 13105 of 2008, July 3, 2009, 7–13.

Badrinath, C. 1970. Urban Development of Greater Madras: Report Presented to the Government of Tamil Nadu.

Benjamin, S. 2008. Occupancy Urbanism: Radicalizing Politics and Economy Beyond, Policy and Programs. *International Journal of Urban and Regional Research*, 32 (3): 719–729.

Chennai Metropolitan Development Authority. 2008. Second Master Plan for Chennai Metropolitan Area, 2026. Available at http://www.cmdachennai.gov.in/ SMP_main.html, accessed August 26, 2012.

Coelho, K., and N. Raman. 2010. Salvaging and Scapegoating: Slum Eviction on Chennai's Waterways. *Economic and Political Weekly*, XLV (21): 19–23.

Davis, M. 2006. *Planet of Slums*. London: Verso.

Devasahayam, M. G. 2009. Chennai's Twin Corridors: Are They Sustainable? *New Indian Express*, December 29, 2009.

Ellis, R. 2010. *Who Participates? Rethinking Civil Society in the Context of Competing Definitions of Urban Sustainability*. Washington, DC. http://siteresources.world-bank.org/INTURBANDEVELOPMENT/Resources/336387–1272506514747/ Ellis.pdf, accessed April 7, 2012.

Gandy, M. 2004. Rethinking Urban Metabolism: Water, Space and the Modern City. *City*, 8 (3): 363–379.

Koolhas, R. 1994. The Generic City. In *S, M, L, XL,* ed. R. Koolhas and B. Mau. 1238–1264. New York: Manacelli Press.

Lakshmi, K. 2006. Mylai Balaji Residents Demand Civic Amenities. *The Hindu*, December 27, 2006.

Manikandan, K. 2008. Scheme to Provide Houses for Resettled Residents Yet to Take off. *The Hindu*, January 14, 2008.

———. 2009. Development in Thoraipakkam Leaves a Lot to be Desired. *The Hindu*, February 20, 2009.

Neeraja, S. 2009a. City's Suicide Point. *New Indian Express*, July 28, 2009.

———. 2009b. Pallikaranai Marsh Turns Dumpyard. *New Indian Express*, December 9, 2009.

Oppilli, P. 2007. Garbage Burning Continues at Pallikaranani. *The Hindu*, April 20, 2007.

———. 2009. Restoration Eluding Pallikaranai Marsh. *The Hindu*, April 13, 2009.

Raman, N. 2008. The Politics and Anti-Politics of Shelter Policies in Chennai, India. Master's thesis, Massachusetts Institute of Technology.

———. 2009. Government Fails to Learn from Past Mistakes. *New Indian Express*, October 16, 2009.

Ranganathan, M., L. Kamath, and V. Baindur. 2009. Piped Water Supply to Greater Bangalore: Putting the (Cost Recovery) Horse before the Cart? *Economic And Political Weekly*, 44 (33): 53–62.

Roy, A. 2003. *City Requiem, Calcutta: Gender and the Politics of Poverty*. Minneapolis, MN: University of Minnesota Press.

Seabrook, J. 1996. *In the Cities of the South: Scenes from a Developing World*. London: Verso.

Sustainable Cities Programme. 2002. *Sustainable Cities Programme, 1990–2000: A Decade of United Nations Support for Broad-Based Participatory Management of Urban Development*. UN-HABITAT.

Swyngedouw, E. 2004. *Social Power and the Urbanization of Water*. Oxford: Oxford University Press.

Tamil Nadu Slum Clearance Board. Undated. *Tamil Nadu Slum Clearance Board Project Report for Rehabilitating 6,500 Families Living in Objectionable Areas in Chennai by Utilizing the Special Problem Grant Recommended by the Tenth Finance Commission: Project Coast Rs. 60 Crores*, Chennai.

Vencatesan, J. 2007. Commentary: Protecting Wetlands. *Current Science*, 93 (2): 288.

Wilbur Smith Associates Private Limited. 2008. *Final Feasibility Report for 4-Lane Elevated Expressway from Chennai Port to Maduravoyal On Nh-4*. National Highways Authority of India (NHAI).

7
Value Struggles: Waste Work and Urban Ecology in Delhi

Vinay Gidwani

> On the sidewalks, encased in spotless plastic bags, the remains of Leonia
> await the garbage truck. Not only squeezed tubes of toothpaste, blown-
> out light bulbs, newspapers, containers, wrappings, but also boilers,
> encyclopedias, pianos, porcelain dinner services. It is not so much by
> the things that each day are manufactured, sold, bought that you can
> measure Leonia's opulence, but rather by the things that each day are
> thrown out to make room for the new. So you begin to wonder if Leonia's
> true passion is really, as they say, the enjoyment of new and different
> things, and not, instead, the joy of expelling, discarding, cleansing itself
> of a recurrent impurity . . . Nobody wonders where, each day, they [the
> street cleaners] carry their load of refuse. Outside the city, surely; but
> each year the city expands, and the street cleaners have to fall farther
> back. The bulk of the outflow increases and the piles rise higher, become
> stratified, extend over a wider perimeter. Besides, the more Leonia's
> talent for making new materials excels, the more the rubbish improves
> in quality, resists time, the elements, fermentations, combustions. A
> fortress of indestructible leftovers surrounds Leonia, dominating it on
> every side, like a chain of mountains. (Calvino 1974, 114–115)

In Italo Calvino's book of fantastical stories, *Invisible Cities*, the Venetian
traveler Marco Polo regales Kublai Khan with tales of the cities he has seen in
his travels around the Empire, as a way of diverting the aged emperor from
his premonition about the Empire's impending end. The story of Leonia, like
another cinematic fable, the 2008 Pixar animation film, *WALL·E*, tells of a
world overwhelmed by its own commodity detritus. In *WALL·E* a toxic planet,
Earth, has long been abandoned following an ecological disaster. In Leonia,
growing mountains of refuse continuously threaten to invade its boundaries,
forestalled only by the unceasing labors of its street cleaners. Leonia could
be, as Calvino surely intended, our hostile urban future should unbridled

consumerism run ahead of our capacities to recuperate—or at the very least, inoculate—its discards.

For waste is not obviously useless, as the urban planner Kevin Lynch (1990) trenchantly observed in *Wasting Away*, his wide-ranging rumination on waste and value. While decline, decay, and wasting may jeopardize our survival, they are also a necessary part of life and growth:

> Wastefulness can be a burden to one and an advantage to another. The wasteful abandonment of household goods, which may in time impoverish a family, is the rag-picker's livelihood. It was once said that the nobility had a duty to live riotously, so that the lower classes might survive by providing for their wasteful demands. An empty building can be profitable to its owner, even while families are homeless. A profligate use of timber, which denudes the land of forests for future generations, can be the cheapest way of building good houses. The labeling of something as waste must always ask: waste for whom? (Lynch 1990, 148)

Here Lynch illustrates how the invocation of waste is always, simultaneously, a normative invocation of value. The politics of waste—or value struggles, if you will—lie precisely in this boundary work: *What is set on the side of waste and what on the side of value in particular places at particular moments, how, with what implications, and for whom?*

Walter Benjamin (2002) furnishes an acute rendition of this border politics in *The Arcades Project*, as part of his summons to the practice of a "cultural-historical dialectic." He writes:

> It is very easy to establish oppositions, according to determinate points of view, within the various "fields" of any epoch, such that on one side lies the "productive," "forward-looking," "lively," "positive" part of the epoch, and on the other side the abortive, retrograde, and obsolescent. The very contours of the positive element will appear distinctly only insofar as this element is set off against the negative. On the other hand, every negation has its value solely as background for the delineation of the lively, the positive. It is therefore of decisive importance that a new partition be applied to this initially excluded, negative component so that . . . a positive element emerges anew in it too—something different from that previously signified. And so on, ad infinitum, until the entire past is brought into the present in a historical apocatastasis. (Benjamin 2002, 459)[1]

I want to momentarily set aside Benjamin's summons to dwell in the present, to draw attention to a series of extraordinary reports issued by the

National Commission for Enterprises in the Unorganised Sector (NCEUS), a body of the Government of India. Among other things, the reports reveal stark insights on employment growth under India's current liberal economic regime. Based on a comparison of the Employment-Unemployment Survey data from the 55th (1999–2000) and 61st (2004–2005) rounds of the National Sample Survey (NSS), the NCEUS's *Report on Conditions of Work and Promotion of Livelihoods in the Unorganised Sector* concludes that:

> The total employment in the economy has increased from 397 million to 457 million between the two NSS rounds. The change in . . . organised or formal employment has been *nil* or *marginally negative* (i.e., 35 million in both the years). Therefore, *the increase in total employment has been of an informal kind*, i.e., 61 million (from 362 to 423 million) or 17 percent. (NCEUS 2007, 4; emphasis added)[2]

These are startling figures that not only give pause to the common narrative of India's 'growth miracle,' but also pose a further question about the singularity of India's development trajectory. Can it be reconciled with textbook models of economic growth? Do we possess adequate concepts to understand the transformations of the past three decades? A parallel set of data from the NSS suggests that, "the rate of decline in poverty did not accelerate in 1993–2005, the period of intensive opening of the economy, compared to the 1970s and 1980s" (Bardhan 2010, 94). The NSS data also indicates that there was "a decline in the growth of real wages in the period 1993–2005 compared to the previous decade, 1983–1993" (Bardhan 2010, 94). What do these trends imply for future employment prospects and poverty reduction in India, against a backdrop of growing urbanization?

In a recent article that issues a call to "provincialize" Euro-American urban theory, Ananya Roy (2009) underscores the pivotal role of informal economies in cities around the world, and the discursive work of the concept of "informality." She writes:

> Informality produces an uneven geography of spatial value thereby facilitating the urban logic of creative destruction. The differential value attached to what is "formal" and what is "informal" creates the patch-work of valorized and devalorized spaces that is in turn the frontier of primitive accumulation and gentrification. In other words, informality is a fully capitalized domain of property and is often a highly effective "spatial fix" in the production of value and profits. (2009, 826)

Focusing on Delhi's informal waste recycling sector, this chapter mobilizes Benjamin's method of the "cultural-historical dialectic" to explore processes of informality and ongoing urban change in Delhi. I argue that these urban transformations should be properly construed as value struggles—what Massimo de Angelis calls "strategies of enclosure" that attempt to forcibly separate certain urban populations from whatever limited access to social wealth they have in the name of capitalist efficiency (de Angelis 2007, 144). As I have elaborated elsewhere (Gidwani 2008) capital does not have a single template for accumulation. As a social formation it is an articulation of interlaced value-producing activities, which are structured-in-dominance to the dictates of capitalist value production. Pictured so, contemporary urban formations are 'complex wholes' where production activity oriented to profit taking for accumulation interdigitates with and comes to dominate other forms of value production that the late Marxist economist, Kalyan Sanyal, called the "need economy" (Sanyal 2007, particularly Chapter 5). I further propose that by tracing the dialectic of value and waste, or the 'positive' that acquires its valence against the background of the 'abortive' or 'retrograde,' we gain insight into how capital continuously draws its economic vitality and moral sanction from programs to eradicate waste.

How Waste Functions

The *Middle English Dictionary*[3] has a fascinating entry for the noun 'waste' that not only reveals how it mattered AS matter in those unsettled medieval times, but also its charged existence at the interface of the moral, legal, and economic:

wast(e (n.(1)) Also **waist, vaste** & (errors) **waf, wafte.**
1.
Uncultivated or uninhabited land; wilderness, desert; also, a tract of uncultivated, barren, or desolate land; ?also, a parcel of land left fallow or untended [quot. a1467].
2.
Consumption, use; the using up, depletion, or wearing out of some concrete thing; also, the consumption of candles, torches, etc. by their burning; also, expense, outlay; **soden to the ~ of half**, boiled until reduced by half.

3a.

(a) Improvident, excessive, or unnecessary consumption or use, squandering; extravagant expense, prodigality; also in *fig.* context, with punning ref. to sense 5.(b) [quot. c1450];

(b) pointless, misdirected, or improper effort, action, thought etc.; **don (werken) ~;**

(c) inanity, foolishness; that which is pointless; **wordes of ~.**

3b.

In phrase **in ~** [cp. **vein** n. **2a. & 2b.**]:

(a) used adjectivally: futile, ineffectual; worthless, useless;

(b) used adverbially: vainly, futilely, ineffectually; improperly, wastefully; also, idly, emptily [quot. c1450].

4.

Enfeeblement, emaciation.

5.

(a) Destruction, ruin; **maken ~;**

(b) refuse, trash; a useless or worthless residue or by-product; also in *fig.* context; **waxen (to) ~**, to be spoiled.

6.

Law. Damage to or destruction of real property; spoliation or some other action that decreases the value of property; **strepe and (or) ~, stroppe and ~; ~ taxe**, a fine assessed for damage to property; **accioun ~**, a lawsuit seeking compensation for damage done to real property; **empechement (pechement) of ~**, liability for damage to property held by a tenant; **permissive ~**, consensual damage or devaluation; **ple of ~**, a lawsuit charging a tenant with damaging or failing to maintain property; **quite from (of) ~**, exempt from liability for damage to a tenement; **voluntari ~**, damage or devaluation caused by some deliberate action; **yer dai and waste**, the royal prerogative by which the king enjoyed the profits of property owned by a felon for a year, following which he was entitled to despoil the property.

7.

That which is left over, the remnant; also, that which remains after a process, the product [2nd quot.].

As this catalog of negatives evidences, the meanings of waste range from wilderness and uselessness to misuse of property and time to disease and foolish spending. 'Waste' is both *excess matter* and *material excess that is unruly and improper*. Or, to extend Mary Douglas's now famous characterization of dirt/pollution, waste is objectionable precisely because it poses a "threat to

good order" (Douglas 2002[1966], 197). As disordered matter or matter out
of place, waste is a historical, political, and technical artifact, "which slips
easily between concept, matter, experience and metaphor" (Campkin and
Cox 2007, 1; see also Frow 2003, Hawkins 2006). Its figurative and physical
vitality produces spaces of abjection and comes to invest them with disgust,
repulsion, fascination, and disavowal. In the work of the feminist theorist
Julia Kristeva (1982) bodily waste exposes the fragility of the border between
self and other: the open, fluid female body by disrupting borders becomes
the abject other of the clean, decent, obedient, and law-abiding male body—
hence subject of/to regulation. Zygmunt Bauman, evoking the work of
Giorgio Agamben (1998), presses this line of argument to its logical extreme
to claim that "[h]omo sacer is the principal category of human waste laid out in
the course of the modern production of orderly (law abiding, rule governed)
sovereign realms" (Bauman 2004, 32). "Throughout the era of modernity,"
he writes, "the nation-state has claimed the right to distinguish between
order and chaos, law and lawlessness, citizen and homo sacer, belonging and
exclusion, useful (= legitimate) product and waste" (2004, 33). Homo sacer is,
here, the life that is devoid of symbolic, economic, or political value, neither
significant in the human realm nor the divine.

In a general sense, then, as I intimated at the inception of this chapter,
'waste' can be regarded as the specter that haunts the modern notion of
'value,' which itself operates in two entangled registers: first, 'value' as the
economic coding and logic of wealth in capitalist society (Spivak 1999,
79)—taken up in different but historically related ways by classical political
economy, Marxist political economy, and neoclassical economics; second,
'value' as a normative or moral template for conduct—to not waste, to make
full or best use of, etc. For projects of value, waste is "an enemy to be engaged
and beaten" (Neeson 1993, 30–31).

Thus, the first prime minister of independent India, Jawaharlal Nehru,
made the case for the nation's 'development' by launching a searing
crusade against waste. Speaking in New Delhi in 1954 to a meeting of the
Coordination Board of Ministers for River Valley Projects, he admonished
that "the 360 million people" of India wanted not "words, even though words
may signify much;" rather "they want food . . . they want clothing . . . they
want shelter . . . they want health." Having warned his audience that "[w]ords
are tricky things always" and that they "are thrown at each other as a bomb

might be thrown at a person" he launched a ferocious verbal assault, clearly intended to rouse:

> We have to utilize the experience we have gained, pool our resources and prevent *wastage* . . . We cannot allow the nation's resources to be *wasted*. Democracy has many virtues, but one of its concomitants is wastage of time and energy. Nevertheless, for many reasons, we prefer democracy to other methods of government. That does not mean that we cannot avoid *waste*. We cannot afford *waste*, because the basic thing is that we should go ahead. The devil is at our heels, or as they say, "*Shaitan peechhe ata hai, to bhagte hain* [If the devil follows, you run]." I should like you to have this kind of feeling. To hell with the man who cannot walk fast. It serves him right if he gets out of the ranks and falls out. We want no sluggards . . . I want work and work and work. I want achievement. I want men who work as crusaders. (Nehru 2003, Vol. 2, 148; emphasis added)

Nehru was by no means the only leader to hitch his nation's fate to the elimination of waste. In 1927, Herbert Hoover, then secretary of commerce for the United States, authored a fascinating report called "Progress in Elimination of Waste,"[4] in which he declared:

> It is obviously not the function of Government to manage business, but for it to recruit and distribute economic information; to investigate economic and scientific problems; to point out the remedy for economic failure or the road to progress; *to inspire and assist in cooperative action in reduction of waste* . . . (Hoover 1927, 3; emphasis added)

Much of Hoover's report focuses on how the American people's high standards of living can be further advanced by more productive utilization of natural and industrial resources and "by the elimination of waste in materials and motion in our production and distribution systems" (1927, 3). But some of the more interesting moments of the report lie in Hoover's call to reduce "the great waste of booms and slumps of the 'business cycle' with their intermittent wave of unemployment and bankruptcy" and in the "[r]eduction of waste arising from industrial strife between employers and employees" (1927, 4). In these summons and in recognizing a vital spatial-economic connection between "motion" and "elimination of waste" Hoover uncannily anticipates the insights of Marxist geographer, David Harvey, particularly his penetrating diagnosis of capital as "value in motion" and the crises that wrack capitalism when this motion slows or ceases (see, for example, Harvey 2007[1982]; 2010; also Sheppard and Barnes 1990).[5]

At a time when 'urban reform' is on the policy agenda with a vengeance and cities across the globe, busy reinventing themselves as 'world class,' have launched massive slum demolition and urban gentrification drives to eradicate squalor, it is tempting to read these upheavals as contemporary phenomena, lubricated by "fast policy transfers" (Peck and Theodore 2010) and "mobile urbanisms" (McCann and Ward 2011). All the more reason to recall that urban reform and its prejudice toward the poor has deep roots. The journalist Jacob Riis, author of the lauded book *How The Other Half Lives: Studies Among the Tenements of New York* (1970[1890]), set the tone for subsequent urban-reform literature, equal parts concern and loathing, when he described the tenement dwellers of Mulberry Bend as "shiftless, destructive, and stupid" and advocated "nothing short of entire demolition "as the only way to provide 'real relief'" (quoted in Page 2000, 78–79). In their crusade to clean the city, sanitation reformers of the late nineteenth and early twentieth century instituted municipal trash collection systems, oblivious or, worse, apathetic to the destruction of livelihoods and trades that the city's poor immigrants had painstakingly built around the disposal of urban detritus, from swill to salvage (what Riis disparagingly called "piles of rubbish"). With gentrification now a 'global urban strategy,' to echo the geographer Neil Smith (2002), municipalities from Bogota to Manila, prodded by middle-class ire and activist (frequently anti-poor) court rulings, are once again on a warpath to 'modernize' waste management. Modernization has inevitably meant transfer of waste management functions to private corporations, a process that has caused untold harm to the livelihoods of groups such as the *zabbaleen* of Cairo, the 'reclaimers' of Johannesburg, and the *kabaris* of Delhi: urban commoners who have fabricated intricate and ingenious circuits of waste recycling for incomes (Assaad 1996; Chaturvedi and Gidwani 2010). In short, the exclusionary urbanism and renewed enclosure of the common that is transforming contemporary cities in the global South is repeating with difference a centuries old class war against 'waste.'

The incantatory power of words in this struggle of the propertied to impose propriety is far from trivial. Hoisted at regular intervals by the ruling elite as reason to condemn and transform marginal places and marginal behaviors—and, inevitably, marginal people who are the bearers of such conduct—the rhetorical appeal of the term 'waste' is illustrated, with wit, in a content analysis of language use in UK parliament debates from December 1935 to March 2010.[6] For the propertied, waste continues to function as a placeholder for material excess and excess matter. *Wasteful 'natures' (bodies, spaces, things, and conducts) have to be territorialized for ordered 'society'—the society of law that safeguards property and value—to be possible.*

How Waste Matters

Hoover's dictums on waste elimination in the United States and Nehru's in India may seem distant to our contemporary existence, but it should be apparent that they are not. The moral and political crusade against waste that was upheld as the cornerstone of economic advancement has found succor in conservative screeds against government expenditures on common goods and programs for the poor. 'Austerity' for the have-nots is a recurring dictum in modern conservatism's economic templates. It is something of a historical twist therefore that a model of economic prosperity that portrays itself in a relentless war against waste has been joined, since the 1950s in the United States and more recently in other parts of the world, especially the booming metropolises of China and India, by a companion paradigm that thrives on waste. As the historian Susan Strasser observes: "Economic growth in the twentieth century has been fueled by waste—the trash created by packaging and disposables and the constant technological and stylistic change that has made 'perfectly good' objects obsolete and created markets for replacement" (1999, 15). Strasser's point here is not the newness of 'disposability.' Wasteful conducts and conspicuous consumption have long been staple tactics employed by the rich to signal and guard social status (cf. Veblen 2008[1899]). As Kevin Lynch drily observed, "where material shortage is the norm, discarding things is a notorious way of demonstrating power" (1990, 31). The revolution in the West, post-Second World War, was the emergence of a 'mass consumption society' with the wherewithal and will to embrace the regulative ideal of convenience that underlies disposability.[7] The wealthy went on wasting as before, but now they were joined by a growing middle class that could also afford to waste (albeit less sumptuously).[8]

This escalating spiral of consumption has proliferated globally; and while spatial and class disparities in consumption remain sharp, increasingly it is the rising middle classes of growth centers such as Brazil, India, and China that are its vanguard. According to the Worldwatch Institute, "[w]orldwide,

private consumption expenditures—the amount spent on goods and
services at the household level—topped $20 trillion in 2000, a four-fold
increase over 1960 (in 1995 dollars)."[9] The amount of post-consumer waste
has risen correspondingly, with China's municipalities alone estimated to
be generating 190 million tons of trash per year—a figure that could soar
to 480 million tons by 2030, nearly double the amount the United States is
projected to produce over the same period.[10]

Predictably, the policy response has been to render the phenomenon
as a technical problem rather than confront it as a bio/political issue. Take
Delhi. Since the 1990s, 'efficient management' of the city has emerged as a
prime concern of its municipalities and of the government of Delhi state.
It has also been a growing concern for its residents, although differently
enabled sections of the population harbor different ideals of efficiency. The
wealthy, for example, have been vocal in demanding more reliable supplies
of electricity and water, unclogged roads, and a clean environment. The poor
too want reliable access to drinking water; but they also want reliable public
transportation.

Against this backdrop, 'waste' in its literal and figurative sense has come
to mark both the excessive and the expendable, and also the productive and
the profitable in present-day urban India. As society's excrement, 'waste'
has become an immanent limit to its well-being and reproduction, as well
as a vector of realized and potential value. Consider that Delhi generates
7,500 tons of municipal solid waste—garbage—every day, a figure that
is expected to rise to 16,000 tons per day by 2021.[11] The bulk is collected,
sorted, stored, and sold or disposed of by a socially stigmatized, informal
army of waste-pickers who, as previously noted, number upward of 150,000.
This is beginning to change. Since 2005 the three municipalities that oversee
Delhi have begun to privatize various infrastructural services, including
collection of municipal solid waste. Several large companies have been
awarded contracts to collect garbage from neighborhood collection points
and transport it to landfills. "The privatisation of waste collection in Delhi
was essential as the MCD [Municipal Corporation of Delhi] was unable to
handle the massive volumes of waste generated by the city," explains Rakesh
Mehta, former commissioner of the MCD.[12]

Value Struggles

Predictably, the privatization of waste collection has had an adverse impact on the livelihoods of Delhi's waste-pickers. This has been compounded by the unprecedented demolition of slums, the most visible policy choice in efforts to remake Delhi as a world city. Various estimates suggest that of the 3.5 million people living in slums, unauthorized colonies, and *jhuggi-jhopri* (JJ) clusters across Delhi, up to a million may have lost their homes to demolition. Of these, only 25 percent (if that) have been relocated.[13] According to the Hazards Centre, a Delhi-based NGO that has worked on housing security for the urban poor, a significant number of demolition and eviction requests have been filed by citizens groups, particularly resident welfare associations (RWAs), who do not wish to allow such slum clusters in their vicinity. Some concerns that they have cited include safety, visual pollution, and environmental quality. RWAs in their interactions with municipal officials have also identified scrap dealers' shops and waste segregation activities as undesirable activities.

The ongoing work with waste-pickers and waste-dealers undertaken by the Delhi-based environmental research and advocacy group Chintan suggests that urban renewal policies have had a deleterious impact on the livelihood of these people. A recent focus group discussion with waste-dealers and waste-pickers in the Nizamuddin Dargah area was instructive. The waste recycling activities, clustered around a series of junk shops, were terminated on the basis of a court order, after the Jangpura Residents' Welfare Association filed a case in court. Subsequently, a sealing drive also closed down all junk dealers in the vicinity. The waste-pickers say that instead of their customary two rounds of picking, they had to reduce picking to one round only. This was because there was no space to store waste, since their slum settlements were torn down. Hence, they were required to sort and sell waste the same day. Furthermore, since they did not have the older junk shops nearby, they were forced to sell materials to at least two different dealers, each trading only in separate, mutually exclusive items, both at a considerable distance. The junk shops took advantage of their spatial monopoly and offered rates much lower than the prevailing market rates. Some waste-pickers complained that instead of the Rs. 150 per day they earned previously, they were subsequently left with less than Rs. 80.

Meanwhile, the parallel trend of handing over municipal solid waste functions to corporations has caused poorer segregation of the city's detritus. Whereas waste-pickers gather and segregate anywhere from 15 to 60 percent of the waste depending on their area of operation, municipal contracts allow private companies to segregate at much lower levels. Thus, in the eight years of their contract the private operator is only required to segregate 20 percent of the waste. Concurrently, as private operators have begun to sell waste directly to recycling factories or large dealers, a legion of small junk and scrap dealers—most of whom had risen, as previously noted, from the ranks of waste-pickers—now find themselves out of work. Delhi's recent embrace of trash-to-electricity projects threatens to worsen the plight of waste-pickers. A November 2011 article in *The Washington Post* describes their concerns:

> For five hours every day, Ranjit Kumar and his 10-year-old son rummage through a giant pile of rotting trash with their bare hands, filling bags with pieces of metal, plastic and glass to take by cart to the recyclers market nearby.
>
> But an incinerator under construction not far away may mean that he and other waste workers will lose access to the trash, he said, which fetches his family a little more than $5 a day.
>
> The incinerator is one of two projects in New Delhi aimed at turning the city's trash into electricity and earning carbon credits under the Kyoto Protocol, the global climate pact designed to reduce greenhouse-gas emissions. Local politicians have hailed the projects for addressing the city's chronic problems of excess untreated waste and a shortage of electric power.
>
> But for almost 300,000 workers in the city engaged in waste collection, sorting and recycling, the plants mean the loss of their livelihood.
>
> "If all the trash goes to the plants to be processed, how do we feed our stomachs?" Kumar said as foul-smelling fumes rose from the trash and dark-brown water trickled past him. "My work may look dirty, but it keeps my family alive."[14]

The privatization of municipal waste by various modes is only the latest salvo in a tense relationship between Delhi's waste-pickers and municipal authorities that extends back to 1863, the Delhi Municipal Corporation's (DMC) founding moment. In 1867 a cholera epidemic swept the city, inciting panic among Delhi's native elite (*rais*), who, as law-abiding taxpayers of the British government, "vociferously demanded the right to live in a clean city" (Prashad 2000, 3). The DMC did not repudiate the *rais'* allegations concerning the inadequate provision of municipal services. Instead, as Vijay Prashad observes, it deflected responsibility and "blamed the poor conditions on the sweepers whose strikes, it argued, prevented the DMC from doing its work" (Prashad 2000, 3).

This strategy of pitting the desires of the urban elite against the unruly conduct of its poor continues in the present, as municipalities plot their modernizing agendas. There is evidence that it worked in 1871, as Delhi's native elite unleashed their misdirected ire against the city's Dalit sweepers, who cleaned Delhi's *mohallas* (neighborhoods) in return for daily dues in food and monthly dues in cash, as well as the right to household waste—whether discarded items or human and animal excrement—which they sold for cash to cultivators in villages abutting Delhi's boundary walls. The *Urdu Akhbaar*'s December 1, 1871 edition fulminated:

> The haughty and overbearing behaviour of sweepers is another nuisance. In all cities, they have divided mohallas among them so that each is the sole and hereditary lord of his circle, and troubles poor persons by refusing to remove filth from their houses, and in many cases leaving them uncleaned for several days till his demands are satisfied . . . This conduct of sweepers is the cause of the houses of the people constantly remaining in a dirty state. (*Urdu Akhbaar* 1871, 6)

The *Akhbaar* went on to claim that the "wicked behaviour of the sweepers" had left the houses of people "in a filthy state, in consequence of which children contract diseases and die in numbers." It was a declaration of class war: *who* had superior rights to the city?

The DMC had no doubts as to the answer. It was strategic in planning its strike against sweepers, concluding that the most effective way to undercut their power was to annex its economic source: nightsoil. Prashad (2000, 6–7) unpacks the DMC's reasoning: "If the DMC took charge of the nightsoil, it would both undermine the sweepers' independence (their earnings from the sale of manure and other . . . recyclable trash) and enable the DMC to profit from the sale of manure." As advance planning, the DMC assembled a supply of carts to remove refuse and allocated warehouses to store the nightsoil. Then, in 1884, it passed a resolution to "enforce their right to the monopoly of all the nightsoil and sweepings of the city proper" (Prashad 2000, 7). The sweepers resisted.

To thwart "surreptitious removal of nightsoil" by the sweepers, the DMC urged its native overseers to exercise renewed vigilance over the *mohalla's* sweepers, and erected *dhalaos* (trash depots) on each street as a means of regulating the movement of nightsoil. Sweepers were required to deposit filth in *dhalaos*. The *dhalao*, now ubiquitous in Delhi, was born as a disciplinary instrument designed to regularize, in both space and time, human conduct and non-human flows of waste. Alongside, the DMC pursued a more conventional strategy of cooptation: sweepers were gradually inducted as salaried municipal employees and wrenched from their previously personalized work relations in *mohallas*. Over a period of forty odd years a relatively independent population of service providers was transformed into servants of the state.

Over a century later the class tussle between the urban elite who generate the bulk of waste and waste-pickers who gather it, and efforts to regulate the latter, are repeating with difference in Delhi. In the late 1990s Delhi's middle classes began to protest the inadequacy of municipal waste collection and advocate for better waste management with upgraded technologies, in order to achieve a 'modern' city. These elite protests were registered via public interest litigations (PILs), a judicial device that was originally intended to "reach legal and constitutional rights to a 'person or determinate class of persons (who) by reason of poverty, helplessness or disability or socially or economically disadvantaged position (is) unable to reach the court for relief'" (Ramanathan 2006, 3194; cf. Rajamani 2007). One of the most significant outcomes of the PILs was to push municipalities to re-examine their delivery mechanisms.

Delhi's municipalities concluded that their existing waste management capacities were inadequate for handling the delivery standards mandated by courts in response to PILs. Oddly, they did not consider upgrading them. Instead, they determined that only segments of the private sector, with large capital outlays at their disposal, were in a position to meet the delivery goals mandated in judicial orders. Capital requirements that were stipulated in the eligibility criteria for municipal waste management contracts sparked a form of capital-intensive privatization that excluded lesser private entrepreneurs from the fiscal concessions granted by Delhi's municipalities as part of public–private partnerships (PPPs), an institutional arrangement that has become the dominant vehicle for urban 'reform' initiatives the world over. In Delhi, PPPs in the waste management sector have had the salutary effect of evicting the informal recycling sector from several pockets of economic activity that it has historically pioneered and occupied. What used to be nominally 'informal'—an arbitrary demarcation to begin with (Roy 2009)—has now become 'illegal' under the new regime of urban governance. How did this unfold?

Judicial Overreach?

The plague of 1994 was a turning point in urban waste management. Blamed on the lack of adequate waste management in the city of Surat in south Gujarat, where it originated, the plague provoked a series of official responses to waste management—particularly by the informal sector. In Delhi, the DMC's initial reaction was to ban waste-pickers. The ban was lifted after the plague subsided and vigorous NGO protest drew attention to the unfairness of the ban and the livelihoods jeopardized by it. The Planning Commission of India's response, by contrast, was more positive. In 1994, it established a high power committee—the Bajaj Committee—to study how waste management practices in urban India could be improved. The Bajaj Committee was unusually attentive to the role of waste-pickers: it recognized both the health hazards associated with their work and the service their work provided to the city. It recommended improving their working conditions. Unfortunately there was no follow-up; and waste-pickers were not discussed again in national policy on solid waste until 2006.

The Bajaj Committee's report did, however, instill a sense of urgency in planning for waste. After years of indifference, authorities and civil society actors were spurred to action. Shaken by media images of garbage and fleeing populations, the renewed specter of a medieval disease, and fear of international ridicule, there was a flurry of activity to 'clean up' India's cities. Ironically, it was the haste to overhaul urban waste management systems that prompted neglect of waste-pickers. In spite of the Bajaj Committee's recommendations to the contrary, municipalities and civil society groups failed to see waste-pickers as critical relays in cities' attempts to manage their multiplying waste. Instead, in a repetition of tired prejudices, waste-pickers were typecast as 'inefficient,' 'unhygienic,' and ultimately 'superfluous' to modern waste management solutions. The wisdom that prevailed saw the technological upgrading of existing municipal waste management systems as the quickest route to success. This prescription was based in part on an important cognitive shift among decision-makers, who now came to perceive waste not as 'filth' but rather as a form of commodity 'wealth.' Inevitably, their discussions involved considerations of technologies and products that would allow waste to be profitably harnessed.

Powerful political and private interests influenced this agenda, and its terms of participation meant that a vast pre-existing system of informal-sector waste recyclers (Figure 7.1) would be excluded from access to waste.

Concurrently, as the judiciary's understanding of 'public interest' shifted—coming to encompass agendas as disparate as corruption, abuse of public power, and environmentalism by the early 1990s—the original constituency of PILs, the poor and the vulnerable who were to be afforded constitutional and legal rights, receded in importance. PILs rapidly became the preferred channel of remediation for middle-class grievances around urban amenities. Two in 1996 pertained directly to the issue of solid waste—*B. L. Wadehra v. the Union of India and Others* (1996) and *Almitra Patel v. Union of India* (1996).

In *Wadehra V. the Union of India*, the plaintiff, Dr Wadehra contended that the "MCD and the NDMC [New Delhi Municipal Corporation] had been totally remiss in the performance of their statutory duties to scavenge and clean Delhi city, as it was their mandatory duty to collect and dispose of the garbage/waste generated from various sources in the city." He also argued, "there were inadequate facilities to dispose of hospital wastes and only a handful of hospitals had incinerators to burn the hospital wastes." Lastly, the petitioner claimed that his "constitutional rights guaranteed under Articles 21, 48A and 51A(g), which place responsibility on the state to provide for protection and improvement of the environment were also being violated."[15]

The Wadehra petition led to the enactment of the Bio-Medical Waste (Management and Handling) Rules, 1998. It also produced several dramatic moments in court, when top-level functionaries were summoned to explain the non-performance of their municipalities. Such public humiliation of municipal officials had a salutary effect. It drew unwelcome attention to the under-performance of public bodies (an issue of persistent concern at a time when India was unrolling its New Economic Policy) and, by the same token, ratcheted pressure on municipalities to find new answers to their cities' compounding waste. Privatization of waste handling, an option broached in the court's decision, became a real possibility for the first time.

The court's decision, issued on March 1, 1996 by Justices Kuldip Singh and S. Saghir Ahmad, is noteworthy for its self-righteous indignation. It begins with a lament about Delhi's deteriorating environment: "The ambient air is so much polluted that it is difficult to breathe," "River Yamuna—the main

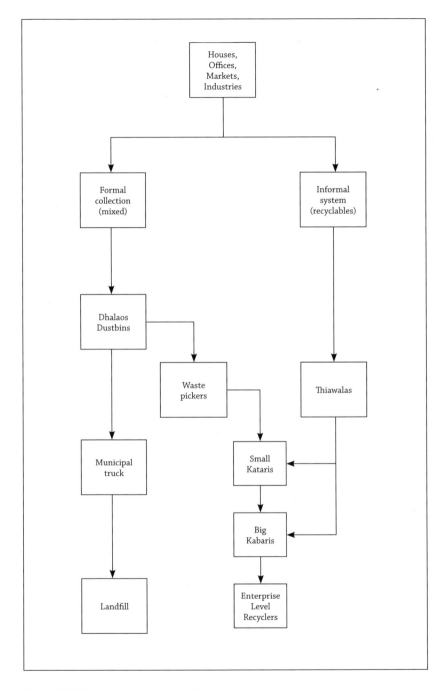

Figure 7.1 The waste processing chain

source of drinking water supply—is the free dumping-place for untreated sewage and industrial waste," and "the city is virtually an open dust-bin" (1996 SCC (2) 594, § 1). The court then upbraids the MCD and the NDMC for being "wholly re-miss in the discharge of their duties under law." Causality is quickly established: "It is no doubt correct that rapid industrial development urbanization and regular flow of persons from rural to urban areas have made major contribution towards environmental degradation . . ." (§ 1). Be that as it may, the court admonishes "the Authorities—entrusted with the work of pollution control—cannot be permitted to sit back with folded hands on the pretext that they have no financial or other means to control pollution and protect the environment" (§ 1). The court order then directs the NDMC and MCD, as well as the Delhi Development Authority (DDA) and the Delhi Administration, to "perform their statutory duties" with respect to "collection, removal, and disposal of garbage and other waste." "Apart from the rights guaranteed under the Constitution the residents of Delhi have a statutory right to live in a clean city," (§ 23) the court proclaims. The order reminds the respondents that on October 12, 1995 the court had directed "officers/authorities" to provide "a final date by which these officers/ authorities shall sort out the problem of collection and disposal of garbage in the city of Delhi" such that "not a drop of garbage is to be seen anywhere in the city of Delhi on early morning each day" (§ 13(2)(a)).

The court proceeds to note that "inadequacy or inefficiency of the [municipal] staff" is an unacceptable defense: "It would be useful to mention that the MCD has a very large force of Karamcharies working for it . . . The simple arithmetic shows that there are 27 Safai Karamcharis and one Sanitary Inspector for one Sq. Km. of area. We are of the view that with such a large manpower at its disposal there can be no excuse with the MCD for not controlling the disposal of garbage and keeping the city Clean" (§ 20; cf. § 23). The NDMC is similarly implicated. In the concluding segments of the order, the court thunders: "Why drive common people to public interest action? Where Directive Principles have found statutory expression in Do's and Don't's the court will not idly sit by and allow municipal government to become a statutory mockery. The law will be relentlessly enforced and the plea of poor finance will be a poor alibi when people in misery cry for justice" (§ 24).

In the same year that the court handed down its decision in *B. L. Wadehra v. the Union of India and Others*, Almitra Patel, a retired MIT-educated engineer running a family-owned business in Bangalore, filed a petition before the court for a violation of Article 21, the right to life and a healthy environment (Writ Petition No. 888 of 1996). The petition argued that "various government agencies had neglected to discharge their constitutional and statutory obligations in relation to the proper collection, handling, transportation and hygienic ultimate disposal or recycling of municipal solid waste (MSW)" (Rajamani 2007, 297). Patel's own account of her decision to go to court underscores the middle-class concerns (and aesthetics) that have guided environmental PILs:

> The frogs stopped singing, on our lovely village road outside Bangalore, because the city began dumping its garbage there, outside the city limits for want of dedicated space for waste management. We found this repeated all over India on a Clean India Campaign led by Exnora's Late Capt Velu after the Surat plague. INTACH's Dahanu eco-warriors urged me to file a PIL for hygienic eco-friendly waste-processing, and the results, with the Supreme Court's full support, have been gratifying.[16]

In January 1998, several months after admitting Patel's writ petition, the Supreme Court constituted an eight-person expert committee under the chairmanship of Asim Barman, the municipal commissioner of Calcutta. The expert committee, which included the petitioner Almitra Patel, was ordered to take stock of the status of municipal solid waste management (MSWM) practices in Class 1 cities. The expert committee—popularly known as the Asim Barman Committee—submitted its final report to the court in March 1999 and made a number of recommendations for improving MSWM.

The court issued its decision in *Almitra Patel v. Union of India* on February 15, 2000.[17] Writing for the court, Justice B. N. Kirpal directed MCD, NDMC, and "other statutory authorities" to "ensure proper and scientific disposal of waste in a manner so as to subserve the common good" and in this "endeavour to comply with the suggestions and directions contained in the report prepared by the Asim Burmon [sic] Committee" (§ 21(4)). As with its predecessor *B. L. Wadehra v. the Union of India and Others, Almitra Patel v. Union of India* resulted in a new law: in this instance, the Municipal Solid Wastes (Management and Handling) Rules, 2000—the first set of rules ever on solid waste, and the most widely used and important ones to date. The Municipal Solid Wastes (MSW) Rules emphasize the need for recycling, but conspicuously fail to acknowledge the right to livelihood of informal recycling sector workers.[18] The importance of incorporating these workers in urban waste management initiatives, thereby granting legitimacy to their skills and toil, appears not to have been a strong priority either for the petitioner or the Supreme Court Justices B. N. Kirpal, M. B. Shah, and D. P. Mohapatra who presided over the *Almitra Patel* PIL.

While the Asim Barman Committee Report contains a brief nod to the work of informal sector waste pickers—"NGOs and the informal sector of rag pickers are not optimally utilized in tackling the ever-growing problems of waste management in urban areas" (GOI 1999, 9); "For the collection of recyclable waste from the doorstep, NGOs may be encouraged to organize the rag-pickers" (GOI 1999, 11)—its recurrent emphasis is on technical solutions to the problem of MSWM. The court order omits even token acknowledgment of the informal recycling sector. In so doing it effaces the contributions of these workers to the urban economy and environment, and thereby ensures their scant consideration in future policy debates. Municipal workers once again incur the court's ire. Hence the court reminds respondents that: "The local authorities are constituted for providing services to the citizens . . . Tolerating filth, while not taking action against the lethargic and inefficient workforce for fear of annoying them, is un-understandable and impermissible" (§ 12).

But the most astonishing moment, as several commentators have noted, comes midway through the decision when Justice Kirpal, writing for the court, attributes Delhi's garbage problem to its slums and slum-dwellers. He starts by lamenting the large areas of public land that "are usurped for private use free of cost" through "passive or active connivance of the land owning agencies and/or municipal authorities." Condemning this "promise of free land, at the taxpayers cost" he not only endorses "Slum Clearance" over "Slum Creation" but also appears to suggest that there is no legal obligation to resettle those evicted. In righteous language he declares: "Rewarding an encroacher on public land with free alternative is like giving a reward to a pickpocket." "It is the garbage and solid waste generated by these slums which require to be dealt with most expeditiously and on the basis of priority," he concludes (§ 14). What is entirely absent in this judicial logic is any recognition of a longstanding structural problem, namely that Delhi's chronic—and according to some, deliberate—undersupply of low-cost housing, combined with unaffordable rents in authorized neighborhoods, often leaves its urban poor, including the army of waste-pickers who serve the city, no option but to become pavement dwellers, squatters on public land, or renters of a sliver of space in unauthorized slums from slumlords (Dupont 2000; Verma 2002).[19]

It seems almost perfunctory to point out that the court's order in *Almitra Patel v. Union of India* underscores the prejudicial workings of judicial activism in advancing an anti-poor agenda in Delhi (Batra and Mehra 2008; Baviskar 2003; Ramanathan 2006, 2008; Sundaram 2010). The process envisions a "clean and green city" for those propertied citizens who are not squatters. Thus, the 2021 Master Plan for Delhi (hereafter MPD 2021) calls for a "slumless" city as part of a vision to transform Delhi into "a global metropolis and a world-class city, where all the people would be engaged in productive work with a better quality of life, living in a sustainable environment" (Puri 2007, 1). Over 40 percent of the city's residents who live in slums are effectively excluded from this frame of reference. Middle-class environmentalism criminalizes Delhi's urban poor—its unwanted inhabitants—in the name of cleaning the city of unwanted effluents, industries, and built structures. Within this exclusionary agenda, waste recyclers have been forced to bear the brunt of injustice twice over: first as workers whose contributions to the city are de-valorized; and second, as a lower rung of citizens whose political claims to the city are suppressed in favor of upper-class demands.

Where Detritus Goes to Live

In recent years the content of everyday garbage has changed too with the increasing use of cardboard and paper in mail advertising, as well as plastics in consumer packaging (Table 7.1). Much of this plastic ends up in peri-urban outposts like Mundka, where an army of laborers and petty entrepreneurs do the quotidian work of recycling the city's ever-expanding detritus.[20] Until a massive fire ravaged the area in April 2010 (authorities suspect arson), Mundka was the largest informal plastics market in Delhi. Mundka is a nondescript locality, and like so many others on Delhi's peripheries it is uneasily urban, still deeply entangled in its rural upbringing. Low buildings—many unpainted, several just exposed brick, some with storefronts—line the main road. Dirt streets, at times wide but typically narrow, with patchy strips of tar, slice deep into the neighborhood, interrupted every few hundred feet by narrow intersections bearing names like Ajay Chowk, Milan Chowk, and Balwant Chowk. Mundka is a warren of small enterprises, warehouses and mini-factories, devoted to finding afterlives for Delhi's discarded pla

used to function, until the fire struck—and may do so again in the future—
as a site of reincarnation not just for Delhi's detritus, but the entire world's
(lately the Middle East had been a large source).[21] One warehouse owner a
friend and I met in January 2010 claimed that Mundka was Asia's largest
plastics recycling market: a cluster economy with over 5,000 businesses—
small and large, licit and illicit—engaged in the plastics trade. We had no way
of ascertaining the truth of this claim, but it was hard not to be impressed
by the hillocks of laboriously sorted plastics that we saw dotting the
landscape. Some of these consisted entirely of footwear. Unwanted footwear
of all kinds—sneakers, shoes, sandals, and *chappals*—arrived in places like
Mundka. Not to die but to be disfigured so that they might enter new circuits
of value.

Table 7.1
Shifts in physical composition of solid waste in India (%)

Year	Biodegradable	Paper	Plastic/ Rubber	Metal	Glass	Rags	Other	Inerts
1996	42.21	3.63	0.60	0.49	0.60	–	–	45.13
2005	47.43	8.13	9.22	0.50	1.01	4.49	4.016	25.15

Source: D. Zhu et al. 2008. *Improving Municipal Solid Waste Management in India: A Sourcebook for Policy Makers and Practitioners*. Washington, DC: The World Bank.

If scavengers/waste-pickers/scrap collectors[22] constitute the bottom end
of various value chains of waste, including plastics, enterprises that process
waste into re-usable forms sit at the top. The nature of processing can be more
or less involved, organized at varying scales of operation—from one-room
affairs to mini-industries—depending on the volume of capital investment
and the type of waste that is handled. When plastics are recycled on a mass
industrial scale they are first sorted according to their resin identification
code, a taxonomic category for polymer types that was developed in 1988.
Polyethylene terephthalate, or PET as it is commonly known in the trade,
has a resin code of 1. These codes are, of course, foreign to the *kabaris* who
are the backbone of India's informal recycling sector. But say, 'PET,' and
they know exactly what you mean. PET is a common packaging material
used in water and soft drink bottles, as well plastic jars for food items. In
the intricate afterworld of waste, purity matters for discarded objects to
re-enter the universe of capitalist value. To obtain pure PET, recycled items

such as plastic bottles and containers are first inspected for the presence of non-PET materials. These materials are then removed and the PET items are sorted into different color fractions, cleaned, and prepared for processing. The sorted post-consumer PET waste is crushed, chopped into flakes, and pressed into bales for sale.[23]

PET along with high density polyethylene (HDP), polyvinyl chloride (PVC), polypropylene (PP), and polystyrene (PS) are plastic polymers that are commonly found in Delhi's consumer waste. Plastics have low entropy of mixing, which is due to the high molecular weight of their large polymer chains. Compared to other materials like glass and metals, plastic polymers require greater processing in order to be recycled. Because heating alone is not enough to dissolve the polymer macromolecule, plastics must often be of nearly identical composition in order to mix efficiently. If different types of plastics are melted together they tend to phase-separate, like oil and water, and set in these layers. These phase boundaries cause structural weakness in the resulting material, meaning that polymer blends are only useful in limited applications. Hence, the process of segregation is crucial in extracting value from detritus, whether discarded plastics or other types of waste. For a *kabari* the economics are simple. The finer the category of recyclables into which he is able to sort his purchases from waste-pickers, and the more he is able to build up volumes and store each sub-category of waste until sufficient to overload a truck, the greater his income. For precisely this reason the *kabari* trade reserves the title of *kalakar* (artist) for that rare sorter who has managed to elevate segregation to an art, transforming backbreaking labor into an artisanal skill bordering on virtuosity.

Just as there is virtuosity in labor, so too is there virtuosity in business. Meet Ajay Balian.[24] He runs a small factory in Mundka that cuts and grinds HDP waste into flakes that can be down-cycled for various uses. Balian is a Jat from an agricultural family in Uttar Pradesh (his family continues to cultivate land). It was his father's idea to join the plastics recycling trade in the mid-1980s, when the sector was still young. It is not clear what inspired his father to buy a cutting machine and enter this aspect of the plastics business, but first-comer advantage served him well, and one machine soon became two. However, the domestic machines, which cost about a *lac* each, were noisy and slow. Once Balian and his brother took over from their father, they set about transforming the family firm from a plodding enterprise into a business school's model of efficiency. Their aim was to purge uncertainties that might cause business to fluctuate and adversely affect profits. They identified the sources of uncertainty: erratic supplies of raw material, electricity, and labor; unreliable machines; and lack of buyers for their product, resulting in sub-optimal capacity utilization as well as high inventory costs. As Ajay Balian describes it, they quickly realized that the answer was vertical integration and pre-production purchase agreements with buyers. The younger brother now runs a *godown* (warehouse), which sends regular truckloads of HDP to the Mundka factory. Agents of the *godown* rove around Delhi and its hinterland purchasing the required *maal* (stuff) from *kabaris* and small traders. The *maal* is washed, then readied for dispatch. Last year Ajay Balian imported a European cutting machine (cost: Rs. 30 *lacs*) that is both faster and quieter than its domestic counterparts. The factory operates three shifts a day, and Balian has pre-orders for his flakes from a company in Rajasthan that manufactures agricultural pipes. The entire operation, from top to bottom, is designed as a closed system that minimizes uncertainty: cut out uncertainty and you have guaranteed profits, Balian says with quiet assurance.

Behind the hillocks of sorted plastics that used to bring topographic variation to Mundka, before fire leveled the landscape, stood tin sheds. Stretched on the floor in these makeshift sheds you were apt to find rectangular open ovens with grills, and arrayed in zigzag pattern along these ovens young women (occasionally men) placing sandals, slippers, and sneakers on the hot grills. As the soles heat up, along with the adhesive that binds them to the body of the footwear, plumes of noxious grey smoke waft into the air. The smoke catches the back of the throat, so acrid that it's difficult to suppress a staccato of coughing. "Dioxins," my colleague murmurs. The women, who have no safety gear at hand, merely cover their noses with a *chunni* or *pallu*. When I ask, "Doesn't it burn your throat?" they stare at us incredulously, both startled and bemused by the obviousness of the question. "Of course it does," one of the women answers with a shrug. "What can we do?"

The women tell us they are from Alwar, in Rajasthan, and grateful to have any work at all—even this. As the late Joan Robinson, a Cambridge economist, once wrote, "the misery of being exploited by capitalists is nothing compared to the misery of not being exploited at all" (her quip, written in 1962, was inspired by underemployment in South East Asia) (Robinson 2006 [1962], 45). As the glue loosens the women grasp the sneaker with a *chimta* and peel its sole off with a pair of pliers. One of them tells us that they remove anywhere from 100 to 150 kilograms of PVC soles daily.

At this point the PVC outsoles and the leather/rubber constituents of the sneaker's upper body are severed into distinct secondary commodities, bound for different destinations. This would have been our journey's end had the proprietor of a plastics *godown* in Mundka not introduced us to a visiting business acquaintance, who operates a plastics re-processing factory in the nearby Udyog Nagar Industrial Area. The industrial area is laid out in a grid with small-scale enterprises tightly packed, one next to the other, masked from the outside by high walls. We were allowed into the factory after the supervisor on duty confirmed our credentials with the owner.

It was not what I had imagined. Steep steps lined on either side by a smooth, sliding surface descended into a dark basement lit by two dim yellow light bulbs and a strip of dirty, white fluorescent tube lighting. Squatting at the bottom of the stairwell was a line of women with saris drawn across their faces, hacking an assortment of outsoles into small chunks (they told us that the smooth strips of concrete, which resembled fat railroad tracks, were used to wheel heavy iron machinery into the basement). The dirt floor was littered with PVC remainders. In the background I could see what looked like a vat belching acrid grey fumes; another next to it lay idle. My eyes were smarting from the smoke, but there was no ventilator in sight—only a thin window with grills on one side, where the exposed brick wall of the basement met the ceiling. The supervisor led us to the vat. He explained that PVC chunks were first coarsely ground in an adjacent grinder, then melted in the vat, removed in buckets and finally poured into a machine with a large funnel at the top that squeezed the viscous substance out like toothpaste. The column of paste was led on a flat conveyor belt to a trough of cold water, immersed, and, after hardening, cut into even pieces, packed in plastic pouches, and sent out, for re-use and re-incarnation, into the world of commodity production. This grim factory, reminiscent of nineteenth-century machinofacture, is one of myriad nodes in the intricate circuits that organize the afterlives of waste. It is invisible to most city dwellers, yet critical to their well-being as citizens and consumers—ensuring not only that the city does not drown in its detritus but also churning out recycled waste as input for new rounds of commodity production.

Conclusion

Unlike the mythical city of Leonia conjured up by Calvino, where the residents welcome street cleaners "like angels" and observe their "task of removing the residue of yesterday's existence . . . by a respectful silence, like a ritual that inspires devotion," (Calvino 1974, 114) the non-fictional city of Delhi displays casual disregard for its cleaners. Poor appreciation of the informal sector's contributions to the urban economy combined with the social stigma attached to waste-pickers, ensures that recognition of informal sector recyclers will remain a slow, laborious, and ongoing process. Assigned *space to store and segregate* waste, *security of housing* in the proximity of areas of work, provisions for *mobility* (such as cycle rickshaws or trollies) that expand the waste catchment area and ease the physical toll of the job, *right of first access* to municipal waste, *guarantees from police and municipal authorities that waste pickers will not be harassed* by field personnel and that their legal rights will be respected, *enforcement of extended producer responsibility* (EPR) regimes that minimize the exposure of waste-pickers to toxic materials in waste products, *access to subsidized healthcare* and medicines, and *incentives for children's education* are some of the goals that urgently demand confrontation.

Regrettably, informal sector livelihoods such as vending, street hawking, waste collection, scrap dealing, petty industry, and reprocessing have been either stigmatized within urban policy or, lately, celebrated in the business management and economic policy literatures as sites of untapped entrepreneurship and consumer demand (see, for example, London and Hart 2010; Prahalad 2009). Such assessments notwithstanding, courts, municipal authorities, and urban planners in cities like Delhi continue to harbor visceral mistrust of the urban poor and small-time entrepreneurs who engage in informal sector livelihoods. Public unwillingness to acknowledge their labors as essential to enabling the urban economy as well as the lifestyles the urban elite demand is deep-seated.

To wit, the global trend towards privatization and formalization of informal sector activities such as waste collection, in which the cities like Delhi are active participants, is misguided for a number of reasons. Not least among these are that it fails to confront the issue of employment generation and urban poverty; cavalierly ignores that the urban poor—despite their precarious access to employment and housing—have equal right to make claims on city resources as the urban elite; and that they are economic actors and entrepreneurs whose work sustains the urban economy in crucial ways. How different might India's cities look if its ruling classes learned to recognize the sprawling universe of people, places, activities, and things that they currently scorn as marginal, peripheral, illicit, or annoying as the enabling conditions of possibility of their own lives?

Notes

1. The translators clarify the word "apocatastasis" as "restoration of all things." See Benjamin (2002, 989, n5).
2. More precisely, the informal sector absorbed an additional 52.3 million workers, 86 percent of total employment generated between 1999–2000 and 2004–2005. The number of protected formal sector jobs declined marginally from 33.7 to 33.4 million while informal jobs in the formal sector—consisting of regular, casual, and contract workers without any job security or social security benefits—increased by 8.5 million between 1999–2000 and 2004–2005. Thus, while employment in the informal sector increased by 52.3 million, informal employment increased by 60.9 million (see NCEUS 2007, 4; Table 1.1).
3. http://quod.lib.umich.edu/cgi/m/mec/med-idx?type=id&id=MED51853, accessed April 12, 2012. See also Scanlon (2005, 22) on the etymology of 'waste.'
4. I am grateful to Marvin Taylor, PhD candidate in the Department of Geography, University of Minnesota, for bringing Hoover's report to my attention.
5. It is instructive to recall Karl Marx's rumination on value in "The Chapter of Money" (Notebook I of the *Grundrisse*): "Considered as values," he writes, "all commodities are qualitatively equal and differ only quantitatively, hence can be measured against each other and substituted for one another (as mutually exchangeable, mutually convertible) in certain quantitative relations. Value *is their social relation*, their economic quality" (Marx 1993 [1973], 141; emphasis added). During capitalist crises the jeopardy to value in the form of devaluation—or waste of accumulated capital—lies precisely in the breakdown of the "economic quality" and "social relation" that allows commodities to be "mutually exchangeable, mutually convertible." In periods of economic lull some workers are brutally reminded of their pared-back existence as commodities: "labor power" that can find no buyers and, since it is a living commodity that cannot be stored, must suffer the pain and ignominy of devaluation.
6. I am grateful to Steve McFarland, PhD candidate in Geography at CUNY Graduate Center, for alerting me to this analysis. See the first figure here: http://contentini.com/an-analysis-of-uk-parliamentary-language-1935-2010/

7. It was precisely this 'mass consumption society' that was reviled by Max Horkheimer and Theodor Adorno in their *Dialectic of Enlightenment* (2002[1947]) and celebrated by W. W. Rostow in his *The Stages of Economic Growth: A Non-Communist Manifesto* (1991[1960]).

8. Consumption (demand) accounts for two-thirds of US GDP. Alarms about a shrinking middle class, a process that has evidently intensified in the wake of the 'Great Recession of 2008,' could cause a long-term decline in mass consumption (and levels of commodity detritus) in the West; but it could also, simultaneously, aggravate the condition of a growing surplus population that is redundant or irrelevant to the capitalist economy: the debris of mass consumption displaced by the debris of wasted lives (see Bauman 2004; Nun 2000).

9. The State of Consumption Today, http://www.worldwatch.org/node/810, accessed June 28, 2011.

10. Jones (2007).

11. These estimates are from Chapter 12, "Solid Waste Management," in "City Development Plan Delhi," prepared by IL&FS Ecosmart Ltd for the Department of Urban Development of the Delhi government in 2007 as part of funding guidelines stipulated under the Jawaharlal Nehru National Urban Renewal Mission (JNNURM). http://ccs.in/delhicdp.asp, accessed April 12, 2012.

12. Quoted in Sethi (2006).

13. See Hazards Centre (2007).

14. R. Lakshmi, Indian Waste Workers Fear Loss of Income from Trash-to-Electricity Projects. *Washington Post*, November 20, 2011. http://www.washingtonpost.com/national/health-science/indian-waste-workers-fear-loss-of-income-from-trash-to-electricity-projects/2011/11/18/gIQACCB7fN_story.html, accessed April 12, 2012.

15. Dr B. L. Wadehra v. Union of India and others, 1996 SCC (2) 594, JT 1996 (3) 38, decided in the Supreme Court of India on 01.03.1996; www.ielrc.org/content/e9604.pdf, accessed April 12, 2012.

16. Patel, A. 2007. Solid Waste Management. http://www.almitrapatel.com/, accessed April 12, 2012.

17. Almitra H. Patel v Union of India, Writ Petn (C) No. 888 of 1996, D/- 15-2-2000 in the Supreme Court of India. http://www.elaw.org/node/1420, accessed April 12, 2012

18. The Ministry of Environment and Forests, Government of India, notified the MSW Rules on September 25, 2000. The notification is available at http://envfor.nic.in/legis/hsm/mswmhr.html, accessed April 12, 2012.

19. Dupont (2000, 106) notes: "Some small private entrepreneurs, perceiving the shelterless situation of so many as good business opportunity, rent out sleeping place and bedding facilities to pavement dwellers. Quilts are available for hire for an average rate of Rs. 5 per night, and cots with bedding for an average rate of Rs. 15 per night."

20. This section draws on Gidwani (2010). See also Gill (2010).

21. The Supreme Court Monitoring Committee revealed that despite directives and orders from the Bench, Indian firms have been illegally importing hazardous waste, including plastic. In 2006–2007, 9.92 million tons of plastic bottle scrap was imported for recycling.
22. Although there are internal gradations as previously noted, for simplicity of exposition I use these terms interchangeably.
23. One use for recycled PET that has recently started to become popular is to create fabrics to be used in the clothing industry. The fabrics are created by spinning the PET flakes into thread and yarn.
24. Ajay Balian is a pseudonym. I met him in Mundka on his factory premises on January 12, 2010.

References

Agamben, G. 1998. *Homo Sacer: Sovereign Power and Bare Life*. Stanford, CA: Stanford University Press.

Assaad, R. 1996. Formalizing the Informal? The Transformation of Cairo's Refuse Collection System. *Journal Of Planning Education and Research*, 16 (2): 115–126.

Bardhan, P. 2010. *Awakening Giants, Feet of Clay: Assessing the Economic Rise of China and India*. Princeton, NJ: Princeton University Press.

Batra, L. and D. Mehra. 2008. Slum Demolitions and Production of Space: Delhi. In *Inside the Transforming Urban Asia: Processes, Politics, and Public Actions*, ed. D. Mahadevia. 319–414. Delhi: Concept.

Bauman, Z. 2004. *Wasted Lives: Modernity and its Outcasts*. Oxford: Polity.

Baviskar, A. 2003. Between Violence and Desire: Space, Power, and Identity in the Making of Metropolitan Delhi. *International Social Science Journal* 55(175): 89–98.

Benjamin, W. 2002. *The Arcades Project*, ed. R. Tiedemann, trans. H. Eiland and K. McLaughlin. Cambridge, MA: Belknap Press of Harvard University Press.

Calvino, I. 1974. *Invisible Cities*. Orlando, FL: Harcourt, Inc.

Campkin, B. and R. Cox. 2007. Introduction: Materialities and Metaphors of Dirt and Cleanliness. In *Dirt: New Geographies of Cleanliness and Contamination*, ed. B. Campkin and R. Cox. 1–8. London: I. B. Tauris.

Chaturvedi, B. and V. Gidwani. 2010. The Right to Waste: Informal Sector Recyclers and Struggles for Social Justice in Post-Reform Urban India. In *India's New Economic Policy: A Critical Analysis*, ed. W. Ahmed, A. Kundu, and R. Peet. 125–153. New York: Routledge.

de Angelis, M. 2007. *The Beginning of History: Value Struggles and Global Capital*. London: Pluto Press.

Douglas, M. 2002 [1966]. *Purity and Danger*. London: Routledge.

Dupont, V. 2000. Mobility Patterns and Economic Strategies of Houseless People in Old Delhi. In *Delhi: Urban Space and Human Destinies*, ed. V. Dupont, E. Tarlo, and D. Vidal. 99–124. Delhi: Manohar Publishers.

Frow, J. 2003. Invidious Distinction: Waste, Difference, and Classy Stuff. In *Culture and Waste: The Creation and Destruction of Value*, ed. G. Hawkins and S. Muecke. 25–38. Oxford: Rowman & Littlefield Publishers.

Gidwani, V. K. 2008. *Capital, Interrupted: Agrarian Development and the Politics of Work in India*. Minneapolis, MN: University of Minnesota Press.

———. 2010. Remaindered Things and Remaindered Lives: Travelling with Delhi's Waste. In *Finding Delhi: Loss and Renewal in the Megacity*, ed. B. Chaturvedi. 37–54. Delhi: Penguin Books.

Gill, K. 2010. *Of Poverty and Plastic: Scavenging and Scrap Trading Entrepreneurs in India's Urban Informal Economy*. Delhi: Oxford University Press.

Government of India. 1999. *Solid Waste Management in Class 1 Cities in India*. Final Report of the Asim Barman Committee. New Delhi: Government of India.

Harvey, D. 2007 [1982]. *The Limits to Capital*. London: Verso.

———. 2010. *The Enigma of Capital and the Crises of Capitalism*. New York: Oxford University Press.

Hawkins, G. 2006. *The Ethics of Waste: How We Relate to Rubbish*. Oxford: Rowman & Littlefield Publishers.

Hazards Centre. 2007. *A Fact-Finding Report on the Eviction and Resettlement Process in Delhi*. New Delhi: Hazards Centre, October.

Hoover, H. 1927. *Progress in the Elimination of Waste: An Extract from the Fourteenth Annual Report of the Secretary of Commerce*. Washington DC: United States Government Printing Office.

Horkheimer, M. and T. Adorno. 2002 [1947]. *Dialectic of Enlightenment*, ed. G. S. Noerr, trans. E. Jephcott. Stanford, CA: Stanford University Press.

Jones, S. L. 2007. Environmental and Health Challenges of Municipal Solid Waste in China. Washington DC: Woodrow Wilson International Center for Scholars, February 1. http://www.wilsoncenter.org/publication/environmental-and-health-challenges-municipal-solid-waste-china, accessed April 12, 2012.

Kristeva, J. 1982. *Powers of Horror: An Essay on Abjection*, trans. L. S. Roudiez. New York: Columbia University Press.

London, T. and S. L. Hart. 2010. *Next Generation Business Strategies for the Base of the Pyramid: New Approaches for Building Mutual Value*. Upper Saddle River, NJ: FT Press.

Lynch, K. 1990. *Wasting Away—An Exploration of Waste: What It Is, How It Happens, Why We Fear It, and How To Do It Well*, ed. M. Southworth. San Francisco: Sierra Club Books.

Marx, K. 1992. *Capital, Volume 1: A Critique of Political Economy*, trans. B. Fowkes. London: Penguin.

———. 1993 [1973]. *Grundrisse: Foundations of the Critique of Political Economy*, trans. M. Nicolaus. London: Penguin.

McCann, E. and K. Ward, eds. 2011. *Mobile Urbanism: Cities and Policymaking in the Global Age*. Minneapolis, MN: University of Minnesota Press.

National Commission for Enterprises in the Unorganised Sector. 2007. *Report on Conditions of Work and Promotion of Livelihoods in the Unorganised Sector*. New Delhi: Dolphin Printo Graphics for NCEUS.

Neeson, J. M. 1993. *Commoners: Common Right, Enclosure, and Social Change in England, 1700–1820*. Cambridge: Cambridge University Press.

Nehru, J. 2003. Building India. In *The Essential Writings of Jawaharlal Nehru*, Vol. II, ed. S. Gopal and U. Iyengar. 47–48. Delhi: Oxford University Press.

Nun, J. 2000. The End of Work and the Marginal Mass Thesis. *Latin American Perspectives* 27 (1): 6–32.

Page, M. 2000. *The Creative Destruction of Manhattan, 1900–1940*. Chicago, IL: University of Chicago Press.

Peck, J. and N. Theodore. 2010. Mobilizing Policy: Models, Methods, and Mutations. *Geoforum* 41: 169–174.

Prahalad, C. K. 2009. *The Fortune at the Bottom of the Pyramid: Eradicating Poverty Through Profits*, revised and updated 5th anniversary edition. Upper Saddle River, NJ: Prentice Hall.

Prashad, V. 2000. *Untouchable Freedom: A Social History of a Dalit Community*. Delhi: Oxford University Press.

Puri, V.K. 2007. *Master Plan for Delhi, 2021*. Delhi: JBA Publishers.

Rajamani, L. 2007. Public Interest Litigation Environmental Litigation in India: Exploring Issues of Access, Participation, Equity, Effectiveness, and Sustainability. *Journal of Environmental Law* 19(3): 293–322.

Ramanathan, U. 2006. Illegality and the Urban Poor. *Economic and Political Weekly* 41 (29) (July 22, 2006): 3193–3197.

Ramanathan, U. 2008. Ostensible Poverty, Beggary and the Law. *Economic and Political Weekly* 43 (44): 33–44.

Riis, J. 1970 [1890]. *How the Other Half Lives: Studies Among the Tenements of New York*. New York: Dover.

Robinson, Joan. 2006 [1962]. *Economic Philosophy*. New Brunswick, NJ: Aldine Transactions.

Rostow, W. W. 1991 [1960]. *The Stages of Economic Growth: A Non-Communist Manifesto*, 3rd ed. Cambridge: Cambridge University Press.

Roy, A. 2009. The 21st-Century Metropolis: New Geographies of Theory, *Regional Studies* 43 (6): 819–830.

Sanyal, K. 2007. *Rethinking Capitalist Development: Primitive Accumulation, Governmentality & Post-Colonial Capitalism*. New Delhi: Routledge.

Scanlan, J. 2005. *On Garbage*. London: Reaktion Books.

Sethi, A. 2006. Waste and Wealth. *Frontline*, 23 (7), April 8–21. http://www.hindu.com/fline/fl2307/stories/20060421002508600.htm, accessed April 12, 2012.

Sheppard, E. and T. Barnes. 1990. *The Capitalist Space Economy: Analysis After Ricardo, Marx, and Sraffa*. London: Unwin Hyman.

Smith, N. 2002. New Globalism, New Urbanism: Gentrification as Global Urban Strategy, *Antipode* 34 (3): 427–450.

Spivak, G. 1999. *A Critique of Postcolonial Reason: Toward a History of the Vanishing Present.* Cambridge, MA: Harvard University Press.

Strasser, S. 1999. *Waste and Want: A Social History of Trash.* New York: Holt.

Sundaram, R. 2010. *Pirate Modernity: Delhi's Media Urbanism.* New Delhi: Routledge.

Veblen, T. 2008 [1899]. *Theory of the Leisure Class.* New York: Oxford.

Verma, G. D. 2002. *Slumming Delhi: A Chronicle of Slums and their Saviors.* New Delhi: Penguin.

8
Housing in the Urban Age: Inequality and Aspiration in Mumbai

Nikhil Anand and Anne Rademacher

Introduction*

The problem of inadequate housing—often referred to simply as 'slums'—has long occupied policy attention in Mumbai.[1] In the last decade, the city's housing stresses have attained a particularly global visibility, as special 'urban' issues of scholarly journals from *Social Text* (2004) to *Science* (2008) supplement a wealth of recent literature on the contemporary global urban condition. Books like *Planet of Slums* (Davis 2004), *Shadow Cities* (Neuwirth 2006), and *Maximum City* (Mehta 2004), and the film *Slumdog Millionaire* (see Echanove and Srivastava 2009, details in note 2) have constructed and reinforced understandings of a global, and yet simultaneously Southern, urban predicament marked by seemingly intractable problems of poverty, marginality, and uncontrolled growth (Zeiderman 2008; Dawson and Edwards 2004). With remarkable consistency in this literature, Mumbai is invoked as an iconic example of the problem of urban slums in the twenty-first century.

In early November of 2007, Maharashtra State Housing Secretary S. S. Kshatriya addressed a transnational group of urban policymakers, activists, and scholars assembled for a conference called "Urban Age India." In his introductory comments, he announced,

> We'll plan for making cities without slums. That does not mean bulldozers will be there . . . We have moved far . . . a long way from that, and our policy is that we are going to provide in-situ housing for slum dwellers

---

*   An earlier version of this chapter appeared in N. Anand and A. Rademacher (2011), Housing in the Urban Age: Inequality and Aspiration in Mumbai. *Antipode* 43 (5): 1748–1772.

wherever they are residing, except for where the land is required for
a vital public project, like an airport, road or railway line. (Kshatriya
2007)[2]

The secretary went on to describe an enlightened government that
regarded all city slum-dwellers (hereafter, settlers)[3] as entitled to humane
resettlement. He invoked bulldozers as if they were relics, suggesting that
violent or unannounced evictions were a thing of the past. Forced evictions,
he suggested, were no longer a condoned official practice. Yet the bold, semi-
public declaration was only partly true.

Indeed, as the secretary pointed out, the state government has formulated
a slum development program to give developers clear incentives for providing
apartments to qualified settlers (Coelho and Raman, this volume; Doshi, this
volume). This program is generally referred to simply as 'SRA,' a reference to
the official agency through which it is administered, the Slum Rehabilitation
Authority. As Doshi points out in the next chapter, the SRA administers
several different kinds of urban housing interventions. Depending on their
political and geographic location, when settlers have their homes demolished,
they may be provided housing on an adjacent piece of land, or be provided
housing on the city's periphery. Doshi points to some critical and troubling
effects of the SRA housing policy for those displaced to the city's margins,
that is, the latter type of program. In this chapter, we focus on the former
type, the *in situ* rehousing initiatives of which Secretary Kshatriya spoke
above. In this case, settlers receive apartments free of cost, in a location
adjacent to where their homes existed previously.

In contrast to gated communities and enclaves in other cities, that
spatialize and separate inequality (Caldeira 2000; Low 2003), *in situ* SRA
developments highlight, and in some ways, concentrate the experience of
urban inequality. In addition to apartment buildings for rehoused settlers,
private developers are given lucrative development rights for construction
on the same site. Since high real estate values generally characterize the
settlement areas that are redeveloped in this manner, the opportunity to
produce SRA rehousing schemes tends to excite developers and many of
the city's informal settlers alike. For the latter, who are living on valuable
land, it presents an opportunity to negotiate the terms of resettlement, and
to acquire formal housing free of cost in the general neighborhood in which
they already reside.

Contrary to Kshatriya's claim, however, *in situ* SRA initiatives have not fully replaced state-initiated demolitions and evictions. In fact, on the very day that the Maharashtra state housing secretary declared them to be a thing of the past, bulldozer demolitions took place in a nearby suburb of Ghatkopar (Doshi, personal communication). Furthermore, only three years earlier, the secretary's own administration had overseen Mumbai's most extensive demolitions in decades, in which tens of thousands of informal homes were bulldozed (Anand 2006; Mahadevia 2006). Secretary Kshatriya's declaration therefore met with considerable contest at the conference, and among activists in the city.

SRA resettlement projects have been described as neoliberal housing interventions (Nijman 2008) insofar as the cost of their construction is borne by private developers rather than the state; it is a system in which state agencies manipulate regulations, approvals, zoning, FSI (floor space index; a measure of air-rights) ratios and the like, often to benefit the interests of developers. The state's role distinguishes SRA from many other conventional forms of low-income housing. Yet this observation alone does not explain why *in situ* rehousing in the specific form of SRA initiatives occurs in Mumbai and in no other Indian city, nor does it explain why state bulldozers continue to operate in certain locations. Moreover, neoliberalism cannot explain why bulldozers *do not* operate on tenements constructed before 1995. How has it come to be more politically and/or economically 'costly' to bulldoze these settlements than to house their residents in SRA high-rise structures? In this chapter, we suggest that while the diagnostic of neoliberal restructuring is important, it is also inadequate to fully understand housing and urban inequality in Mumbai. We point here to particular forms of political empowerment, NGO movements for political rights, and real estate markets that have converged to produce a housing intervention that is both specific to its time and place, and consistent with broader movements toward urban inclusion despite persistent inequality.

In this chapter, we use *in situ* SRA developments as an optic through which to demonstrate how the housing access practices of settlers elude conventional theoretical approaches to housing rights. Drawing on the work of activists, politicians, and private developers, we demonstrate how many settlers in Mumbai actively seek inclusion in this housing regime. Their doing so does little to shift sedimented patterns and processes of inequality. Yet, *in situ* projects also create opportunities for Mumbai to move toward being a more 'inclusive' city, contributing to a contemporary urban condition in which inclusion has partially *supplanted* equality as a guiding policy aspiration. Since in this sense inclusion and equality are not co-constitutive, the new forms of settler mobility captured by SRA rehousing are neither fully consistent with logics of accumulation by dispossession (Harvey 2008), or with logics of market-based inclusion through mass *in situ* titling (De Soto 2000).

We begin by recounting histories of settler politics in Mumbai over more than three decades of formal rehousing interventions (see also Doshi, this volume). We then suggest that the genealogy of SRA policies enables a distinction between 'new' practices and rationalities of government (such as urban policy recommendations crafted in times of neoliberalism), and older ones (such as urban demolitions undertaken by the Maharashtra state's bulldozers). We emphasize the critical importance of voting practices and settler mobilization, noting postcolonial contrasts with the colonial period (Chatterjee 2004). We suggest that specific political practices, together with changing legal regimes and powerful city developers, operate simultaneously to enable a form of urban citizenship that is both unequal, and yet more inclusive, in contemporary Mumbai.

Capital Cities

Mumbai is a city of many meanings and myths. It is a place of spectacular cash, commerce, consumption, and cinema (Appadurai 2000) that may be understood as a site of profound uncertainty and profound possibility. It is a city of many layers and layered experiences; this is as true in issues of housing as it is in other facets of its urban life. Today, over half of Mumbai's population lives in settlements that occupy only 8 percent of the city's area (McFarlane 2008). Eighty percent of these people live in homes of less than 100 square feet (Sanyal and Mukhija 2001).

Over the last century, the Maharashtra state and Mumbai municipal governments have addressed inadequate housing through simultaneous strategies of accommodation, regulation, and demolition (Chatterji and Mehta 2007). Its officials have vacillated between providing municipal services to urban settlements *in situ*, and building *ex situ* resettlement colonies at the city's margins (Durand-Lasserve 2006; Payne 1997; Sharma 2000; Tarlo 2000).

Over the last two decades, a new housing paradigm has developed. It seeks to rehouse settlers in 225 square foot apartments in mid-to high-rise buildings on a portion of the same land they already inhabit. Unlike other *in situ* projects that provide municipal services and upgrading to settlers in their existing 'slum' homes, *in situ* SRA projects require qualified settlers to move out of their homes during a reconstruction period. They then move back to the same area and into a new apartment, free of cost, in a designated SRA high-rise building. Developers who agree to provide slum-dwellers with these new apartments are in turn granted development concessions that authorize construction of luxury housing on the land made vacant by verticalizing previous slum housing stock. The high profit margins guaranteed through this policy make it appealing to many of Mumbai's most powerful real estate investors and builders.

Not all settlers are eligible for these *in situ* rehabilitation projects; only those who can prove continuous residence since 1995 qualify. Moreover, if the land is required by the government for any 'public purpose'—such as an airport, road, or railway project—or if it is in an ecologically sensitive area (Coelho and Raman, this volume; Doshi, this volume), even 'qualifying' settlers can be evicted from their homes and exiled to *ex situ* housing at the city's margins, in areas like Chandivali and Mankhurd (see Doshi, this volume). Such housing is also provided free of cost, and the developer receives incentives. However, because *ex situ* SRA housing is constructed a considerable distance from the social infrastructure of the previous settlement, it is far less popular, and far more contentious (Doshi, this volume; Roy 2009).

According to the director of the housing advocacy group the Society for the Promotion of Area Resource Centres (SPARC), as of February 2008, approximately 50,000 *in situ* and 80,000 *ex situ* tenements were completed under the SRA (Sheela Patel, personal communication). While some argue that both forms of housing improvement are delivered on a small scale given the magnitude of Mumbai's settler population, they are nevertheless the most significant housing interventions that have been undertaken in Mumbai in the last two decades.[4] Several researchers have therefore taken notice (e.g., Chatterji and Mehta 2007; Mahadevia and Narayanan 1999; Mukhija 2003; O'Hare, Abbott, and Barke 1998; Weinstein and Ren 2009), and pointed to the asymmetrical power relations that SRA projects both draw upon and produce.

In their account of SRA projects in Dharavi, Sanyal and Mukhija (2001) show the perils and pretensions of SRA projects by describing how settlers bypassed the NGO that sought to represent them, and dealt directly with relevant politicians and private developers. They also highlight the contentious and uncertain aspects of SRA redevelopment. Indeed, as the wide gap between the number of SRA projects approved and those completed suggests, most SRA projects are rife with contestation, connivance, and conspiracy and are never brought to fruition.[5] Doshi extends Mukhija and Sanyal's insights in her contribution to this volume, showing that even groups that oppose SRA through rights-based mobilization are compelled by the residents they represent to negotiate with the state for SRA-style developments. These accounts point to the considerable interest settlers have in SRA projects; many constantly and consciously seek out the transformative opportunities that SRA projects promise.

In this chapter, we take settlers' claims and aspirations to *in situ* SRA housing seriously (Appadurai 1999), and ask what they might suggest about inclusion and inequality. As a particular hybrid that sits between more common *in situ* upgrade projects and *ex situ* resettlement strategies (Bromley 2008; Calderon 2004; Payne 1997; Sjaastad and Cousins 2008), we suggest that *in situ* SRA projects are neither a neoliberal solution to the problem of urban housing (Nijman 2008), nor a continuation of historically repeating processes of accumulation by dispossession determined by the new interests of international financial capital (Harvey 2008). Instead, the histories of informal housing in Mumbai (Chatterjee 2004; Chatterji and Mehta 2007) compel us to suggest that SRA projects are politically situated, specific arrangements that emerge at the intersection of housing rights mobilization, political patronage, developer power that accrues from the city's high real estate values, and the neoliberal housing policies of the Maharashtra state government.

Heterogenous Histories

Housing struggles have long been a central political, social, and environmental issue in Mumbai. Since the beginning of the twentieth century, the city government has permitted the poor to inhabit, settle, and convert previously uninhabitable wetlands in the city's frontier regions. Through such 'urban pioneering,' Mumbai's poor have made the city's wetlands habitable

(Doshi, this volume; Sharma 2000; Tindall 1982). Informal settlers have consistently invested material and financial resources to transform these areas; it is generally only *after* this process has taken place that the state begins to exercise its sovereign power by employing brutal demolition and eviction tactics (Sharma 2000). Settlers, in turn, have historically been exiled to new urban margins to begin the process afresh, creating a pattern in which settlements precede, and literally make possible, the formal urban development in much of Mumbai today.

Nevertheless, in this chapter we also draw attention to the ways in which settlers in the postcolonial period have made resilient and somewhat effective claims to remain in, and *improve*, their settlements. In the late 1970s and early 1980s, we note that the government responded to these demands to extend urban services (water, electricity, roads) into many settlements via slum upgrade projects. Through gradual shifts in housing policy, qualified settlers were assured legal protection from demolition, which many used as justification to make improvements to their homes.

This pattern today constitutes a form of improvement that settlers themselves have undertaken. In this sense, SRAs may be considered as the latest iteration of a longer trajectory of urban land improvement in which settlers have played an active role. Attention to this history further complicates a reading of SRA projects as exclusively neoliberal interventions.

In the colonial and early postcolonial periods, settlers had few avenues of recourse through which to object to state intervention (Chandavarkar 2007). In the postcolonial period, however, some have achieved a significant degree of political power through a combination of large mobilization, political party advocacy, and NGO collaboration (Chatterjee 2004; Sanyal and Mukhija 2001). Thus, even as Mumbai's housing policy has shifted with the changing prerogatives of multilateral development institutions, settlers have also made these policies progressively—though *not sufficiently*—more responsive to, and inclusive of their needs.

The postcolonial city's first slum clearance plan, passed in 1956, continued the colonial era preoccupation with regulation by 'eradication.' It authorized aggressive bulldozing, eviction, and subsequent police surveillance of 'reclaimed' government lands (Burra 2005). Evicted settlers were entitled neither to resettlement nor to rehabilitation under this policy. As Mumbai grew rapidly in the 1960s, the Municipal Corporation realized that it could not respond to the problem of housing exclusively through 'clearance'-oriented policy. In 1971, the state government passed the Slum Areas (Improvement, Clearance and Redevelopment) Act, which reauthorized 'clearance' for some slum communities, but promoted municipal infrastructure development in specific 'declared' slums (O'Hare, Abbott and Barke 1998). The act remained in effect through much of the 1980s.

The slum improvement component was largely a response to popular pressure from elected representatives, NGOs, and housing rights movements. This included pressure from people such as the rights activist Mrinal Gore, who in the 1960s and 1970s led marches demanding water and sanitation services in Mumbai's settlements. After a series of neighborhood victories consolidated her reputation, Gore decided to march on the headquarters of the Bombay Municipal Corporation (BMC) in the early 1970s. Many settlers—who by that time called her *Paniwalli Bai*, or 'water woman'—participated in her protests by arriving at BMC offices en masse, brandishing rolling pins. In a summer 2009 interview with Anand, Gore remembered:

> We took out big *morchas* [protest marches]. First, because we brought water [to Goregaon], people had confidence in us. So when we went to the BMC for other work, we decided to take *morchas* there . . . The BMC had never seen such big *morchas* till then. I remember the view of Azad Maidan from the BMC building. Officers would see the sight and say, "*arre baba* so many women have come, we will have to listen to their demands." Also I was there [inside] as an elected councilor. So inside I raised my voice in the assembly, and outside the *morchas* . . . We asked [the BMC administrators]: "Do you think people living in slums want to live there, and not in buildings? It is not like that. If you can give *pucca* [permanent] homes they would definitely live there. But can you afford it? If you can't give everyone a house, then let's talk about improving the slums at least. Take care of the three responsibilities—water, sanitation, and roads. Slums are bad because they lack these facilities . . . Slum eradication *nahi, slum sudharane ka kaam karo* [don't do slum eradication, do the work of slum fixing/solving]." (field interview, June 2009)

In such protests, slum residents learned and articulated strategies for framing and demanding housing entitlements. Gore argued that settlements were not a problem of the poor, but rather the result of state failure to provide universal housing. In the 2009 interview, Gore described how she amplified protestor demands in city council meetings. Simultaneous protests outside the municipal council building gave her the legitimacy and authority to speak inside the building as a city councilor.

In the 1970s, councilor demands to extend urban infrastructure to slums converged with objectives espoused by the World Bank, which began to fund slum improvement and slum upgradation projects as a component of their development assistance to the city (O'Hare, Abbott, and Barke 1998). Since that time, the World Bank has consistently pressured the city to acknowledge that problems of informal settlement are related to inadequate land tenure regimes and infrastructure. By the late 1970s, the World Bank required the municipal administration to extend water infrastructure into slum settlements as a precondition for funding Mumbai's larger water infrastructure projects. In response, the state and municipal governments began a program intended to measure, count, and map populations living in settlements on government land. As Burra (2005) explains:

> Legislation was developed to provide civic amenities in slums, and it became a matter of policy that when slums were demolished, some form of resettlement should be provided. In 1976, a census of huts on government lands was conducted and "photopasses" were issued to all those found eligible by certain criteria. Those who received photopasses had, for the first time, some security. (Burra 2005, 70)

Slum residents counted in the 1976 census could expect a measure of tenurial security and public services as well. Yet the census also created a constitutive split between those settlers who were deemed entitled to services and rehabilitation and those left uncounted; the latter remained vulnerable to forced eviction and demolitions (see Chatterji and Mehta 2007).

The legacy of this classificatory split is evident in recurrent patterns of settlement demolition. After a wave of demolitions in the 1980s, new housing rights organizations formed. NGOs like YUVA (Youth for Unity and Voluntary Action), *Nivara Hakk*, and SPARC called large protests, and began to organize official tenurial documents for settlers. These included the ration cards, voting cards, and water connections that furnished settlers with a degree of formality in the eyes of the state while also reifying a state-constituted division between those settlers who were eligible for services and those who were not.

Working with and through government, then, NGOs were not only hailed for their use of the practices of statemaking (Sivaramakrishnan 1999), but also became critical intermediaries who negotiated housing policy on behalf of settlers (Sanyal and Mukhija 2001). They realized some compromised gains: they successfully argued that it was necessary to provide *in situ* resettlement through the SRA regime, and they also succeeded in securing entitlement to alternative (*ex situ*) housing for those living on sidewalks and footpaths. NGOs were unable, however, to guarantee a right to rehabilitation for all settlers. Instead, together with municipal councilors and state legislators hailing from the settlements, they pressured the state government to bring forward the "cutoff date to 1995" (Hansen 2001). To date, the cutoff date remains at 1995, a politically negotiated artifact that determines which settlements can be 'declared' eligible for public services and rehabilitation in the city today.[6]

Settlers have therefore worked provisionally with civil and political society—NGOs, elected representatives, *and* social movements—to realize housing security and prevent demolitions (cf. Chatterjee 2004). By compelling the government to progressively extend the cutoff date, many settlers have achieved conditional access to state services and have therefore made tentative yet effective claims to the city (Appadurai 2002; Chatterjee 2008). Through large-scale mobilization, political representation, and a moral economy of petitions and favors, they have been able to secure relatively reliable social and infrastructural services in many settlements. These afford direct benefits, and they also constitute grounds for future claims (Chatterji and Mehta 2007).

Mumbai's latest housing policy, the Slum Rehabilitation Scheme, was formulated in 1995. It established a Slum Rehabilitation Authority (SRA) to oversee the private redevelopment of declared slums (Mukhija 2003). In return for constructing and providing residential apartments for settler families free of cost, the SRA grants builders extremely lucrative development rights which they may then use to construct luxury housing on the land released by consolidating settlement residences in high-rise apartment buildings. Providing cost-free (excluding monthly building maintenance charges), *in situ* apartments constitutes a new, but now relatively established, experience of slum 'rehabilitation' in Mumbai. It marks a critical shift in the state's role, from bulldozing certain tenements and constructing public housing, to 'facilitating' the private construction of low-income housing by manipulating Mumbai's complex zoning and density regimes to ensure development rights and protecting the promise of maximum profits for private builders. This happens at virtually no cost to the government (Nijman 2008).

We have drawn on the city's longer history of housing to show that the SRA program is not simply a techno-managerial neoliberal policy from 'above' that emerged in the 1990s. It developed in part from a specific history of settler marginalization *and* mobilization; settler enfranchisement and political action played a significant role.

Popular Aspirations

Critics of the new SRA regime point to its many problems, which include forged development proposals and widespread coercion of settlers unwilling to sign development agreements (Guzder 2002; Nijman 2008). The buildings are often of poor quality and design, and construction involves a contentious process in which entitled residents, developers, NGOs, and politicians all exercise their financial power and moral legitimacy (see Sanyal and Mukhija 2001 for a description of this process). Further, the state's redevelopment regulations and builders' interests often produce housing that may be too inflexible to accommodate the diverse forms of sociality and domestic economy that horizontal slums enable. SRA buildings rarely offer residents expansion options in the event of growing families or paying tenants, and they make no provisions for renters or other settlers who may have recently shifted to the settlement in question.

Yet, what critics, activists, and scholars often fail to fully acknowledge is that the SRA regime has nevertheless been unexpectedly popular, not just among builders, but—crucially—among the large number of settlers entitled to rehabilitation. To paraphrase Vinay Gidwani, the urban poor view market-based solutions far more ambivalently than the scholars who write about them (see Gidwani, this volume). It is precisely the popularity of *in situ* SRA opportunities among Mumbai's settlers that must be taken seriously, for it complicates any singular and homogenous category implied through the conventional usage of, or aspirations to produce, universal housing rights.

Anand's field research points to the importance of settlers' aspirations to access SRA housing. Between 2007 and 2009, in areas including Kurla, Santacruz, Jogeshwari, and Goregaon, residents had formed, or were forming, housing committees that would facilitate direct negotiation with builders in the event that an SRA opportunity arose. Field notes detail how rival politicians regularly arrived with specific preferred builders to 'convince' residents of the merits of a proposed private development/SRA project. To convince settlers of the legitimacy of their respective schemes, SRA developers competed by hosting large parties for slum residents. These featured free food, alcohol, and images of future homes to be built in the settlement.

In 2007, Anand interviewed Rakesh, a settler who lived in a recognized settlement in Jogeshwari (fieldwork interview, November 2007). Rakesh enthusiastically described securing entitlement to a home in an adjacent settlement that was scheduled for redevelopment as an SRA project. The previous year, he explained, he'd heard that this particular settlement was on the verge of signing an SRA redevelopment agreement with a builder. Rakesh consequently 'sold' his home in a settlement with reliable municipal services to quickly buy a small house in the settlement where an SRA project was imminent. At the time of the interview, the negotiations had yet to conclude, but Rakesh remained confident and eager, if also a bit restless, to realize the promise of an SRA flat. His expectations were buoyed by examples of settler experiences in other developments; he cited 'Housing Board,' for example, where residents negotiated for their cost-free flat in a new on-site building, but also received an astonishing one-time payment of Rs. 3 million (approximately USD 65,000).

At the time of writing, both 'Housing Board' and Rakesh's settlement have yet to be redeveloped. But regardless of their status, we point to Rakesh's aspiration, and subsequent strategic pursuit of SRA resettlement. The logic of accumulation by dispossession fails to fully capture this desire and effort for *in situ* SRA housing.

In a process rife with power asymmetries, settlers are emboldened by the promises of SRA resettlement. They sometimes argue for, and reap, more than the SRA laws provide, and, depending on the settlement location (and its real estate value), builders generally engage in such negotiations with a willingness to subvert the law if it facilitates the settler consent that state policies require.

Conversations with the city's real estate developers confirmed this. While meeting a senior state administrator for a midday interview, Anand was introduced to the administrator's friend—a real estate developer by the name of Sathe. A conversation about an SRA project in which Sathe was engaged ensued. Sathe described forging documents on behalf of eighteen settlers who would have otherwise been ineligible to receive a cost-free flat, in order to gain their consent for the project. The senior state administrator was visibly upset, and asked why Sathe had not excluded the ineligible settlers as per government policy. The developer responded by pointing to the community opposition that would follow if they were excluded. "It would be a big headache," he said, one that could endanger the entire project. Sathe also had a financial interest; by including more of the initial settler population, the developer would himself receive additional development rights to sell on the private market (fieldwork interview, June 2009).

SRA policies thus align the interests of certain settlers with developers seeking to maximize profits from the market. For every additional apartment allocated to settlers, developers get additional development rights to sell on the open market or utilize in their own projects. Where these rights are far more valuable than the cost of construction, developers try to construct as many tenements as possible, and to house as many people as the regulations allow. In a curious twist, when developers mobilize illegal means to include the maximum number of flats in their projects, NGOs and state bureaucracies seek to restrict their number (Sanyal and Mukhija 2001).

The desirability and potential financial benefits of SRA projects are contingent on the value of the land in question, the organizing abilities of settlers, and the kind of rehabilitation package to which the parties agree. Few projects are actually completed. Nevertheless, the promise of living in a building, and having the right to do so, functions as an incentive for millions of qualified settlers to leave unopposed the contemporary, and yet quite unequal, processes of urbanization and settlement redevelopment through which their formalized housing materializes. Instead of mobilizing against displacement by state administrators, private developers, and local politicians, settlers often seek better terms of redevelopment by working strategically with these same groups. 'Development' for millions of recognized settlers may therefore be less about persistent cycles of displacement, and more about the strategic pursuit of what are perceived to be transformative opportunities to participate in a thriving real estate market.

At this point, we must restate that legal entitlement to a free *in situ* SRA flat is by no means universal. State policies mandate that beneficiaries of SRA redevelopment must prove residence in particular settlements for over fifteen years. The large populations of renters who live in nearly every settlement in Mumbai often have difficulty claiming sufficient tenurial status, in part because their landlords, who are also settlers, prevent them from accessing government documents.[7] For residents who cannot access forged documents that show otherwise, SRA projects can have catastrophic effects. While creating transformative opportunities for some, then, SRA projects continue to re-inscribe state-constituted differences between those who are eligible for and can claim rehabilitation in alternative housing, and those who cannot (Doshi, this volume; Holston 2008). The new SRA policy continues to subject residents who cannot claim *in situ* SRA housing—renters, recent migrants, and those without documents—to the disciplinary strategy of bulldozers, displacement, and dispossession. For these settlers, accumulation by dispossession has unquestionable resonance and clear experiential content.

Compromising Rights

Today, millions of settlers find themselves recognized as political subjects occupying potentially valuable land. Their engagement with the state is as much a matter of financial and material *incentive* as it is a matter of rights. As circumstances have changed, so too have politics and political patrons. For activists who have a history of sympathizing and working with settlers, contemporary settler politics and strategies are often deeply troubling. Many settlers, motivated by the promise of financial gain, no longer align themselves with the long-term goals for which activists have long fought on their behalf.

For instance, in July 2007, activists from various Mumbai housing rights groups met to discuss legislative revisions to the state's housing policy at the College of Social Work. Many spoke of how the policy would only exacerbate the marginalization of the city's poorest. Datta Iswalkar, a twenty-year veteran activist on behalf of mill-workers and their housing rights, characterized the challenge:

> We have to realize that the amounts of money are so large for all these redevelopment projects. Builders are paying the poor large sums of money. Vilasrao [the chief minister] says he has nothing to do with this . . . How can we stop the poor from taking this money? [If they are getting] 2 lakhs, 3 lakhs ($5000) . . . their income is nowhere near this amount . . . (Meeting on New Housing Policy, July 2007)

Redevelopment incentives have produced deep divisions among activists and NGOs that were once united in demanding settlers' tenurial rights to the city. Millions of settlers benefited when the official cutoff date for redevelopment eligibility was pushed forward to 1995. In its aftermath, as local politicians and builders validate their newfound status with large amounts of cash, many settlers are happy to reap the material benefits (see Sanyal and Mukhija 2001).

Pratibhatai is one of the many housing activists disillusioned with the current state of housing politics. She is seeking other channels of legitimacy these days, as she explained in a 2007 interview:

> Our NGO does not work directly in *bastis* anymore. After working for so many years organizing people, *morchas* [protest marches], getting them ration cards, starting groups, our work got appropriated by political parties . . . They [settlers] were smarter than us. They took our help for ration cards, got papers and now tell us it's ok—that we are not needed—they will handle their matters on their own. (field interview, October 2007)

Pratibhatai conveyed an acute sense of betrayal and disappointment that after spending years helping organize the residents of Sitawadi, they seemed to have abandoned her NGO for political parties. Yet embedded in her narrative of a weakened housing rights movement was also some evidence of its own compromised successes.

Having achieved documentation for settlers through countless protests, marches, and negotiations, NGOs have indeed been instrumental in helping many settlers achieve substantive rights to the city. They have also done so by 'participating' in state committees to promote subtle shifts in state policy (Chatterji and Mehta 2007; Li 1999; Rahnema 1992). It is precisely because of these partial rights that many settlers can now approach developers and local politicians directly. Most settlers no longer need NGOs to access state entitlements; instead, they do so through social workers and the grassroots activists affiliated with political parties.[8]

Pratibhatai also stated that many settlers with whom she had worked no longer live in the city. Many have sold their homes and gone away, she explained (field interview, October 2007). Indeed this is a common story, shared particularly by those in Mumbai's housing sector. Of course, while the reasons for their move have to do with the value they can extract from their new housing, it is also striking that many who have earned SRA flats also stay, desiring in part to remain in their neighborhoods for the social ties, services, and infrastructure that they provide.

When settlers 'cash in' on the very homes that have been the central demand and focus of intense, sustained social movements, activists like

Pratibhatai are inevitably disappointed. This is due in part to the fact that those settlers who 'sell out' can be understood neither through a logic of 'deserving' citizens *nor* one of resisting subjects. And although government officials have attempted to prevent SRA flat sales by making them illegal, their attempts have met with limited success.[9] Pratibhatai conveyed her sense of betrayal by saying, "They were smarter than us." Hers is a common disappointment, based on a politics in which settlers are imagined as agents of revolutionary change rather than the recipients of compromised gains (Conklin 1997; Tsing 1999).[10]

Scholars and activists often explain settler decisions to sell their new SRA homes in terms of gentrification, in which hegemonic capitalist structures of domination and marginalization are reproduced via the peripheralization of the poor. Indeed accelerated gentrification is an important effect of the settler practices we have discussed in Mumbai, and it is an indispensable analytical tool across many contemporary forms of urbanization. For example, David Harvey writes the following on the critical structural inequalities in which policies that confer property rights to favela residents in Rio de Janerio are embedded:

> The problem is that the poor, beset with income insecurity and frequent financial difficulties, can easily be persuaded to trade in that asset for a relatively low cash payment . . . I wager that within fifteen years, if present trends continue, all those hillsides in Rio now occupied by favelas will be covered by high-rise condominiums with fabulous views over the idyllic bay, while the erstwhile favela dwellers will have been filtered off into some remote periphery. (Harvey 2008, 36)

Harvey will undoubtedly win his wager. Yet, as our discussion of Mumbai's housing politics suggests, the market-effected marginalization that occurs when settlers sell the cost-free flats that they have secured through SRA policies has rather different effects for settlers than the state's bulldozers have had in other (simultaneously existing) periods.

With real estate values in Mumbai at astronomical highs for much of 2008, settlers stood to gain approximately ten to twenty years of their annual income by selling their SRA flats in certain neighborhoods. And why not? While choice is always already circumscribed by deep structural inequalities, and never 'free' and rational as liberal theorists assume, it may also be a mistake to overlook the significance and meaning of settlers' aspirations *because* of inequality. As Ananya Roy notes, the "politics of compensation" that Mumbai's SRA regime has mobilized "cannot be simply dismissed as coopted or compromised forms of insurgent citizenship. Indeed, it must be taken seriously as a modality of inclusion, one that makes possible resettlement, rehabilitation and dialogue" (Roy 2009, 173; see also Holston 2008). Like everyone else, settlers in Mumbai have contradictory and multiple relations with capitalism that simultaneously marginalize *and* enable them. Like most urban citizens, their decisions to retain rights to the city hinge less on structural transformation, and more on other conditions, like the desire to make life better for their children, to access work, and to cultivate the range of social and infrastructural relations on which their social worlds depend.

Though compromised and unequal, rights to SRA housing have been secured through a history of struggle by social movements, the electoral compulsions of political parties, and the policy interventions of the World Bank and other multilateral development agencies. They have also been powered by the peculiar costs of land in Mumbai. They mark the latest iteration in a history of government slum policies that try to manage Mumbai's inadequate housing. To recognize this history and its measured achievements in Mumbai is more than a simple scholarly gesture. It forces us to recognize the critical differences between the spatial marginalization effected by the 'bulldozer state' and the spatial practices underway when settlers sell their tenements. Both these sets of governing practices coexist in Mumbai today. But by conflating them, and situating them in impact narratives of displacement and marginalization, activists and intellectuals risk obfuscating the compromised achievements of settlers, NGOs, and political movements alike (see Gibson-Graham 1996; Hart 2002).

Conclusion

In Mumbai, *in situ* SRA projects afford *some* settlers the opportunity to participate in a housing scheme that privileges capital accumulation for the developer and housing consolidation for the settler. Employing a mode of *differential inclusion*, the regime confers tenure to a significant subset of the city's settlers, and entitlement to negotiate on-site, cost-free, new high-rise housing (see also Doshi, this volume). Although only some settlers qualify for this hybrid form of rehousing, many *aspire* to it. We point to these aspirations, and their attendant practices, to raise two points. First, while

Mumbai's SRA regime is to a large extent a neoliberal solution to housing the urban poor, it has also emerged over a nearly three-decade history of settler mobilization, advocacy, and negotiation. With settlers' political power multiply constituted across arenas of activism and government, state agents often find it easier and politically necessary to accommodate settler demands than to bulldoze their homes.

Second, although many slum-dwellers are unable to qualify for SRA housing, it is nevertheless analytically imperative that we take their SRA-related practices and aspirations seriously. As they negotiate with builders and politicians, many settlers engage in a 'politics of compensation' that suggests important disjunctures between equality and inclusion in Mumbai. Settlers negotiate SRA housing agreements despite the knowledge that their own successful resettlement in an on-site high rise flat will reinforce certain forms of housing inequality. These forms may separate them from the upper classes on one hand, and from ineligible settlers on the other.

The promise of inclusion implied by the SRA housing policy in Mumbai thus does little to solve the broader problem of urban inequality. This shift in emphasis from equality as a core urbanization problem to the goal of achieving a general urban state of 'inclusion' is not unique to Mumbai. For example, as Teresa Caldeira (2009) has recently observed, Sao Paulo's latest development plan incorporates and assumes inequality in its very design by accommodating separate building codes for those who live in favelas.

We recognize, albeit quite uncomfortably, that the SRA approach of accommodating inequality is not only endorsed to different degrees by city administrators, property developers, and development banks, but also, quite crucially, by those among the poor and marginalized who actually live in the settlements in Mumbai. The differential inclusion enacted through SRA housing projects builds on older histories of differentiating settlers in the city so that some settlements were recognized and protected while others were deemed liable for demolition. The SRA perpetuates longstanding patterns through which the homes of certain settlers become eligible for improvement while those who may be renters or who occupy public lands deemed critical to the city (on which airports, railways, or roads might be built) become vulnerable to eviction and exile. Differential inclusion has long enabled the state government to more effectively manage the magnitude of the city's housing problem, and the SRA perpetuates this.

With this in mind, we urge attention to the history of struggles for inclusion and equality to better understand why and how SRA housing has emerged as an aspiration and goal for many in Mumbai's settlements. Such desires, shared both by settlers who qualify for SRAs today, and those who *might* qualify for it in the future, confound most conventional notions of housing rights and housing politics. The aspirations and practices recounted in this chapter require many of us who organize our research toward promoting rights to the city to consider an uncomfortable proposition: in order to achieve certain kinds of inclusion and equality, we might be called upon to institutionalize other forms of exclusion and inequality. This is not a proposal set forth by the authors; it is an already emergent and articulated set of political practices among Mumbai's settlers today.

Notes

1. See, for example, M. Echanove and R. Srivastava, Taking the Slum out of Slumdog. *New York Times*, December 2, 2009.

2. S. S. Kshatriya (2007), Reforming the Housing Debate, Introductory Comments. Housing the Urban Poor I, Urban Age India Conference, Mumbai, November 2, 2007.

3. Because they are marked by the imaginaries of dirt, criminality, and vice, we chose not to use the labels 'slum' and 'slum-dweller,' unless we are referring to government programs for improvement and eradication (see Echanove and Srivastava 2009 [details in note 2]; Ghannam 2002; Ghertner, this volume). We instead use the terms 'settlement' and 'settler' in this chapter. 'Settlement' is also a better translation of the Hindi word *basti*, which is also a better representation of the process through which urban habitation has been made.

4. In comparison, the Maharashtra Housing and Area Development Authority (MHADA) has constructed only 4,000 flats a year in Mumbai since its inception in 1977, with the number decreasing in the last two decades. In an interview given to the *Mumbai Mirror* MHADA officials point to the difficulty of acquiring land as the prime reason for this shortfall ("Mass housing: Mhada fails to shine in report card," Mumbai Mirror, February 2, 2009).

5. Of the 211,000 *in situ* SRA tenements approved, only 50,000 have been completed (Sheela Patel, personal communication).

6. As a result of engagement, pressure, and negotiation, the cutoff date has been revised roughly every five years, from 1980, to 1985, to 1990, to 1995 (Mahadevia and Narayanan 1999; McFarlane 2008), to include and recognize more recent settlements in the city. Once a slum is 'declared,' its residents are

entitled to receive formal municipal water and electricity services, as well as rehabilitation in the case of eviction. Yet the services that accompany 'declaration' are
not instantaneous or even wholly assured. State entitlements are provided very
slowly. Nevertheless, the benefits that accrue as a result of declaration-based
policies are real; they mark, as noted above, a significant break with the past.

7.   In settlements, the landlord's approval is necessary for renters to gain connec-
     tion to different urban services including food subsidies, electricity, and water
     services.

8.   It is noteworthy that local politicians and social workers also require settlers
     to provide state documents to effect their requests for water connections or
     housing societies. They do this not only because these documents are required
     by the water department, but also because by arranging the necessary paper-
     work for those who lack it, they are at times able to extract more money or other
     personal obligations (see Anand 2011).

9.   As per SRA regulations intended to ensure that slum-dwellers do not profit
     from their housing, they are not permitted to legally transfer their housing for a
     period of ten years.

10. Anthropologists have often pointed to the demands placed on marginalized
     people to be noble, resisting subjects, unaffected by materials and money.
     Conklin writes of how Amazonian Indians were compelled to "act in a certain
     way that is natural and beyond material goods" so ask to fit environmental activ-
     ists' conceptions of them as "authentic" (Conklin 1997, 724). This is no easy
     task. As Tsing points out, "It is an enormously complex skill to reproduce the
     dominant group's stereotypes so beautifully that they only see their imagined
     Other" (1999, 81).

References

Anand, N. 2006. Disconnecting Experience: Making World Class Roads in Mumbai.
     Economic and Political Weekly, 41 (31): 3422–3429.
———. 2011. Pressure: The Polytechnics of Water Supply in Mumbai. *Cultural
     Anthropology*, 26(4): 542–563.
Appadurai A. 1999. Grassroots Globalization and the Research Imagination. *Public
     Culture*, 12(1): 1–19.
———. 2000. Spectral Housing and Urban Cleansing: Notes on a Millennial Mumbai.
     Public Culture, 12: 627–651.
———. 2002. Deep Democracy: Urban Governmentality and the Horizon of Politics.
     Public Culture, 14: 21–47.
Bromley, D. 2008. Formalising Property Relations in the Developing World: The
     Wrong Prescription for the Wrong Malady. *Land Use Policy*, 26: 20–27.

Burra, S. 2005. Towards a Pro-Poor Framework for Slum Upgrading in Mumbai, India. *Environment and Urbanization*, 17: 67–88.

Caldeira, T. 2000. *City of Walls: Crime, Segregation, and Citizenship in São Paulo*. Berkeley, CA: University of California Press.

———. 2009. Peripheries: Spaces in the Making. Conference paper presented at Peripheries—Decentering Urban Theory, University of California, Berkeley, February 5.

Calderon, J. 2004. The Formalisation of Property in Peru 2001–2002: The Case of Lima. *Habitat International*, 28: 289–300.

Chandavarkar, R. 2007. Customs of Governance: Colonialism and Democracy in Twentieth Century India. *Modern Asian Studies*, 41: 441–470.

Chatterjee, P. 2004. *The Politics of the Governed: Reflections on Popular Politics in Most of The World*. New York: Columbia University Press.

———. 2008. Democracy and Economic Transformation in India. *Economic and Political Weekly*, 43 (16): 53–63.

Chatterji, R., and D. Mehta. 2007. *Living with Violence: An Anthropology of Events and Everyday Life*. New York: Routledge.

Conklin, B. 1997. Body Paint, Feathers and VCRs: Aesthetics and Authenticity in Amazonian Activism. *American Ethnologist*, 24: 711–737.

Davis, M. 2004. Planet of Slums: Urban Involution and the Informal Proletariat. *New Left Review*, 26: 5–34.

Dawson, A., and B. Edwards. 2004. Introduction: Cities of the South. *Social Text*, 22 (4 81): 1–7.

De Soto, H. 2000. *The Mystery of Capital: Why Capitalism Triumphs in the West and Fails Everywhere Else*. New York: Basic Books.

Durand-Lasserve, A. 2006. Informal Settlements and the Millennium Development Goals: Global Policy Debates on Property Ownership and Security of Tenure. *Global Urban Development*, 2 (1): 1–15.

Ghannam, F. 2002. *Remaking The Modern: Space, Relocation, and the Politics of Identity In A Global Cairo*. Berkeley, CA: University of California Press.

Gibson-Graham, J. K. 1996. *The End of Capitalism (As We Knew It): A Feminist Critique of Political Economy*. Cambridge: Blackwell Publishers.

Guzder, C. 2002. The Free for All City. *Seminar*, 528: 28–30.

Hansen, T. 2001. *Violence in Urban India*. New Delhi: Permanent Black.

Hart, G. 2002. *Disabling Globalization: Places of Power in Post-Apartheid South Africa*. Berkeley, CA: University of California Press.

Harvey, D. 2008. The Right to the City. *New Left Review*, 53: 23–40.

———. 2008. *Insurgent Citizenship: Disjunctions of Democracy and Modernity in Brazil*. Princeton, NJ: Princeton University Press.

Li, T. 1999. Compromising Power: Development, Culture and Rule in Indonesia. *Cultural Anthropology*, 14: 295–321.

Low S. 2003. *Behind The Gates: Life, Security, and the Pursuit of Happiness in Fortress America*. New York; London: Routledge.

Mahadevia, D. 2006. NURM and the Poor in Globalizing Megacities. *Economic and Political Weekly*, 41 (31): 3399–3403.

Mahadevia, D., and H. Narayanan. 1999. *Shanghaing Mumbai: Politics of Evictions and Resistance in Slum Settlements*. Ahmedabad, Gujarat: Centre for Development Alternatives.

Mehta S. 2004. *Maximum City : Bombay Lost and Found*. New York: Alfred A. Knopf.

McFarlane, C. 2008. Governing the Contaminated City: Infrastructure and Sanitation in Colonial and Post-Colonial Bombay. *International Journal of Urban and Regional Research*, 32: 415–435.

Mukhija, V. 2003. *Squatters as Developers: Slum Redevelopment in Mumbai*. Burlington, UK: Ashgate.

Neuwirth, R. 2006. *Shadow Cities: A Billion Squatters, A New Urban World*. New York: Routledge.

Nijman, J. 2008. Against the Odds: Slum Rehabilitation in Neoliberal Mumbai. *Cities*, 25: 73–85.

O'Hare, G., D. Abbott, and M. Barke. 1998. A Review of Slum Housing Policies in Mumbai. *Cities*, 15: 269–283.

Payne, G. 1997. *Urban Land Tenure and Property Rights in Developing Countries: A Review*. London: IT Publications/ODA.

Rahnema, M. 1992. Participation. In *The Development Dictionary: A Guide to Knowledge as Power*, ed. W. Sachs. 155–176. Hyderabad, Andhra Pradesh: Orient Longman Limited.

Roy, A. 2009. Civic Governmentality: The Politics of Inclusion in Beirut and Mumbai. *Antipode*, 41: 159–179.

Sanyal, B., and V. Mukhija. 2001. Institutional Pluralism and Housing Delivery: A Case of Unforeseen Conflicts in Mumbai, India. *World Development*, 29: 2043–2057.

Science. 2008. Special Issue: Cities. 319 (5864). February 8.

Sharma, K. 2000. *Rediscovering Dharavi*. New Delhi: Penguin.

Sivaramakrishnan, K. 1999. *Modern Forests: Statemaking and Environmental Change in Colonial Eastern India*. Oxford: Oxford University Press.

Sjaastad, E., and B. Cousins. 2008. Formalisation of Land Rights in the South: An Overview. *Land Use Policy*, 26: 1–9.

Social Text. 2004. Special Issue: Global Cities of the South. 22 (4 81).

Tarlo, E. 2000. Welcome to History: A Resettlement Colony in the Making. In *Delhi: Urban Space and Human Destinies*, ed. V. Dupont, E. Tarlo, and D. Vidal. 51–74. New Delhi: Manohar.

Tindall, G. 1982. *City of Gold: The Biography of Bombay*. London: Temple Smith.

Tsing, A. 1999. Becoming a Tribal Elder, and Other Green Development Fantasies. In *Transforming the Indonesian Uplands: Marginality, Power and Production*, ed. T. Li. 157–200. Amsterdam: Harwood Academic Publishers.

Weinstein, L., and X. Ren. 2009. The Changing Right to the City: Urban Renewal and Housing Rights in Globalizing Shanghai and Mumbai. *City and Community*, 8: 407–433.

Zeiderman, A. 2008. Cities of the Future? Megacities and the Space/Time of Urban Modernity. *Critical Planning*, 15: 23–40.

9
Resettlement Ecologies: Environmental Subjectivity and Graduated Citizenship in Mumbai

Sapana Doshi

Introduction

Mumbai's overcrowded trains, traffic-jammed roads, and sprawling underserviced slums undergird the paradigmatic Malthusian imaginary of the Indian city living beyond its means. Efforts to redevelop the city's informal 'slum' settlements into world-class infrastructure and residential and commercial real estate promise a remedy for these urban ills. Such slum redevelopment projects have unfolded through social and material processes in which the 'environment'—as spatial experience, discourse, and geographical imaginary—has figured centrally. Most notably, redevelopment has entailed what Amita Baviskar (2003) calls "bourgeois environmentalism," a set of discourses and interventions aimed at remaking and ostensibly cleaning the city through the removal of the poor. This is an environmental politics in which the subjective desires and material interests of the upper and middle classes, business owners, and financiers are secured through state-facilitated slum demolitions, an instantiation of "accumulation by dispossession" (Harvey 2003). Yet, as this chapter argues, redevelopment in Mumbai has not unfolded in a simple top-down fashion where elites and a bulldozing state serve as the only agents of spatial transformation. Rather in a city with a strong history of social mobilization, slum-residents and their representatives also play a critical role in facilitating, negotiating, and thwarting projects of urban environmental transformation in the service of capital accumulation. Slum clearance in Mumbai entails a complex ecology of state force, accommodation, and negotiation, as well as diverse and changing understandings of space and belonging. Slum-residents are making claims to space as citizens and environmental subjects in highly differentiated ways with significant implications for whether and how the city is remade.

Focusing on collective actions of slum-residents, this chapter examines how urban subjectivity is produced through the intersecting experiences and politics of redevelopment, displacement, and ecology. I take as a point of departure the works of Amita Baviskar (2003) and Colin McFarlane (2008), who argue that urban environmental citizenship is often rife with hierarchy: it either seeks to erase the 'polluting' poor from the space of the city or relegates them to sub-standard environmental conditions. My project develops this line of reasoning by investigating how evicted slum-dwellers and their representative organizations have advanced new forms of environmental politics that negotiate or challenge displacements that occur as a result of redevelopment. This work takes seriously the call made by a number of political ecologists to engage more deeply with questions of subject formation and cultural politics, in addition to questions of urban political economy, infrastructure, and urban nature (Agrawal 2005; Braun 2002; Grove 2009; Peet and Watts 2004). In Mumbai, slum-dwellers emerge as environmental subjects through complex spatial processes in which relations of class, ethnicity, religion, and gender are articulated in diverse and politically salient ways.

Highlighting the environmental subjectivities of the urban poor, this chapter also engages recent scholarship on new citizenship formations in Third World cities that has sought to challenge commonly held notions of modern democratic political participation (Appadurai 2002; Chatterjee 2004; Holston 2008). The chapter departs from these works, however, by emphasizing the relational and differentiated nature of subject formation—in the space of a single city—and the political implications of such processes for urban environmental change. The Mumbai case demonstrates that environmental subjectivity operates through the terrain of what Ong (2007) has called "graduated citizenship," where class-based, gendered, and ethno-religious identities fracture and remake experiences of citizenship and claims to legitimacy. Here environmental politics is shaped by a political ecology of redevelopment that privileges capital accumulation through slum clearance. Differentiated environmental subjectivities emerge through the uneven distribution of resettlement compensation as well as a contentious cultural politics of urban belonging. Resettlement compensation is thus a central arena for the formation and recalibration of urban environmental citizenship.

This analysis of differentiated slum citizenship is not merely an effort to expose the complexity of neoliberal politics in 'actually existing' cities like Mumbai. Rather, I argue, it is precisely the production of difference, or what Ruth Wilson Gilmore, following Stuart Hall, has called the "fatal couplings of power and difference" (2002, 16), that provides the contradictory spatial experiences that incite displaced slum-inhabitants to engage in global city projects. Drawing on environmental discourses and situated experiences of unequal access to resources, slum-residents have made new claims to legitimacy and belonging. Paying attention to these multiple, relational subjectivities shows us how slum-residents both reinforce and challenge elite projects of urban environmental transformation in cities like Mumbai.

Accordingly, this chapter specifically explores spatio-environmental conflicts and subjectivity in and around Mankhurd, an area on the suburban northeastern coast of Mumbai that has become a major slum resettlement hub for the city. I consider three moments in which Mankhurd served as a frontier site for producing new forms of environmental subjectivity among evicted slum-dwellers. The first examines an off-site participatory resettlement project where NGO mediation harnessed particular forms of gendered environmental subjectivity to enable cooperation with slum clearance. In the second case, river basin slum evictees contested resettlement countering the ecological justifications of eviction embedded in "bourgeois environmentalism." The third moment pertains to the ways that discourses of the urban periphery—as a vast and empty space of resettlement opportunity—belie the violent erasure of those who already occupy those lands. In this instance, North Indian and Muslim minority evictees of a slum in Mankhurd have—with the assistance of a social movement—struggled to negotiate rights to slum land demolished to make way for evicted slum-dwellers from other parts of the city, the latter of whom were eligible for compensation.

These examples show how the politics of eviction and resettlement on the urban fringe have shaped environmental experiences, subjectivities, and problem framings that are differentiated according to the specific positionings of slum-dwellers in relation to each other, and to agents of neoliberal urban transformation. Mediating groups including NGOs, social movements, and advocacy lawyers further shape political possibilities through highly partial representations of evicted slum-dwellers' experiences. Examining these ethnographic cases in "relational comparison" (Hart 2002), I suggest that the environmental subjects in question form not in social isolation, but in ways that are deeply interconnected both spatially and politically in relation to each other, and to powerful, translocal forces of urban development. Resettlement compensation and legitimate belonging in the space of the city have emerged as key signifiers of symbolic and material struggle invigorated by the political and economic transformations of the 1990s. The following overview of slum redevelopment policies and identity politics during this period helps to situate the current geographies of environmental politics and the ethnographic cases to follow.

Violent Environments: Neoliberal Redevelopment and Graduated Slum Citizenship

The decade of the 1990s represents a period of significant change in redevelopment and resettlement policy and practice in the city. In the early part of the decade, Mumbai's real estate markets surged as economic liberalization in India created new demand for urban land among the local middle and upper classes and transnational elites (Banerjee-Guha 2002; Nijman 2000). Flows of foreign capital and increasing middle-class incomes fueled elite desires for a city with world-class transport infrastructure, spaces of consumption and leisure, and upscale residences (Fernandes 2004). Such processes resulted in upper-class impatience with slums while low-income residents faced an intensified squeeze in affordable housing. Under these conditions, the Shiv Sena, a political party and populist movement known for its unique brand of Hindu nationalism and regionalist xenophobia, won the state of Maharashtra elections. The Shiv Sena campaign promised to beautify the city, expand transportation infrastructure, eradicate slums, and provide 'free' resettlement flats to 4 million slum-dwellers, which appealed to a broad set of constituents. The Shiv Sena-led state government subsequently established the Slum Rehabilitation Scheme (SRS), a neoliberal policy that aimed to promote real estate and infrastructure redevelopment through mass slum clearance. The scheme would facilitate slum clearance by leveraging the market to resettle slum-dwellers evicted by state projects. Elite and middle-class resistance to spending tax revenue on so-called 'encroachers' would be quelled by the promise that the state would not spend a rupee on providing 'free' flats. Rather, the market would create a 'win–win' solution, addressing housing for the poor and redevelopment desires for the upper classes.

Resettlement, however, would not be extended equitably to all slum-residents. In the SRS policy, resettlement housing was guaranteed only to evicted slum-dwellers who could furnish documentary proof of residency in Mumbai prior to a 'cutoff date' of January 1, 1995. The cutoff date helped to limit resettlement by excluding ostensibly freeloading populations attracted by government giveaways. Furthermore, resettlement compensation would be financed entirely by the market; a newly created Slum Rehabilitation Authority (SRA) would offer incentives to private developers to build tenements for slum-dwellers free of cost in exchange for coveted transfers of development rights to build taller buildings throughout the city. All other public housing and slum improvement schemes would be phased out and replaced entirely by this market-oriented model. The SRS not only increased the role of the private sector in low-income housing construction, it also dramatically expanded the space available for market-rate redevelopment and created a vigorous market for transferable development rights. Both the release of cleared slum land and transferable development rights for high-value neighborhoods offered a windfall of opportunities for developers. Slum rehabilitation thus merged the imperatives of a booming real estate market with the political management of slum clearance and the tightening supplies of affordable housing.

Exclusions embedded in the resettlement policy, which belied its win-win image, must be understood in relation to the ethno-religious, political violence gripping Mumbai during the 1990s. In a scenario of intense struggles over space, the housing crisis was articulated through anti-Muslim, regionalist, and xenophobic frames fueled by the right wing Shiv Sena party in diverse arenas. As Arjun Appadurai has argued, the Shiv Sena "sutured a specific form of regional chauvinism with a national message about Hindu power through the deployment of the figure of the Muslim as the archetype of the invader, the stranger, and the traitor" (2000, 646). The Shiv Sena played a central role in the communal riots of 1993, shattering thousands of lives, especially in poor and Muslim neighborhoods (Chatterji and Mehta 2007; Hansen 2001). Shiv Sena leaders like Bal Thackeray fused the utopian promise of a Hinduized global city with a thuggish strategy of scapegoating outsiders for the ills of the city and nation. In the realm of slum redevelopment, the exclusions of Hindu nationalist and regionalist imaginaries became concretely embedded in resettlement policy through the cutoff date eligibility criterion for resettlement mentioned above. The cutoff date discursively invoked a barrier to an imagined migratory tide of invasion by Muslims and North Indians. As one bureaucrat said in an interview: "We cannot keep allowing Mumbai to turn into a 'mumbaiabad,'" (fieldwork interview, July 2005) referring to an imagined Islamicized, North Indian colonization of the city. The vilification of the slum-dweller as an encroaching outsider—while actively disregarding his or her actual ethno-religious background—was compounded under the Shiv Sena and the xenophobic climate in Mumbai, further justifying the curtailment of public benefits like resettlement. Thus, slum clearance and resettlement compensation practices have undergirded powerful real estate interests and violently exclusionary class and identity-based ideals regarding who rightfully belongs in the space of the city. The contradictions of differentiated spatial politics of resettlement eligibility and public imaginaries of legitimacy were brought into sharp relief in the demolition sweeps of the next decade.

Eviction and resettlement practices reflecting both inclusive and exclusionary notions of belonging have contoured the boundaries of urban citizenship among slum-residents. Accordingly, I argue that Mumbai's slum redevelopment exhibits a form of accumulation by differentiated displacement—experienced through graduated forms of urban citizenship— rather than a simple form of dispossession (Doshi 2013). Divisions were created not only by resettlement eligibility criteria, but also by the location of the original slum of residence. While redevelopment policies gained popularity among slum-residents who expected resettlement in newly constructed buildings on the same plot of land, not all displaced residents were to be resettled in their former neighborhoods. The residents of hundreds of slums in areas where resettlement could not be offered on-site due to their location on river basins, railway tracks, or road projects would be relocated off-site. Moreover, given the high cost of real estate in the city and the anxieties of the upper and middle classes over what they considered government handouts to encroachers, off-site resettlement would have to be undertaken as cheaply as possible. Developing low-value land on the urban fringe emerged as the state's principal strategy for resettling slum-dwellers displaced by environmental improvement and infrastructure projects. City officials, planners, and developers have argued that the solution to Mumbai's environmental problems and housing shortages lay in releasing for development 5,000 acres of marshy coastal land, known as the 'salt pans.' Located on the northern fringes of the city, most of these peripheral wetlands have until recent years quietly retained 'no-development' zoning status, and have thus been of little interest to the powerbrokers of the city. Since the mid-1990s, these areas have emerged in the planning imaginary as the ideal locations for resettling slum-dwellers evicted by infrastructure projects. Accordingly, these areas now represent a "new urban frontier" (Smith 1996), an opportunity for the urbanization of the capital in a formerly devalued space.

Redevelopment interventions have significantly altered the landscape of several northeastern coastal neighborhoods, which have now seen the emergence of new colonies of densely concentrated resettlement buildings. Many of these colonies, linked to the resettlement component of a World Bank–supported transportation infrastructure project, have become models for the mass rehabilitation of slum-dwellers. These resettlement interventions have not only transformed the political ecology of the area, but also reflect a set of urban ecological framings of slums and slum-dwellers by non-governmental and neighborhood-based groups. Yet, expansion into the urban fringe is hardly a foregone conclusion: resettlement and redevelopment have incited conflicts often couched in environmental terms. Insofar as the periphery represents a solution for buffering large-scale evictions, it reveals the dynamic and contradictory forms of environmental politics shaping urban citizenship in the city. I now turn to examine three distinct cases of social mobilization around eviction and resettlement in Mankhurd, a neighborhood known for including several of the city's largest resettlement colonies.

Embodied Environments: Resettlement and Feminized Stewardship

If redeveloping the urban fringe today is posited as the principal strategy for relocating slums for infrastructure, it is also true that such resettlement policies have emerged from longstanding struggles over evictions of people generally excluded from adequate compensation (Mitlin and Patel 2005). One of the best-known groups involved in resettlement implementation and policy negotiations in Mumbai is the Society for the Promotion of Area Resource Centres (SPARC), an NGO that has been involved in the resettlement of thousands of slum-dwellers affected by road and rail projects. This section examines the history, strategies, and development discourse advanced by this internationally-known housing and development organization. It culminates in an analysis of the alliance SPARC formed with two other advocacy groups in order to bolster their involvement in resettling slum-dwellers affected by the Mumbai Urban Transport Project (MUTP), a World Bank–funded project that has been hailed as a model for resettlement in transnational development circles. I argue that environmental subjectivity was contoured by gender in ways that facilitated cooperation in a potentially volatile situation of mass off-site displacement. Understanding this gendered environmental subjectivity requires an investigation into the histories and practices of mobilization in slums prior to and during the MUTP resettlement.

SPARC began its work in the early 1980s with women living in shacks along the busy streets of south-central Mumbai. Repeatedly facing the threat of the demolition of their homes by the authorities, these 'pavement-dwellers' were considered by activists to be the city's poorest and most vulnerable population. SPARC leaders recall that the organization grew frustrated not only with government mal-treatment of pavement-dwellers but also with housing organizations and movements in the city. SPARC leaders and staff argued that many housing movements, though well meaning, demonstrated a middle-class bias in their strategies. They asserted that an activists' rights-based approach, which consisted of protesting the government with little follow-up, did not adequately engage the participation of poor women who they claimed were less interested in conflicts with the government than in long-term solutions (D'Cruz, n.d.).

Working with pavement-dwelling women, SPARC developed an alternative and now-famous model of participatory development and non-confrontational negotiation with state bureaucracies. The organization sought to convey the needs of slum-dwellers to state and transnational agents by promoting the participation of women in activities such as savings, housing and sanitation design alternatives, and community surveying. The idea was to demonstrate to state and development agents that the poor had viable and economical solutions to addressing their own problems. These activities soon led to the creation of Mahila Milan, a slum-based women's collective, and a subsequent alliance with the well-established grassroots group, the National Slum Dwellers Federation. Today, these three organizations, known collectively as the SPARC Alliance, are involved in a variety of slum interventions ranging from toilet construction to resettlement. In virtually all of its interventions, the Alliance has focused on the participation of slum-dwelling women in social and environmental improvement. In the Alliance's discursive framing, women's knowledge of the home, role in water provision, and special needs with regard to sanitation make them ideal environmental stewards for the slum. In a context in which slum-dwellers are dehumanized for their ostensibly polluting practices, the reframing of poor women as practical solution-seeking subjects has provided a powerful non-confrontational counter-narrative to bourgeois environmentalism. This mode of engaging with the local state and development agencies around the world has made the group a powerful advocate for many of its members and constituents.

A large range of academic and policy literature has hailed the SPARC Alliance as a model for empowering the urban poor (Appadurai 2002; Mitlin and Patel 2005), though critiques of the limits of SPARC and similar NGOs have arisen from diverse quarters more recently (Benjamin 2008; McFarlane 2004; McFarlane 2008; Roy 2009). Housing activists in Mumbai have also recognized the important influence of the Alliance but have criticized the group for its cozy relationship with developers and the xenophobic Shiv Sena political party. Yet, to date there has been little in-depth, independent ethnographic work on precisely how slum-dwellers have engaged with the organization.

Drawing briefly on ethnographic data collected between 2006 and 2007, I examine the particularly gendered forms of environmental subjectivity in a large-scale resettlement project implemented by SPARC from 1998 to 2007. With its strong, positive relationship with the state, broad grassroots support base, and excellent reputation in international development circles, the SPARC Alliance was chosen as the major NGO partner for implementing community-based resettlement activities for the MUTP. The project involved the relocation of approximately 20,000 slum-dwellers into neighborhoods mostly on the eastern suburban periphery, with the greatest concentration in Mankhurd.

In interviews with SPARC Alliance leaders and in the Alliance's literature on the project, women slum-dwellers are consistently highlighted as both participants and primary beneficiaries of the resettlement. As one SPARC Alliance staff member writes, "the central role that women played in the Kanjur Marg [resettlement] experiment is justified not only on the grounds of gender equity but also upon the demonstration of their skills as managers of the family. With their experience of running households on inadequate budgets, poor women take easily to managing projects when given exposure, training, and opportunity" (Burra 1999). Arputham Jockin, an award-winning leader of the Alliance, has also put the needs of slum-dwellers into a gender-sensitive historical context. During a workshop for British urban planning students that I attended in May 2007 in Mumbai, Jockin explained that early in urbanization processes the need for housing and infrastructure was less acute because single male migrant workers could bathe and sleep freely in public. When these migrants settled with their families, their needs shifted because girls and women required more privacy. Similarly, in a broadly circulated SPARC publication, women slum-dwellers were interviewed about the great difficulties that they faced in accessing water and relieving themselves in the absence of toilets and regular water supplies (Bapat and Agarwal 2003). Appadurai's (2002) compelling notion of the "politics of shit" thus becomes markedly gendered. In SPARC Alliance discourse, the management of formalized resettlement and environmental concerns of sanitation, water supply, and appropriate design were all designated as women's concerns due to their roles in social reproduction. In this narrative, poor women are presented as problem solvers whose participation benefits not only the urban environment but also the lives of poor families. Although the focus on women remained similar in tone to that of the earlier struggles of pavement-dwellers, the actuality of gendered roles and experiences diverged fundamentally from this ideal in the later MUTP resettlement. Here, women's participation in resettlement was geared less to negotiating with the state for their needs and more to facilitating the organized cooperation of residents over years of arduous resettlement processes from slum to transit camp to the Mankhurd resettlement colony (Doshi 2012). Volunteer activities included information transmission, surveying and mapping activities (in some though not all neighborhoods), and facilitation of community social and environmental activities such as neighborhood clean-ups, festivals, and collective water provision in the transit camps and colonies. These activities drew on gendered social-reproductive labor roles in the household and extended them materially and symbolically into the space of the community. Highlighting these feminized activities is not meant to tell a narrative of gendered false consciousness. Indeed, a significant number of women interviewed in this research expressed a sense of accomplishment and growth arising from their participation in resettlement processes. I elucidate these experiences more thoroughly elsewhere (Doshi 2012). Here

I would like to emphasize two key issues that stand out with regard to the resettlement experiences of women residents and an understanding of urban environmental subjectivity.

The first is that women's experiences in participatory resettlement were significantly intertwined with their own social and economic positioning in relation to each other. The women who participated the most tended to have more free time and material resources to sustain themselves, enabling them to engage in the volunteer resettlement and post-resettlement work of Mahila Milan.[1] With few exceptions they identified as housewives able to volunteer in community activities. They reported not needing to work for wages outside the home because their husbands or grown children financially supported the household. For instance, Jyoti, one highly active participant of Mahila Milan, conveyed how much she enjoyed spending her free time attending SPARC Alliance meetings, where she organized activities with others and learned how slum-dwellers could improve their lives (fieldwork interview, October 7, 2007). Another member, Meena, is one of a small group of women leaders who have benefited financially by working on SPARC's toilet construction contracts with the state. Organizational leaders like Arputham Jockin have cited this kind of involvement of women in contracted construction activities as a form of empowerment that taps into women's specific knowledge of housing and sanitation (fieldwork, May 2007). Yet, as one Mahila Milan leader admitted, only a very small number of women have had access to such opportunities (fieldwork interview, November 15, 2007); in fact the loss of work and income is the biggest problem facing most women in the resettlement colonies.

The second key issue concerns the gendered framings of environmental improvements. Piped water, toilets, and *pucca* (solidly constructed) housing are all widely considered to be particularly beneficial for women, as claimed by SPARC staff, project impact evaluations, and several Mahila Milan participants themselves. The amenities were welcomed by most women (and men) despite notable infrastructure problems arising from shoddy construction and water supply constraints (Modi 2009). However, not all women valued these changes to the same extent, a fact that was hardly reflected in SPARC Alliance discourses or independent impact evaluations. Several women who had been recruited to participate expressed the view that they did not have the time or energy necessary to continue participating due to the increased economic and physical burdens of commuting from their new homes in resettlement colonies to their former neighborhoods to work as domestic servants (fieldwork 2007). This view was supported by MUTP impact evaluations which found that many resettled residents either lost their jobs or faced the pressures of increased transport costs or commuting exhaustion (Tata Institute of Social Sciences 2007). Loss of women's income due to fewer employment opportunities in the new neighborhoods also intensified financial insecurity and reduced overall household incomes. As one resident commented caustically, "What good are toilets when we can no longer feed ourselves?" (fieldwork interview, October 2007).

Constructions of environmental subjectivity among resettled slum-dwellers thus relied on gendered discursive practices in which women's participation was hailed both as an environmental solution for the city and as a benefit to the women themselves. However, the gendering of participation relied on a discursive emphasis of women's domestic social-reproductive needs and roles to the exclusion of those who work outside of the home. While women who could afford to participate as volunteers cited more benefits to themselves, women who relied on income sources in their former neighborhoods were either less involved with the SPARC Alliance or experienced increased hardships resulting from resettlement.

In response to the MUTP, several slums have utilized oppositional strategies to resettlement in areas far from their livelihoods, eliciting the support of politicians, as in the case of Mumbai's airport-land slums.[2] Slum-dwellers and advocates have presented cases against distant resettlement based on environmental reasoning, thereby forming counter-narratives to the bourgeois environmentalism that undergirds evictions. For example, slum-dwellers displaced by a later road component of the MUTP presented the World Bank with complaints not only about livelihood and resettlement-process concerns but also about the proximity of the Mankhurd resettlement colony to toxic dump sites. These complaints prompted a suspension in World Bank funding and a contentious independent investigation by the Inspection Panel into the case.

Inverting Anne Rademacher's provocative question "when is housing an environmental problem?" (Rademacher et al. 2009), the following case of organized resistance to resettlement by slum-based shop owners located on the Mithi River Basin in central Mumbai demonstrates that the environment can also be framed as a housing problem.

Flood Politics: River Basin Clean-up and Conflicts over Resettlement

During the monsoon of 2005, a few weeks before Hurricane Katrina hit New Orleans, Mumbai was showered with a record-breaking thirty-nine inches of rain in twenty-four hours, which produced one of the worst floods in the city's history. Hundreds of people died almost immediately due to inundation, and thousands more would continue to suffer from water-borne diseases and homelessness. Although flooding during the monsoons is nothing new for slums located in the city's low-lying areas, the scale of the flood and its impacts on the middle classes led to a vociferous outcry in the local media and among civic groups. Newspaper headlines railed against the incompetent emergency response of the government and hailed the spirit of cooperation among Mumbaikars during a time of crisis (Anjaria 2006). City officials facing public outcry over the poor emergency response attempted to identify a cause, one that was inevitably environmental in nature. Blame was assigned to the informal settlements located in the Mithi River basin, which had flooded. Official accounts claimed that sewage and trash from slums clogged the basin, causing overflows into neighboring low-lying areas. Such narratives resonated well with middle-class frustrations over the pollution, ugliness, and supposed civic irresponsibility of slums and their dwellers. Meanwhile, left-leaning environmentalists suggested that the flooding was less a symptom of informal settlements and more likely one of rapid formal development in ecologically sensitive areas of the city. One scientist estimated that of the 800 million liters of sewage dumped into the river daily, only 2 million liters came from informal settlements. Large-scale industry and formal, modern buildings produce most of this waste (Faleiro 2006). Other activists, like Chandrashekhar Prabhu (2005), blamed developments such as the Bandra-Kurla Complex (BKC), a massive complex built on reclaimed swampland on the Mithi River. The BKC consists of some of the most expensive commercial real estate in Mumbai, is home to several local and transnational banks and corporations, and is therefore not an appealing target for government officials aimed at transforming Mumbai into a "global city."

Despite the contradictory evidence, the state concentrated its actions on slums located along the Mithi River. Soon after the 2005 deluge, former member of parliament Kirit Somaiya filed a public-interest petition calling for the clearance of all illegal structures located in the basin. In March 2006, the Mumbai High Court ordered the demolition and rehabilitation of 3,600 illegal structures found to be within thirty meters of the river. Two months later, the city demolished several hundred structures including those belonging to scrap metal dealers, paper recyclers, and other merchants and small-scale industry owners. A group of shop owners whose structures were demolished filed a counter petition against the head of the newly created Mithi River Development and Protection Authority (MRDPA). Besides drawing attention to the failure of state agencies to follow due legal processes by demolishing structures before providing rehabilitation, the petitioners exposed the government's violations of its own zoning and environmental protection legislation. The petition asserted that the proposed resettlement plot was located on the periphery of Mankhurd in an area zoned for no-development and coastal regulation because of its location on ecologically sensitive marshland.[3]

This brief overview of the Mithi River evictions is a product more of secondary sources and interviews with affiliated activists rather than ethnographic data collected from evictees. Nonetheless, the eviction processes, legal responses, and strategies of evictees reveal much about the multiple possibilities of environmental citizenship. Mithi River evictees' resistance to resettlement was primarily due to the large distance they would have to travel to the relocation site and the corresponding loss of income and social networks (Faleiro 2006). The response of these evictees is not unique. Later evictees of projects such as the MUTP also contested relocation to Mankhurd because of distance and loss of income. But the ecological reasoning of their claims to the city is a significant change in recent years. Raj Awasthi, a neighborhood shop owner and the main activist lawyer involved in the anti-eviction and anti-resettlement petitions for both the Mithi River and the MUTP residents, also saw these actions as an important frontline in the battle against what he called the "corrupt land-grabbing" (fieldwork interview, May 23, 2007) practices undertaken by developers in collusion with state officials. He admitted that some of those resisting resettlement were materially better off than many other evicted slum-dwellers. Nonetheless, oppression is relative in a city where powerful economic interests increasingly dominate central urban space. The environmental and social contradictions of these processes continue to fuel conflicts shaping the rocky trajectory of Mumbai's redevelopment.

In highlighting such contradictions, another important aspect of the Mithi River clean-up deserves attention. Announcements about plans to remove slums along the river occurred in the same month as another violent demolition in Mandala, a slum located on the swampy eastern periphery of Mankhurd. The Mandala plot was to serve as the commercial resettlement area for displaced shop owners from the centrally located Mithi River. Though presented as empty resettlement space, Mandala was in fact already occupied by at least 3,500 homes. Mandala slum-dwellers were, however, deemed illegal in accordance with cutoff date laws, and were therefore more vulnerable to evictions and ineligible for resettlement compensation. In a macabre political ecology, Mandala homes were violently demolished, and debris from the Mithi River basin was transplanted across the city to the site in truckloads to both "clean up" the river and to solidify land for developing the commercial resettlement center. Mithi River shop owners, whose material and political power was strong enough to continue legal battles, were ultimately able to negotiate a more desirable, closer resettlement site. Many of them also continued to remain on-site at the river (Faleiro 2006). Mandala evictees persist in struggles and negotiations with officials to re-occupy their land. Understanding how and why Mandala slum evictees were positioned differently from other resettled groups requires analysis of the politics of recent demolition drives and new social movements in the city.

The Politics of 'Empty' Space: Eviction and Land Struggle in Mandala

In December 2004, bulldozers descended upon 45,000 to 90,000 informal structures[4] deemed illegal by the state, leaving over 300,000 people in Mumbai homeless. The demolitions inaugurated the launching of the Vision Mumbai plan by the newly elected Congress Party government in the state of Maharashtra. In a campaign to clear the city of all illegal slum dwellings, the state proceeded to enforce cutoff date laws with special emphasis on slums settled on no-development zones after 1995. The demolitions were a shock to the evictees as the party's campaign promises to slum-dwellers included regularization and resettlement for all structures existing before 2000. The demolitions also stunned housing activists and NGOs, many of whom had been working within the parameters of resettlement implementation. The demolition drive came to be known as a 'tsunami' in some of the local media for it displaced as many people as that natural disaster which occurred in the same month. Still others in the media applauded the government for aggressively following through with efforts to clean up the city.

Although officials underscored the goal of making Mumbai 'slum free,' not all slums were razed equally. According to housing rights activists and my own observations, the demolition drive focused on illegal slums with a majority of Muslim and North Indian residents. Officials of the Congress Party, normally seen as more tolerant of diversity and secular politics, invoked the rhetoric of ethnic cleansing and security against illegal migrants. For instance, the newly elected chief minister of the state of Maharashtra defended the demolition drive by asserting that the city had no other choice but to "take action against illegal Bangladeshis." It has become commonplace in Indian cities to decry the elusive "illegal Bangladeshis," though rarely have evictees proven to be from anywhere other than India. The identity and class-based constitution of evictees also elicited the approval of Shiv Sena party politicos; in fact the opposition party's leaders, Bal and Udhav Thackeray, praised the actions of their political rivals to rid the city of encroaching slums.[5] Several activists have thus speculated that ethnic targeting helped to make such a large-scale demolition sweep politically feasible (D'Souza et al. 2005).

Evicted residents confirmed ethnic discrimination in their lived experiences as well. For instance, one resident of Mandala slum expressed with frustration, "This would not have happened to us if we were Maharashtrians" (fieldwork, December 9, 2007).The exclusionary discourses that define rightful belonging to the space of the city in terms of class, regional, and ethno-religious identity—and that have animated official justifications of the Vision Mumbai demolitions—raise vexing questions about the possibilities of political action among the evicted. How and to whom have these evictees defended their access to urban space? Have evicted groups mounted counterclaims to legitimacy and belonging? What are the idioms through which legitimate belonging gets reworked? Slum-dwellers evicted during the Vision Mumbai demolitions have undertaken multiple and sometimes contradictory strategies for reclaiming their homes. Although many neighborhood leaders initially engaged in organized protests, several slums were reclaimed by their original inhabitants soon after the demolitions. Residents stealthily re-occupied the land through leveraging contacts and allies in the state, in a process that Solly Benjamin has called "occupancy urbanism" (Benjamin 2008). However, the trajectory of the Mandala slum in Mankhurd was markedly different.

Six months after being evicted in the Vision Mumbai sweep, Mandala's slum-dwellers took the opportunity of the state of emergency caused by flooding in July 2005 to re-occupy the plot. However, the area would be demolished again the following year when it was redesignated for resettling shop owners located on the banks of the Mithi River. The second demolition spurred a violent clash between residents and police, including several cases of police brutality and arson. Since the second eviction, the area remains guarded and fenced; it is used by neighboring residents only for urination and defecation. Currently, neighborhood leaders and some residents remain in informal rental housing along the perimeter of the area; they continue to try to negotiate legal re-occupation and on-site resettlement. They have maintained a close working relationship with a coalition of anti-displacement of groups, the National Alliance of People's Movements (NAPM). The trajectory of Mandala has much to do with its relationship with this activist organization, which has introduced an important voice critical of neoliberal development, exclusionary identity politics, and state land usurpation in urban and rural areas. A brief overview of NAPM will help to situate its role in the Mandala resettlement process.

While housing NGOs denounced the Vision Mumbai demolitions, the most powerful groups engaged in implementing slum rehabilitation contracts with the state fell short of consolidating a collective response to the evictions. Instead NAPM, a group with little prior experience in Mumbai's slum politics, galvanized anti-eviction protests. Led by Medha Patkar, the world-renowned leader of the Narmada Bachao Andolan (NBA, the Movement to Save the Narmada River), NAPM mobilized and coordinated dispersed evicted slum-dwellers and other city groups critical of the state's actions. The coalition deployed a variety of Gandhi-inspired tactics of civil disobedience and coalition building. The movement's framings and idioms of struggle reveal a legacy derived from its roots in the anti-displacement struggles of the Narmada Valley. The antecedent anti-dam movement sutured a strategic, though somewhat romanticized, notion of indigeneity, capitalizing on tribal Adivasis' purportedly traditionally sustainable relationship to the environment, regardless of whether their livelihood practices and circumstances actually corroborated this image (Baviskar 2005). Notwithstanding the cooperation of the SPARC Alliance with the

MUTP in resettlement, slum-dwellers have typically had markedly less access to the kind of cultural capital and claims to authentic legitimacy that often animates environmental politics in rural areas.

Nonetheless, the NAPM leadership has attempted to counteract the socio-ecological vilification of slum-dwellers with notions of sustainability and justice for excluded working-class citizens. The movement has argued that low-rise so-called slum housing is actually more sustainable compared to resource-consuming high-rises and gated communities built by developers. Invoking the history of anti-colonial struggle, NAPM activists have further highlighted the plight of slum-dwellers as excluded and exploited workers, criticizing both state oppression and neoliberal development as forms of neocolonialism. In rallies held at symbolic city places like Azaad Maidan (a park dedicated to the martyrs of Indian independence struggles), activists and displaced residents have given emotionally charged speeches on displacement and development as a violation of the rights of the people. In these and other spaces, NAPM's condemnation of both Hindu nationalist politics and evictions as exclusions of poor Indians from the spaces of the nation has emphasized both class- and identity-based dispossession. Through these idioms NAPM has vociferously protested redevelopment efforts for their biases towards elites, especially real estate capitalists, and instead advocated more decentralized, small-scale forms of development with an "eco-socialist" political ideology.[6] In the urban realm, this stance has ideally meant support for on-site slum improvement and low-rise structures built under the control of residents, who are given tenure security and the financial support of the state. In this manner, NAPM has differed from NGOs like the SPARC Alliance that have supported public–private partnerships in slum redevelopment and high-rise resettlement colonies. Similar to the SPARC Alliance, NAPM leadership has also encouraged women's participation and leadership in mobilization. But the group's discursive practices around poor women's participation highlight women's working class experience (gendered as it may be) rather than their roles as housewives and mothers.

Thus NAPM's discourse of mobilization addresses the processes of exclusion and dispossession that have harmed the urban poor, like the residents of Mandala, who have faced some of the most severe forms of sovereign violence. Yet movement mediation has been limited in its ability to represent all slum-dwellers' views. While neighborhood-based leadership has produced an ideological position similar to that of the NAPM activists, ethnographic participant observation reveals more complex perspectives among residents. For instance, the Mandala slum-dwellers I spoke with during research in 2007 discussed their deliberations and conflicts over how to strategically proceed with attempts to regain their land. Some neighborhood leaders and residents wanted to illegally re-occupy the land by leveraging their contacts in the local police and other state agencies. Others believed that since the first re-occupation ended in a second demolition, the group should follow a more official course of action. Residents ultimately chose the latter approach, but many continue to express concern that official government channels will delay action interminably. Several neighborhood leaders disagreed with eschewal of the developer-led, high-rise resettlement model. As one NAPM activist admitted, "Some of the people do not always agree with the movement's core principles, though they always maintain the necessary image of solidarity" (communication with author).

In its efforts to build strong alliances within the city, NAPM has supported a broad range of anti-eviction struggles including those surrounding the Mithi River cleanup, the MUTP, and other off-site resettlement projects. However, efforts to build solidarity have often elided significant material and political differences among movement members. The majority of Mandala evictees were clearly more vulnerable than the Mithi River evictees in terms of class and the legal status of their slum. While solidarity may be a form of politically "strategic essentialism," following Spivak's (1988) use of the phrase, there has also been a sense of uneasiness among groups with different concerns.

It is also true, however, that the movement leadership has shown significant flexibility in the face of political constraints. For instance, Mandala and NAPM leaders have drawn up a compromise for the 50-acre Mandala plot. In the proposal, which is still under negotiation, Mandala slum-dwellers would agree to resettlement in taller buildings on 15 acres of the site while the remaining 35 acres would remain in the control of the central government. The compromise falls short of the movement's ideal of small-scale, low-rise, low-environmental-impact forms of slum rehabilitation. However, through the strategy of negotiating with the central government's urban development department, the movement has been able to bypass the state of Maharashtra's exclusionary cutoff date laws, thereby giving all of the Mandala evictees access to some form of compensation. It remains to be seen whether and how the resolution will materialize for Mandala residents who have remained in housing limbo for over five years. Delay and uncertainty may indeed be the price for slum-dwellers asserting their rights as working-class citizens through official and legal channels rather than seeking the undercover approval of what Solomon Benjamin has called the "porous state" (2000).

Conclusion: Frontiers of Differentiated Environmental Citizenship

In this chapter, I have attempted to show how neoliberal redevelopment has accompanied diverse and often volatile conflicts over the urban environment. Elite projects to clear slum space for higher-value, globally-inclined real estate and infrastructure development have not simply unfolded as an inexorable and uniform force for demolitions; they have been bound up with simultaneously inclusionary and exclusionary practices and discourses. Market-based resettlement compensation policies engaging the participation of the evicted in the redevelopment process have tempered state and bourgeois forms of urban environmentalism. In privileging market-oriented land use, however, such policies have led to both developmental expansion into the urban periphery and compensation practices that inherently fall short of providing appropriate housing for all of the displaced.

Moreover, resettlement schemes have been forged through re-workings of public imaginaries regarding who among the slum-dwelling poor should legitimately inhabit the space of the city. Such differentiations are inextricably linked to class-and identity-based politics of belonging shaped by periods of sharpening social inequality, neoliberal urbanization, and xenophobic party politics. To the extent that compensatory resettlement is constructed through market-based policies inflected with such exclusionary politics, it is fundamentally constitutive of more severe and violent forms of displacement and dispossession of people ineligible for appropriate resettlement. While off-site resettlement has (more or less convincingly) been framed as an economic and environmentally sustainable solution for Mumbai's housing problems, that framing has been reshaped, appropriated, and contested in diverse ways by evictees and their representatives.

This chapter focused on environmental politics in the eastern fringe neighborhood of Mankhurd, which has emerged as a spatio-political frontier not only for urban accumulation but also for material and symbolic struggles over belonging in the city. The three cases presented here, all located in or relating to the Mankhurd periphery, illustrate how displaced citizens were positioned differently in relation to state redevelopment practices and how mediating agents and slum-residents engaged in or countered elite narratives about slums and urban environmental sustainability. These cases suggest the need to approach redevelopment and environmental politics as embodied politics and to conceive of urban peripheries as productive sites of contradictory and differentiated forms of citizenship and environmental subjectivity.

In the MUTP railways resettlement case, state agents, non-governmental groups, and residents arrived at a market-based, participatory resettlement that was framed as an environmental solution for both slum-dwellers—especially women—and the city. Gendered environmental subjectivity among evictees—cultivated by an NGO and a slum-dwellers' group—highlighted women's embodied social reproductive roles and experiences in the home and community while eliding issues facing residents and women as laborers outside of home. In the second Mithi River eviction case, evictees successfully countered elite environmentalism and distant resettlement on ecological and social grounds. In the third case of violent eviction in Mandala, evictees doubly marginalized along axes of class and ethnicity have attempted to counter a planning imaginary that saw the frontier as empty space for resettling eligible slum-residents to the exclusion of ineligible (and ostensibly undeserving) evictees. Through the mediation of a movement and its eco-socialist inspired ideology, evictees in this case have attempted to assert counterclaims of legitimate belonging in the city and nation. These cases thus demonstrate that the political ecology of eviction and resettlement relies simultaneously on voicing and inclusion, and on the silencing and exclusion of slum-dwellers as subjects of urban environmental transformation. The cases are certainly not exhaustive with respect to the experience of redevelopment, eviction, and resettlement in Mumbai. Nor is the comparative case structure used here meant to demarcate 'better' or 'worse' framings in a political sense, as those involved in each experienced distinct circumstances and histories. Rather, this study demonstrates how the spatial and relational production of environmental subjectivity among evicted slum-dwellers is key to urban spatial transformation and possibilities for social justice.

Notes

1. This was a marked shift from the original members engaged in anti-eviction nego-
    tiations on the pavements in Mumbai in the 1980s who had few such resources.
    Even among the original women members and leaders, it has been mainly those
    who no longer need to work outside of the home or who have attained some
    source of income through their involvement in paid SPARC exchanges and
    training work that have remained active members in the organization over the
    last twenty years.
2. Times News Network, Along Came Some Turbulence. *Times of India*, May 14,
    2007.
3. Kalina Merchant Welfare Association V. T. Chandrashekhar And Ors (Mumbai
    High Court 2006).
4. Official and activist estimates vary.
5. Times News Network, Demolition of Slums Has Sonia's Nod Says CM. *Times of
    India*, April 17, 2005.
6. National Alliance of People's Movements (NAPM). 2010. http://napm-india.org,
    accessed February 15, 2010.

References

Agrawal, A. 2005. *Environmentality: Technologies of Government and the Making of
    Subjects*. Durham, NC: Duke University Press.
Anjaria, J. S. 2006. Urban Calamities: A View From Mumbai. *Space and Culture*, 9 (1):
    80–82.
Appadurai, A. 2000. Spectral Housing and Urban Cleansing: Notes on Millennial
    Mumbai. *Public Culture*, 12 (3): 627–651.
———. 2002. Deep Democracy: Urban Governmentality and the Horizon of Politics.
    Public Culture, 14 (1): 23–43.
Banerjee-Guha, S. 2002. Shifting Cities: Urban Restructuring in Mumbai. *Economic
    and Political Weekly*, 37 (2): 121–128.
Bapat, M., and I. Agarwal. 2003. Our Needs, Our Priorities; Women and Men from
    the Slums in Mumbai and Pune Talk about Their Needs for Water and Sanitation.
    Environment and Urbanization, 15 (2): 71–86.
Baviskar, A. 2003. Between Violence and Desire: Space, Power and Identity in the
    Making of Modern Delhi. *International Social Science Journal*, 55 (175): 89–98.
———. 2005. *In the Belly of the River: Tribal Conflicts over Development in the Narmada
    Valley*. 2nd ed. New Delhi: Oxford University Press.
Benjamin, S. 2000. Governance, Economic Settings and Poverty in Bangalore.
    Environment and Urbanization, 12 (1): 35–56.

———. 2008. Occupancy Urbanism: Radicalizing Politics and Economy beyond Policy and Programs. *International Journal of Urban and Regional Research*, 32 (3): 719–729.

Braun, B. 2002. *The Intemperate Rainforest: Nature, Culture and Power on Canada's West Coast*. Minneapolis, MN: University of Minnesota Press.

Burra, S. 1999. *Resettlement and Rehabilitation of the Urban Poor: The Story of Kanjur Marg*. Mumbai: Society for the Promotion of Area Resource Centres.

Chatterjee, P. 2004. *The Politics of the Governed: Reflections on Popular Politics in Most of the World*. New York: Columbia University Press.

Chatterji, R., and D. Mehta. 2007. *Living with Violence: An Anthropology of Events and Everday Life*. New Delhi: Routledge.

D'Cruz, C. n.d. Demolitions to Dialogue. Mumbai: SPARC India Publications http://www.sparcindia.org/docs/dtod.html, accessed October 16, 2009.

Doshi, S. 2013. The Politics of the Evicted: Redevelopment, Subjectivity and Difference in Mumbai's Slum Frontier. *Antipode*, 45 (3), accessed September 2, 2012, doi: 10.1111/j.1467–8330.2012.01023.x.

Doshi, S. 2012. The Politics of Persuasion: Gendered Slum Citizenship in Neoliberal Mumbai. In *Urbanizing Citizenship: Contested Spaces in Indian Cities*, ed. R. Desai and R. Sanyal. 82–108. New Delhi: Sage.

D'Souza, D., P. Josson, M. Nair, and D. More. 2005. *Bulldozing Rights: A Report on the Forced Evictions and Housing Policies for the Poor in Mumbai*. Mumbai: Indian People's Tribunal on Environment and Human Rights.

Faleiro, S. 2006. A River Runs through Upturned Lives. *Tehelka*, June 24. http://www.tehelka.com/story_main18.asp?filename=Ne062406A_river_SR.asp, accessed February 10, 2010.

Fernandes, L. 2004. The Politics of Forgetting: Class Politics, State Power and the Restructuring of Urban Space in India. *Urban Studies*, 41 (12): 2415–2430.

Gilmore, R. W. 2002. Fatal Couplings of Power and Difference: Notes on Racism and Geography. *The Professional Geographer*, 54 (1): 15–24.

Grove, K. 2009. Rethinking the Nature of Urban Environmental Politics: Security, Subjectivity, and the Non-Human. *Geoforum*, 40 (2): 207–216.

Hansen, T. B. 2001. *Wages of Violence: Naming and Identity in Postcolonial Bombay*. Princeton, NJ: Princeton University Press.

Hart, G. P. 2002. *Disabling Globalization: Places of Power in Post-Apartheid South Africa*. Berkeley, CA: University of California Press.

Harvey, D. 2003. *The New Imperialism*. New York: Oxford University Press.

Holston, J. 2008. *Insurgent Citizenship: Disjunctions of Democracy and Modernity in Brazil*. Princeton, NJ: Princeton University Press.

McFarlane, C. 2004. Geographical Imaginations and Spaces of Political Engagement: Examples from the Indian Alliance. *Antipode*, 36 (5): 890–916.

———. 2008. Sanitation in Mumbai's Informal Settlements: State, "Slum", and Infrastructure. *Environment and Planning A*, 40 (1): 88–107.

Mitlin, D., and S. Patel. 2005. Re-Interpreting the Rights-Based Approach: A Grassroots Perspective on Rights and Development. Global Poverty Research Group Working Paper 022. Oxford: Economic and Social Research Council. http://www.gprg.org/pubs/workingpapers/pdfs/gprg-wps-022.pdf, accessed March 10, 2009.

Modi, R. 2009. Resettlement and Rehabilitation in Urban Centres. *Economic and Political Weekly*, 44 (6): 20–23.

Nijman, J. 2000. Mumbai's Real Estate Market in the 1990s: Deregulation, Global Money and Casino Capitalism. *Economic and Political Weekly*, 35 (7): 575–582.

Ong, A. 2007. *Neoliberalism as Exception: Mutations in Citizenship and Sovereignty*. Durham, NC: Duke University Press.

Peet, R., and M. Watts, eds. 2004. *Liberation Ecologies: Environment, Development, Social Movements*. New York: Routledge.

Prabhu, C. 2005. Why Mumbai Choked. *Frontline*, 22 (17). http://flonnet.com/fl2217/stories/20050826004601700.htm, accessed January 25, 2009.

Rademacher, A., K. Alley, E. Finnis, A. Guneratne, S. Gururani, and A. Mathews. 2009. When Is Housing an Environmental Problem? Reforming Informality in Kathmandu. *Current Anthropology*, 50 (4): 513–533.

Roy, A. 2009. Civic Governmentality: The Politics of Inclusion in Beirut and Mumbai. *Antipode*, 41 (1): 159–179.

Smith, N. 1996. *The New Urban Frontier: Gentrification and the Revanchist City*. New York: Routledge.

Spivak, G. C. 1988. Can the Subaltern Speak? In *Marxism and the Interpretation of Culture*, ed. C. Nelson and L. Grossberg. 271–313. Chicago, IL: University of Illinois Press.

Tata Institute of Social Sciences. 2007. *Impact Assessment and Evaluation of Phase Ii of the Mumbai Urban Transport Project*. Mumbai.

10
Nuisance Talk: Middle-Class Discourses of a Slum-Free Delhi*

D. Asher Ghertner

Introductory Boundaries

"Slums are the culmination of unwanted elements," the secretary of a resident welfare association (RWA)[1] told me in perhaps the most concise statement of the middle-class "theory of the slum" I encountered during my fieldwork in Delhi in 2006–2007. In this chapter, I set out to trace how everyday depictions of slums as dirty, uncivil, and out of place—what I will call 'nuisance talk'—travel into and gain legitimacy in popular representations and state visions of urban space. While scholars have been attentive to the juridical and institutional transformations that have facilitated the rise of middle-class power and the concomitant demolition of slums, removal of hawkers, and broader bourgeoisification of Indian cities (see Baviskar 2003; Chatterjee 2004; Fernandes 2006; Ghertner 2008; Nair 2005), there has been minimal focus on how the mundane, often place-specific constructions of civility of the middle class gain traction in state policy and the popular urban imaginary.[2] This chapter addresses this question by analyzing the cultural politics of Delhi's world-class redevelopment. Following Moore, Kosek, and Pandian, I take cultural politics to mean the processes by which "people and nature are positioned as out of place, disturbing the natural and social order" (2003, 44) and the various forms of "boundary work" through which geographies of inclusion and exclusion, purity and pollution are constituted. Such boundary work creates a bar against which social order can be evaluated, rendering that which falls below/outside the bar visibly deviant and in need of improvement or removal.

---

* This chapter is a modified version of an article previously published in *Antipode* (2012) 44(4): 1161–1187.

Through the frequent narration of 'the slum' as a deviant zone of criminality and defilement, RWA members, I will show, construct slum removal as a process of environmental improvement, a positive form of violence necessary to 'clean and green' Delhi, install a new symbolic order, and further Delhi's march toward world-class city status. My more than fifty conversations with RWA members in Delhi confirm Douglas's arguments about the symbolic meaning of dirt and that with which it is associated: "Dirt offends against order. Eliminating it is not a negative moment, but a positive effort to organize the environment" (1966, 2). Douglas's work has contributed to a lineage of scholarship on symbolic violence that argues that the purpose of demarcating good and evil, pure and polluted, is "to select a certain form of violence and mark it as good and necessary" (Caldeira 2001, 36). I borrow from this work in showing how the rise of RWA power (as discussed in Ghertner 2011a) in the early 2000s has enabled property owners to establish hegemonic norms of urban order and civility that represent slum removal as a purification process, an act of establishing an orderly and beautiful city.

The first goal of this chapter, then, is to trace how RWAs position slums on the 'outside,' both symbolically vis-à-vis idealization of the bourgeois public sphere and private self, as well as materially in terms of property value. Here, I specifically argue that 'nuisance' has become the key principle according to which discourses of the slum are both organized in everyday speech and translated from the neighborhood into official policy and practice. As a lay term, 'nuisance' is widely used to identify forms of aesthetic impropriety or private annoyance. But, because it is a primary element of environmental law in India (Jain 2005; see also Sharan in this volume), it operates discursively as a catch-all category allowing a diverse array of private grievances, often pertaining to the defense of private property, to be expressed in terms of environmental welfare and the public interest. As such, the widening depiction of slums as nuisances—i.e., as illegal environments—reworks the public/private divide, inserting codes of civility once restricted to the home and neighborhood into the core of public life.

More than just showing how slums are symbolically coded in the everyday speech of the property-owning middle class, a second goal of this chapter is to show how tropes of the slum are mobilized through everyday speech and diverse technologies of power, including municipal 'clean-up' campaigns and the media, to construct a repertoire of images and typifications that determine what is considered pleasant and abhorrent for the imagined 'world-class' future. As the aesthetic sensibilities of activist RWAs are rendered routine both in everyday conversations and in governmental and popular representations of the city, residents of Delhi who desire a world-class future adopt certain expectations of how the city should look.

By way of introducing how nuisance talk is mobilized in everyday speech, I begin with an extended account of my first encounter with an RWA actively mobilized against slums. This description demonstrates how nuisance talk operates across multiple discursive registers, linking intimate aversions around hygiene and class difference to state anxieties over security and environmental order. The multiple voices and antagonisms that emerge here provide insight into how nuisance talk pulls multiple speech acts together, cohering them into a discursive formation that identifies the constitutive outside of bourgeois civility. Next, I detail how RWAs evoke specific geographical imaginaries of transgression in everyday neighborhood speech and how these express neighborhood concerns in terms of a broader vision of a 'world-class' city. I finally trace how these geographical imaginaries are transmitted through broader media and government campaigns into a governing rationality of slum removal.

Sant Ravi Das Camp

I had visited Sant Ravi Das Camp numerous times before, both in 2005 and leading up to its eventual demolition in May 2006. In the days before its demolition, I watched Delhi Development Authority (DDA) surveyors count the settlement's households and eventually saw the bulldozers roll in and raze the more than 800 huts settled there. When I came back to Delhi six months after Ravi Das Camp's demolition, I returned to the site, curious to see what the DDA had done with the open space (see Figure 10.1).

A thick, concrete fence had been erected on all sides of the empty land, with yellow signs staked in the ground which read "Property of the DDA: Do not enter." Dotted with mounds of rubble and scattered brick, the site lay vacant, except for a Hindu temple still nestled in the corner of the lot (see Figure 10.2). After I pulled out my camera, a shopkeeper approached me from the housing society across the street. We began talking about the scene before us.

Figure 10.1 The demolition of Sant Ravi Das Camp

The left and right photographs show two settlements, outlined in black, before and after (respectively) the DDA demolished them on May 4, 2006. The larger of the two settlements, located on the left side of each of the photographs, is the site of Sant Ravi Das Camp. Both photographs were captured from Google Earth showing the space in September 2004 and September 2006, respectively. The small "x" on the photograph on the right shows the position from which the photograph shown in Figure 10.2 was taken. © Google 2009.

Figure 10.2 A slum no more

Former site of Sant Ravi Das Camp, which was demolished on May 4, 2006. The temple is visible in the top right of the image. Photograph by author.

I told the shopkeeper that I had visited months before when a *basti* (settlement) was here and wondered what had happened. With this subtle prompt, he launched into a tirade,

> Those people were a major problem in the area. They made lots of noise, spread filth, and disturbed the area. They just sat in the road and smoked cigarettes. They screamed a lot and made all kinds of noise. They were always drunk and would fight for no reason. The space was such a mess. There were 1,000 huts here and many thousands of people. They were such dirty people . . . But don't think they were poor. They just occupied the land, took rent on it, and got rich . . . We filed a petition in court, and the court had them removed. The place is better now, no?[3]

Pointing across the vacant lot, he asked me how things looked. I was not sure what to say. It appeared quite ruinous, with the foundations of huts and other signs of the previous inhabitants still visible. "Seems okay," I said, to which he quickly shot back, "Yeah, it is nice. It is good place now. It is clear and peaceful and quiet. There is no filth, no more noise and troubles. The air is totally clean. It's beautiful, no?" He then offered to walk me around and introduce me to his neighbors.

The first person we met as we strolled around the neighborhood was a man in his early 70s, perched against the housing society's boundary fence. The shopkeeper addressed him as 'Uncle.' "Uncle can tell you about all the problems we had." "Oh my," Uncle began, "these people troubled us so much. They would just come into our park and do *latrine*," as he looked over his shoulder to a small playground. "There was filth everywhere. We couldn't use our own park. It was so bad we wanted to sell our homes and leave, but we couldn't sell. The price fell so much, and it took a lot of time. As soon as anybody saw the huts here, they weren't interested. The stench of fish and meat destroyed the atmosphere." Uncle then said the value of his flat had increased threefold after the demolition, "But, what's the reason to leave?" he said, "Now this will become a *posh* area."

Our next encounter was with a carpenter who was renting a flat in the housing society and used to rent a hut in Ravi Das Camp for storing his supplies. The shopkeeper joked that the carpenter, like the slum-dwellers, had earned excessive profit through his slum business, a claim the carpenter disputed, as he did the shopkeeper's repeated suggestion that the slum residents were actually rich due to the free government services they received. As a participant in the slum economy, this man challenged the shopkeeper and Uncle's effort to draw a sharp distinction between the residents of their lower-middle-class housing society and the slum, "I have lived here for thirty-two years. I came here to build for the Asiad [Asian Games in 1982] and applied for an LIG [lower income group] flat, like here. But, it wasn't in my fate. You [residents of the housing society] had good fate. Maybe I'll get one someday."

The shopkeeper and Uncle live in DDA-built LIG flats, constructed by the earliest residents of Ravi Das Camp who were recruited, employed, and settled by a government contractor in the early 1980s. Through the 1970s and 1980s, DDA flats were the primary means to access land in Delhi, but the DDA failed to provide the amount of housing mandated by the Delhi Master Plan, leading to the gross under-provision of planned housing in the city, especially in the LIG and EWS (economically weaker section) categories—the two lowest income classifications the DDA uses (Verma 2002). Due to the shortage of housing, competition to obtain a DDA flat was (and still is) fierce; fewer than 10 percent of applicants receive flats. Most lower-income groups that are denied DDA housing either rent or move to slums and unauthorized colonies. The carpenter's "bad" fate, he hinted, was based on this fact. If

Uncle and the shopkeeper had not been in the lucky 10 percent, they would have been like the carpenter and slum-dwellers, unpropertied.

After Uncle and the carpenter took their leave, the shopkeeper walked me through the gate into the housing society, where we met three men who had just returned from work. The shopkeeper introduced me and said I wanted to know about the old slum; he then retreated to his shop. The four of us sat for tea on plastic chairs directly in front of the large iron gate that enclosed the society's inner road from the main street, our backs to the park where Uncle had been standing and the former site of Ravi Das Camp a stone's throw away. After introductions, we returned to the topic of the slum. One man began, "Before, we wouldn't have been able to sit here like this. There would have been so much crowded. Those people walked straight in and used our park and bothered us so much. Our own children couldn't play here."

The three men looked out across the empty lot, as if it were a picturesque landscape, "It is so clear. The weather is also nicer now. You feel the wind, right? Before, we didn't have such wind," one of the men declared.

When I asked what they did to avoid the trouble of the slum, they said they installed the gate to prevent the slum-residents from entering, but "they threatened us, so we had to open it in the day," one of the men said. The man hosting us, whose flat was on the ground floor and just two doors down from the main road, pointed at the iron grilling in front of his veranda and said he built this wall with a roof and locking gate to prevent theft, "I have valuable things out there. Without this, those people would have just taken it all . . . For security, I built this cage and locked my own family in, like animals, but the real animals were out there!" Turning to the other men, he laughed at his joke, "Imagine the state we were in!" The other men nodded in approval, watching me laugh at what seemed a familiar line to them.

Later in our conversation, I asked about the temple still erect on the empty plot. One of the men said the DDA could not clear it because it is religious, adding, "The land there is worth *lacs* of rupees. They run a guesthouse out of it so people from Bihar can come stay. The people who run it are Bihari. Now they are making their own little Bihar here! The rest of the people, we had them thrown out. They lived in trash; wherever they went, our roads, our parks, filth also came . . . They were filth. We had them tossed."

While Ravi Das Camp had been cleared many months before, the symbol of the slum continues to operate in these narratives as the constitutive outside against which property bearing and middle-class selfhood is defined.

Against the filth and disorder of the slum, the housing society emerged as 'posh.' Against the violence and decay of slum life, the men found the caring and secure home. The stories the shopkeeper and his neighbors told me that day had been recited time and time again, supplying a generative symbolism for distancing self from slum, even in moments of categorical mixture, as presented, for example, by the status of the carpenter.

I begin with an extended description of this encounter because it highlights the metonymic associations RWAs in Delhi frequently make between dirt and slums (e.g., "they were filth"), as well as how such associations are used to enforce the social and physical boundary between private property and slum (inside and outside). Following Douglas's (1966) formulation of dirt as "matter out of place," scholars have long noted how talk of dirt and excrement is used to represent residual people and places, "excrement and its equivalents (decay, infection, disease, etc.) stand for the danger to identity that comes from without" (Kristeva 1982, 71). As Sibley remarks on the symbolic distancing of rich from poor that accompanied spatial segregation in the nineteenth-century capitalist city, "the middle classes have been able to distance themselves from their own residues, but in the poor they see bodily residues, animals closely associated with residual matter, and residual places coming together and threatening their own categorical scheme under which the pure and the defiled are distinguished" (1995, 56). Stallybrass and White (1986) similarly trace how nineteenth-century schemes to reorder the city operated as purification processes, designed to either exclude groups associated with pollution—slum dwellers, prostitutes, the unemployed—or morally reform them through close surveillance and disciplining, a practice deepened in the colonial context (see Gooptu 2005; Legg 2007; Prakash 1999; Prashad 2001).

This "unattainable desire to expel those things which threaten the boundary" (Sibley 1995, 19) is what Kristeva has theorized as abjection, where the abject is "everything that the subject seeks to expunge in order to become social" (McClintock 1995, 71). I am interested here not so much in psychic processes of abjection (revulsion, disavowal, fetishism) by which the self-encounters and affectively registers the other, but rather in showing how such processes are transformed into political processes of abjection—in this case the large-scale removal of slums as abject objects/ outsiders. Nuisance talk, as the above narrative demonstrates, attributes the aesthetic annoyances and daily hassles of urban life to a particular 'outside' subject—the slum-dweller, the migrant, the street vendor. But, although most speakers engage it only in this way, nuisance talk's effect, as a discourse, does not stop here. As it circulates, gains a larger 'coalition' of speakers, and produces agreed-upon 'truths' about the proper organization of space, it also articulates the 'unbelonging' of that outside subject to a broader urban politics. That is, the 'truth' of slum illegality and unbelonging operates beyond the influence and even intentions of those engaged in nuisance talk, gathering political force through its taken-for-grantedness in popular, and even state and legal, contexts. To provide an initial glimpse into how this works, which I elaborate on in the remainder of the chapter, I now turn briefly to the legal case against Ravi Das Camp.

The men with whom I sat at the housing society that day were members of the local RWA that, along with two neighboring RWAs, filed a public interest litigation (PIL) in the Delhi High Court in 2002 that led to Ravi Das Camp's demolition in 2006. I obtained a copy of the RWAs' petition later, through which the same description of slum filth enters the domain of the judiciary:

> . . . the encroachment [Ravi Das Camp] . . . has now grown and taken a mammoth shape threatening the natural environment in the area and has started jeopardising the life of the residents of the area by posing problems . . . like pollution of all sorts, health hazards, insanitary conditions due to garbage dumping . . . blocks of roads and entry points . . . and also giving rise to social problems like theft, robbery etc. and has threatened the security of the residents.[4]

Like in the RWA members' conversation with me, the slum emerges in the petition as an illegal environment based purely on its aesthetic impropriety and the nuisance it causes to property-owning residents of the city. Yet, as I have demonstrated elsewhere (Ghertner 2008), the courts, in response to a surge in RWA-filed PILs, have since the early 2000s begun to accept such arguments about 'the nuisance of slums' as a legitimate basis for slum removal. In the case against Ravi Das Camp, the High Court thus concurred with the RWAs' nuisance argument, ordering the slum's demolition because it "deprives the rights of citizens of Delhi" to civic amenities and degrades public space.[5] How has 'nuisance talk,' an often particularistic set of speech acts expressing local environmental anxieties and social aversions, moved from everyday neighborhood conversation into state discourse and urban strategy? How do such specific statements of disgust circulate, become commonsensical, and gain official legitimacy?

Nuisance Talk

After my encounter with the RWA members adjacent to Ravi Das Camp, I began contacting other active RWAs in Delhi to ask them about their perceptions of slums and urban space. Most RWA members were enthusiastic to meet me, inviting me to their homes or offices after I reached them by phone. Across a diverse array of neighborhood-specific concerns, most RWA members, especially those in wealthier South Delhi colonies, expressed a clear desire for Delhi to become 'world-class.' When I asked what a 'world-class' city meant to them, they often gave examples of the Delhi Metro Rail, a new shopping mall, or the Commonwealth Games, but they most often expressed a general sense of a clean, comfortable, and what I will describe as a 'nuisance-free' public life. Regardless of how optimistic they were that Delhi would become 'world class,' residents agreed that Delhi required a significant upgrade in infrastructure, services, and visual appearance.

In an in-depth survey of twenty-five RWA members that I conducted in 2006, all respondents agreed that a "slum-free Delhi" was either "very important" or the "most important" factor in Delhi becoming a world-class city.[6] All RWAs with whom I spoke stressed the value of their neighborhood-specific efforts in terms of their contribution to increasing the quality of life in, and appearance of, Delhi as a whole. For example, the secretary of an RWA in one of South Delhi's wealthiest colonies said, "Our goal is to maintain and enhance the posh character of [the colony]," an effort that he directly linked with the image of Delhi as a whole:

> I had a friend whose boss was visiting from Germany. They were driving in [the colony], and he had just told his boss how [it] is one of Delhi's poshest areas. Just then, some pigs crossed the street. He was so embarrassed! No matter what we do, this city is still a mess. We have to do more to change things and put the proper systems in place. Everyone needs to get together and make Delhi look like a planned city.[7]

One of the main problems his RWA worked to solve in both his colony and in Delhi as a whole was the presence of hawkers and other "street encroachments," as he called them:

> . . . the hawkers that operate under the Tehbazari scheme [a license program granting temporary vending rights] are a big problem. They aren't supposed to cook in the open, but they do. They create filth, causing danger to human life and making the colony unsightly. They sit

> in an unauthorized way, cook and create filth . . . Near "D block" . . .
> 20–25 rickshaws stand there and eat breakfast. People taking morning
> walks have to see this. It's not a pleasant sight to see auto drivers eating
> their breakfasts and then easing themselves, just taking a leak on the
> street. We aren't against the poor people trying to live, but are against
> the creation of filth and unhygienic living conditions.

We see here how grievances of a primarily aesthetic nature—the hawkers
as eyesores, as stains on an otherwise "posh" landscape—gain expression
through a rhetoric of public health, hygiene, and public nuisance. His main
complaint was not about illness in the neighborhood or noxious smells, but
rather the appearance of "filth" and a general revulsion of the senses. This
statement also demonstrates the manner in which RWAs frequently depict
their interventionist efforts to structure and discipline public life as a struggle
to secure the 'inside' from the alien and impure threats of the 'outside.'
This RWA secretary went on to say, "Overall, we are against traffic flow and
outsiders entering into the colony unnecessarily"—thus marking his move
from the identification of an abject object (hawkers) to the formulation of a
spatial politics of abjection (displacing outsiders in order to "maintain and
enhance the posh character" of the colony).

Most RWA members with whom I met similarly attributed neighborhood
deficiencies to external forces, whether visible or remote—an effort to
not only define external threats in need of disciplining, but also forge a
community (the 'inside') in which incivility is necessarily exogenous. After
I asked a South Delhi RWA member, a retired man in his 70s, what the main
problems his RWA faced were, he responded with his own question, "Did you
smell the *nallah* [drain] on your way in?" I had noticed the strong smell of
sewage in his otherwise upscale neighborhood, but was unsure whether I
should conceal this fact out of courtesy. I hesitated, and he proceeded, "There
is a *nallah* outside our boundary wall and slums and their fecal matters and
foul materials ruin things here." I asked him where the slum was located, and
he said his RWA had won a three-year court battle that eventually led to the
slum's demolition earlier in the year.

> The problem was that the DDA was letting people occupy the land. In
> the city there are 35 lakh [3.5 million] slum-dwellers . . . This has given
> rise to crime because they are mostly unemployed and coming from all
> states. A car was stolen here even . . . They occupy public land, set up
> *jhuggis* [huts] and create health hazards. Because the infrastructure in
> the city isn't even enough for [real] inhabitants, so they should stop

immigration from these countries, Nepal, Bangladesh, West Bengal, Bihar . . . These people used to roam into this area; their children played here. Our children couldn't even go outside. These people are a different lot.[8]

He went on to describe how neighborhood crime had gone down after the slum's removal and how the quality of public services in the city would only improve by demolishing the city's remaining slums. When I asked him why the stench of the *nallah* remained even after the slum's demolition, he conceded that the environment of the colony had not improved with the removal of the slum, but attributed the sewage not to other formal colonies, most of whose untreated sewage flows through such *nallahs* across the city and directly into the Yamuna River, but rather to an upstream slum, "The root cause for the filth is the slum. Delhi is infested by this problem." Referring to the problem of open defecation, he continued, "Just travel by train and you'll see along the tracks how people behave. It's shameful." Despite the physical distance between slums and his residence, this man attributed waste in his social environment to the slum problem, bolstering his claim by referring to the aesthetic impropriety of the poor who, in their compulsion to openly defecate, he argued, were the source of urban decay. When I asked him about the legal basis for his RWA's court petition against the old slum, he replied, "Basically, these people do not belong in Delhi . . . They ruin Delhi's environment. They don't follow any of the rules and create so much nuisance. This is a posh colony. How can we have such slums nearby?"

Even in colonies with no nearby slum, RWA members often described slums as a source of disease and danger that, if not controlled, would spread into purer spaces like the neighborhood and home. One man exemplified this in describing how a scorpion had crawled out of the drain in his kitchen sink while his wife was using it, "She was very frightened. This is a dangerous thing! I mean, it can't kill you, but it's dangerous. Now how does a scorpion come out of a drain like that?" I said I did not understand where the scorpion came from, and he proceeded to answer his own question, "All these sewers are connected. Our waste flows into them, and the slum waste flows into them before ours. It is all mixed. This scorpion just climbed through the sewer and came into our house."[9] Here, he was signaling the invisible risk of the slum through the city's subterranean and public infrastructure. The scorpion represented a violation of the bourgeois inside, the perceived threat that the sanctity of the home could be punctured at any moment by external risks. Although no slum was within miles of his home, the mere presence of such degraded spaces in the same city posed the threat of contamination. Whereas this man had begun his conversation with a partial recognition that the degraded state of slums was the product of social conditions for which slum-residents were not themselves responsible (namely, a shortage of low-income housing), the social origins of slum degradation were quickly elided in his move to refer to the natural, animal essence of the slum. It is here, in stories about invasion and savagery, that the metonymic associations of filth with slums are often displaced by a metaphoric language of the slum-dweller as animal, a theme that emerged in a number of my interviews. As one RWA president proclaimed, "These people live with dogs and pigs. Of course their habits will be like that only." He went on to say, "Slums aren't part of society; they aren't integrated. And, anything not integrated into society can't last forever . . . They have to be removed. They are all bound to be relocated." When he realized that I might find his words unethical, he said, "Slum-people are used to going from place to place. It's natural for them."[10] Animalized slums, naturalized dispossession.

If not through the transgression of the boundary separating human and animal, then RWAs seeking to justify their aggressive stance vis-à-vis slums evoked transgressions of 'natural' boundaries dividing the urban from the rural, educated from uneducated, and Indian from alien. As one RWA president told me:

> The people who have encroached on parks here by habit don't develop a taste for sanitation . . . We haven't yet changed the culture of these people to be urban. We need to change the rural mindset. We need to change the attitude to cleanliness and responsibility. All people in Delhi were once migrants. These people need to change or else they don't belong in the city.[11]

My argument is not that this type of neighborhood speech is in some way new, as social constructions of class and caste have always rested on constructions of taboo and unbelonging. Rather, what is significant here is the way in which this everyday speech is molded into a larger discursive formation as it is taken up by the media, the state, and juridical representations. That is, nuisance talk becomes part of a discourse of world-class city-making, where the category 'nuisance' provides the key pivot combining bourgeois claims to the moral and aesthetic value of private property with an environmental claim to public welfare. Nuisance talk hence articulates with and is picked up by other ongoing interventions to civilize public space, such as heightened state concerns about crime and public order, as well as increased middle-class worries about the 'origins' of domestic servants and associated police efforts to monitor the 'floating population.' Nuisance talk often slides between these different registers, depicting slums as spaces of both environmental and social decay, a topic discussed by Doshi (this volume) in the Mumbai context.

It is in this way that the trope of the slum-dwelling migrant unhabituated to urban life dovetails with a more deeply rooted neo-Malthusian concern about resource scarcity, overpopulation, and government handouts. Delhi's second largest RWA federation, called People's Action, has hence staked out an explicitly anti-immigrant political platform, drawing popular support from the widespread belief that shortages in electricity and water supply are caused by overpopulated slums, and not by rising middle-class consumption. As Sanjay Kaul, a savvy media professional and the spokesman for People's Action, told me in an interview in his office, "the biggest problem for Delhi is that 500,000 people come here every year . . . Delhi can't become world class if it lets 5 LAC people in tattered clothes come to the city . . . It can't be world class without security." He continued, saying,

> In Delhi, those who legitimately own land, pay taxes, and those with papers are getting pushed out of the city to the satellite cities because the prices are going up so much from letting illegal occupation go on for political benefit . . . The culture of illegality is crowding out the good, working man who buys land and pays taxes . . . You are marginalized if middle-class and educated.[12]

This "culture of illegality," according to Kaul, contaminates not only physical space, sullying neighborhoods and street sides, but also political space, producing 'vote bank' politics and corruption. The response to the slum problem, then, requires measures both to insulate important decision-making processes from the poor, as well as to bolster physical security within colonies.

Nuisance on the Move

A primary strategy that individual RWAs deploy to reclaim 'their city' is to fortify and securitize their neighborhoods by building fences, closing colony entrances at night, increasing the number of hired security guards, and requiring domestic workers to register with the police. Such efforts are considered necessary to ensure neighborhood security, a primary concern among RWAs with whom I spoke during my fieldwork. An RWA secretary in West Delhi thus stated that the main goal of his RWA was to turn his residential block, a pocket of 400 houses and approximately 2,000 residents, into a 'sub-city'—a vision of a privatized, urban utopia shared by many RWAs:

> . . . we would have our own small market with only approved vendors and shops so the residents don't have to go outside for daily requirements. There would be a food supplier, a *dhobi* [clothes washer], milkman, daily rations, all these things. We would have the colony fully developed and maintained by the RWA only. So the RWA would be in charge of services and oversight; it could also manage the primary school and childcare for young children. We would build gates and have permanent security guards to monitor who could enter and when . . . We are now trying to work with the police to start a checking system for security enhancement. We want to check domestic workers and record their information.[13]

Unlike other cities that have experienced new forms of urban segregation in the wake of economic liberalization (see Caldeira 2001; Davis 1990), Delhi has not seen a marked increase in violent or property crime. After asking Pankaj Agarwal, the secretary of Delhi's RWA Joint Front, the largest RWA federation in Delhi with over 400 member RWAs, about why there is so much opposition to slums, he said,

> they drain resources, create security problems, and create [a] negative impression in the minds of tourists when they see beggars on the streets . . . You see, today, a house costs some 3–4 crore rupees [$750,000–$1,000,000]—for a small house. The middle class has to pay so much to live here, and then to have all these security problems. The middle class is discriminated against.

I interjected and asked what security problems slums cause, and he replied, "The feeling is there that crime is a problem, even if it is not true. It is a psychological feeling."[14]

These feelings are enhanced by sensational media coverage of violent crime and dangerous slums, which depict an increasingly violent city in need of securitization, despite significant declines in crime over the past decade.[15] Without any empirical backing to its claim, *The Hindustan Times*, for example, reported that the "[p]olice's annual crime report attributes the incidence of sexual abuse to a number of sociological factors, including mushrooming of

JJ clusters [slums] and sub-human living conditions. Last year, about 80 per cent of the accused belonged to the poor strata."[16] It further drew upon the fallacy of rising crime to justify RWA securitization when it stated in the same article, "With murders and burglary increasing by the day, security concerns have led RWAs to build more gates around colonies." Elsewhere, the paper suggested that "[h]iring a domestic help, especially a Nepalese or Bangladeshi, is fraught with dangers, say the police."[17]

An interview with Ravi Bajpai, an RWA beat writer for *The Hindustan Times* and the author of the previous quote, explained the source of the English-language media's pro-middle-class stance, "My job is to cover RWA concerns. We cater to that segment. We are a medium to put peoples' grievances forward to the government."[18] A writer for *The Times of India* expressed a similar view, "The [weekly] supplement [catering to the middle class] is a link between communities and civic agencies. It is an outlet for expressing concerns and problems of a civic nature in neighborhoods . . . Government officials also read and respond to these articles."[19]

Police support for neighborhood securitization further fuels RWA rhetoric of outside intruders. As the police chief said during a large state-sponsored conference with RWA leaders in the city,

> The attacks that took place in Ayodhya were organized by people staying in Delhi.[20] There are many anti-social elements that stay in Delhi, its slums and unmonitored places. We have to watch out for suspicious people, terrorists, and criminals. This is the duty of RWAs. RWAs need to restrict and control this movement with security to remove anti-social elements and security risks. They must contact the police, monitor workers, build security mechanisms to achieve [this].[21]

Thus, the rhetoric of slum illegality is mutually reinforced by the middle-class public and the state, rendering discussion of slums as criminal, polluting spaces a routine part of neighborhood and public speech. A South Delhi RWA president justified his successful court petition to demolish a nearby slum in the same terms, saying the slum was inhabited

> by illegal immigrants and anti-social elements. They had big brawls with the cops and a month and a half back stole a cop's gun . . . They also could have been involved in the terrorist issues. There were many Pakistanis and Bangladeshis there. I don't believe that all Mohammedans are terrorists, but all terrorists are Mohammedans. Pakistan is the root of all problems. You can never trust Pakistan.[22]

Unlike in Ravi Das Camp, we see here how perceived threats to the bourgeois inside are read beyond home and neighborhood, across the city (and sometimes nation) as a whole. The efforts of activist RWAs are thus not just about reclaiming local parks and neighborhoods, but the entire city, controlling the entry of workers and servants into both the residential colony and city at large.[23] The anxiety about immigration hence operates as an extension of the boundary of the bourgeois inside beyond the neighborhood to the borders of the city itself. Nuisance not only serves as a coherent discourse for uniting the diverse geographic imaginaries of transgression we have considered here, but also represents a vehicle through which broader efforts to restructure the land economy and visual landscape are advanced.

The Propriety of Property

In both their internal meetings and in conversation with me, RWA members consistently raised concerns about slum sanitation and cleanliness, most often by arguing that behavior they consider distinctly 'private'—for example, washing, bathing, drinking, and defecating—is unpleasant, morally degrading, and harmful when conducted in public. Seeing public land as the material foundation for urban order and an aesthetically gratifying life, the spatial imaginary RWA members expressed to me opposed the use of such land for subsistence purposes. As Pankaj Agarwal told me, "We want gardens in front of our houses, but there's all kinds of filth there now. They [slum residents] wash clothes there. How can I enjoy my balcony?"[24] Thus, while couched in the language of danger and insalubrity, nuisance talk often betrayed more of a concern with property value than with environmental risk or crime. A wealthy South Delhi RWA member candidly conveyed this sentiment while giving me a tour of his house:

> We have a back entrance also. It was on the side [of the house] with the
> *jhuggis* [huts], so until we had them removed we never even opened
> the door . . . Why would someone in a posh colony want to walk that
> way [near the slum]? This house is worth so much, and to just see these
> people squatting on free land! One wants to be reminded of the value of
> his property, not faced with encroachment and nuisance.[25]

"Nuisance" here has a striking resemblance to colonial applications of the concept under British rule. As "the coercive arm of property rights" (Anderson 1992, 17), the doctrine of nuisance "was closely wedded to a regime of private property . . . affording [property owners] a promise of protection against extrinsic interferences" (Anderson 1992, 4). The law of nuisance also "played an important role in the appropriation and reconstitution of a specifically 'public' social space" (Anderson 1992, 16), curtailing previous modes of "common access" by "introducing a fresh geopolitical ordering" that "permitted new entrepreneurial and middle class groups to sustain an attack on the customary rights of those with limited access to [and ownership of] productive resources" (Anderson 1992, 17). That is, the colonial distinction between public and private—as in urban India today—had to be actively constructed and maintained so that, for example, "while it was perfectly legal to urinate in the open on one's own property (if one had property), it was not legal alongside a public thoroughfare" (Anderson 1992, 16).

Like these colonial applications of nuisance law, contemporary mobilizations of 'nuisance' do not aim to eliminate public space. Rather, where they are successful, they enact a redefinition of public-ness, which also restructures the relationship between rights and property. For example, in responding to a batch of sixty-three cases filed mostly by RWAs demanding the removal of neighboring 'nuisance-causing' slums, the Delhi High Court found it necessary to distinguish between different forms of 'the public':

> The welfare of the residents of these [RWAs'] colonies is also in the realm of public interest which cannot be overlooked. After all, these residential colonies were developed first. The slums have been created afterwards which is the cause of nuisance and brooding [sic] ground of so many ills. The welfare, health, maintenance of law and order, safety and sanitation of these residents cannot be sacrificed . . . in the name of social justice to the slum dwellers.[26]

In its order against Ravi Das Camp in 2006, the court took this argument further, arguing that "the right of honest citizens . . . cannot be made subservient to the right of encroachers," where the former were defined as those who "pay [a] handsome price for acquiring land" and the latter as "unscrupulous elements."[27] As the defense of property has been elevated as a 'public interest' priority, the courts have accepted the RWA petitioners' claim that property ownership is the requirement of substantive citizenship. Private property owners' neighborhood-specific efforts to extend bourgeois civic codes into public space have hence been codified at the city level, signaling the re-emergence of a conception of waste that Gidwani (this volume) identifies in medieval law, waste/nuisance as "spoliation or some other action that decreases the value of property."

Here then, we see how nuisance talk entangles the economic with the biopolitical, signifying a theory of value as much as it indexes biological risk. As a full-time RWA activist told me, "You have to create space for the rich. I don't know what you think about the US, but we think capitalism isn't a bad word. Rich people only spread goodness. Poor people spread dirt." Arguing against the new Master Plan's approach to densifying residential space, he continued, "It [densification] will squeeze out the rich making posh colonies too tight. They want to make the whole city for the poor. You need to encourage rich people to live here because they bring good things . . . If you make things too tight, they'll go outside the city and it will crumble like a slum." While his reference to things being "too tight" certainly refers to comfort and the use value of space, his claim also clarifies that the "good" of the rich depends on their separation from the poor—value accrues through the sequestration of degraded people (cf. Bauman 2004), or as Gidwani (this volume) writes, "Wasteful 'natures' (bodies, spaces, things, and conducts) have to be territorialized for ordered 'society'—the society of law that safeguards property and value—to be possible."

While such stark binaries of wealth-virtue and poverty–degradation may appear extreme, the media and government have launched various public campaigns couched in similar terms. The Delhi Government's "Clean Delhi, Green Delhi" campaign, for example, is a city-wide public information drive aimed at instilling a sense of civic pride in the city's cleanliness and appearance, primarily through aesthetic projects (e.g., roadside landscaping, park rejuvenation) that do little to address underlying sources of environmental stress.[28] The "Clean Delhi, Green Delhi" phrase has been specifically used to criminalize public urination and littering and to fence and beautify road medians to remove space for begging and resting, efforts that constrain the daily survival strategies of those without nearby shelter or services. Under the guise of 'cleaning up' Delhi in preparation for the 2010 Commonwealth Games, the DDA similarly banned approximately 300,000 vendors of street food, and the courts demanded the removal of all beggars from city roads. As the Delhi Government's advertisement, shown in Figure 10.3, attests, the discourse of infestation not only circulates from the middle class to government, as discussed above, but becomes a part of official problematizations of urban poverty that are subsequently conveyed to the

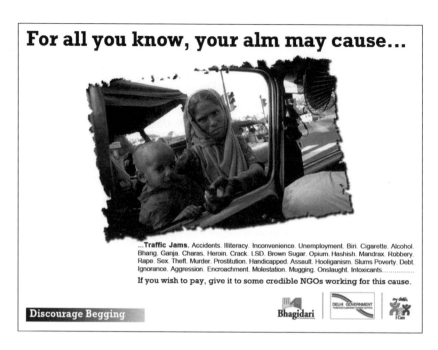

Figure 10.3 Nuisance on the move

Delhi government advertisement appearing in the *Hindustan Times*, November 25, 2006.

public at large. Because nuisance talk establishes a pattern of identifying its problem objects (the slum, the beggar, pollution) as sources, not products, of urban decay, the reader of the advertisement in Figure 10.3 is asked to inhabit a subject position with a particular bourgeois politics vis-à-vis the poor. By drawing upon a shared affective response (guilt, discomfort, abjection), the advertisement interpolates its subject, hailing the reader to respond on the aesthetic terms with which he is familiar. As the advertisement's text brazenly reads, "For all you know, your alm may cause . . . Traffic Jams . . . Unemployment . . . Alcohol . . . Heroin . . . Robbery . . . Rape . . . Murder . . . Slums." Here, the reader is positioned in an automobile facing the onslaught of social ills listed in the text, his senses educated for later embodied encounters with poverty/disorder. The message is clear, the source of social decay is the urban poor, donations to whom encourage their illicit conduct and inhibit urban progress.

The government has perhaps advanced this message most aggressively in attributing high pollution levels in the Yamuna River to the presence of slums, despite the Delhi Water Board's public acknowledgement that the main cause of pollution is the twenty-two open drains that carry untreated sewage from mostly middle-class residential colonies across the city directly into the river.[29] The managing director of the Delhi Metro Rail Corporation thus writes,

> A handful of self-styled environmentalists are stalling this idea [of modeling the Yamuna on the Thames in London and clearing all slum settlements from sight]. The result is rampant encroachments on the riverbed by *jhuggis* which catch fire at regular intervals every summer, often burning alive a few people. Sewage and untreated industrial waste are let into the river without treatment.[30]

The chief minister similarly held "the slums responsible for the condition of the Yamuna," even though the Central Pollution Control Board found "no improvement in the quality of water" following the removal in 2004–2005 of 40,000 *jhuggis* housing approximately 200,000 people from its banks.[31] Here, the evidentiary basis for proving slums as the source of environmental stress and public nuisance is not a techno-scientific rationality—nor, as I have argued elsewhere (Ghertner 2008), is it based on legal precedent or statutory law. Rather, the 'fact' of slum pollution/illegality is known via a shared aesthetic disposition, acquired through subjective engagement with nuisance talk.

Conclusion

This chapter has shown the different geographic imaginaries of transgression that both mobilize and are mobilized by RWAs in Delhi. These imaginaries operate across scales from the neighborhood to the nation, and engage anxieties and aspirations traversing the material, symbolic, and sensate. Nuisance has proven itself equally transmutable, taking on ecological, economic, legal, and aesthetic registers allowing for the easy identification of the abject 'outside' —the excess to be 'tamed' or, as is usually the case with slums, 'exiled' (see Sharan, this volume). As it circulates beyond local settings, becoming incorporated in public service announcements, the mass media, commercial advertisements, and government proclamations, nuisance talk shapes the terms in which poverty and urban space can be described in the city as a whole. By designating the objects of urban disorder and calibrating individuals' perceptions of that disorder to a broader program of social action (world-class city-building), nuisance-as-aesthetic clarifies and confirms the unsightliness of poverty, disclosing its inherent structure to be as it appears, out of place, disturbing the natural order, illegal. "[E]thico-political duty has been internalized as spontaneous inclination"; that is to say, the mechanism of rule has shifted from the head to the heart, "from abstract decisions to bodily dispositions" (Eagleton 1990, 114). Slums are known to be polluting and illegal because they look polluting and illegal; slum removal is a necessary process of urban improvement because it contributes to a more beautiful city.

By routing residents' affective response to urban disorder through an aesthetic field defined in terms of the image of the world-class city, nuisance talk establishes its own rules of order and legitimate opinions. Because nuisance talk makes certain types of disorder visible (e.g., pollution caused by open cooking) and not others (e.g., automobile exhaust), those entering into this aesthetic field embody certain visual dispositions—what Bourdieu (1998) calls "schemes of perception"—in order to gain membership in communities defined in terms of the field. In the case of the lower-middle-class residents adjacent to Ravi Das Camp, it was an effort to claim middle-class status. In the case of the elite RWA members we met, it was membership in a global community of 'world-class' citizens, or a more general desire to 'catch up' with the West. As I have explored elsewhere (Ghertner 2011b), slum residents also seek membership via this field, at times strategically adopting nuisance talk to construct themselves as potential world-class citizens—i.e., worthy of government resettlement and property ownership and critical of 'the nuisance of slums.' In this way, nuisance talk is not just a type of speech. It also actively shapes the social world by projecting aesthetic codes that are indexed to social status, as subjects desirous of a world-class future experience forms of disorder identifiable as 'nuisances,' this aesthetic seems to tell them, 'anyone in a world-class city would find this abhorrent.' In other words, nuisance talk posits a particular form of aesthetic engagement, allowing concrete experiences of disorder to be linked to a broader social project of urban improvement.

As nuisance talk has become legitimated by the media's adoption of 'citizen concerns' and the Delhi Government's efforts to a 'clean and green' Delhi, RWA federations and activists have effectively consolidated their de facto role as nuisance experts. This is not to say that all RWA members embrace an aggressive anti-slum stance, but a vanguard segment of this population has shaped public discourse by advocating a form of propertied citizenship and a vision of the urban future in which occupants of public land have no part. This group not only defines the norm for urban aesthetics, but also now judges what constitutes an infraction of that norm. Without the need to scientifically assess resource degradation, pollution levels, or ecological health, middle-class quality-of-life concerns and aesthetics have become the proxy for environmental quality in Delhi. As experts, then, activist RWAs' goal of removing slums is construed as a legitimate social cause, the valiant and award-worthy effort of local civic activists struggling for a cleaner, greener city.[32] Removing slums and other visible blotches from the landscape, they suggest, is a necessary and politically progressive step in the transformation of the city.

Late in 2006, the Delhi Government, for the first time, began strict enforcement of child labor laws.[33] In a week of aggressive raids across the city, the police drove around in lorries collecting barefooted, raggedy children working in hotels, restaurants, and other commercial establishments, shipping them out of the city, out of sight, and fining their employers. While celebrated by many as a human rights victory, this action might be better read as one in a series of acts of aesthetic disciplining, in line with the DDA ban on informal food vendors, the Supreme Court's 2001 order banishing industry to the city's peripheries, the criminalization and round-up of beggars, and the broader aesthetic reconstitution of the urban core. Nuisance, I have shown, provides the aesthetic framework that unites these disparate actions as part of a rational process of urban improvement, despite their adverse livelihood implications for the numerically dominant urban poor.

Notes

1. Resident welfare associations (RWAs) are neighborhood-based organizations of property owners often mobilized around quality of life issues. Although residents of informal settlements can form RWAs, I here use 'RWA' to refer only to associations located in formally planned colonies, as these are the groups that have been empowered via the judiciary and local state to intervene in local land use decisions (see Ghertner 2011a).

2. 'Middle class' is the term used consistently in the literature to designate that
    class driving the bourgeoisification of Indian cities. Despite its conceptual ambi-
    guity in the Indian context (Deshpande 2006), I retain usage of the term here to
    indicate my engagement with this literature. I often add the label 'property-own-
    ing' to 'middle-class' to specify that I mean property owners in state-planned
    colonies (i.e., not those in slums).

3. This encounter took place in Hindi. Translations are my own. All conversations
    described after this section took place in English unless otherwise noted. While
    I interacted with RWA activists from diverse neighborhoods and class back-
    grounds during my research, most of my interlocutors lived in wealthier colonies
    dominated by English speakers. These were the people who could afford the addi-
    tional time to mobilize against slums and who had the cultural capital to garner
    media and judicial recognition. I would not have encountered the neighbors of
    Ravi Das Camp had I not already been studying Ravi Das Camp.

4. Civil Writ Petition No. 593 of 2002 in the Delhi High Court.

5. Civil Writ Petition No. 593 of 2002 in the Delhi High Court, order dated March
    8, 2006.

6. This data was collected using a mail-in survey sent out to 85 randomly selected
    RWA members (response rate of 29 percent) using a database provided by the
    Bhagidari Cell of the Chief Minister's Office. I made initial contact over the
    phone and sent surveys to those who expressed a willingness to participate. The
    data I present here indicates responses from a part of the survey in which I asked
    respondents to evaluate the relative importance of various civic grievances on
    a scale of 1 to 5, where 1 was "not important at all," 2 was "of minor impor-
    tance," 3 was "somewhat important," 4 was "very important," and 5 was "most
    important."

7. Interview date: November 10, 2006.

8. Interview date: October 18, 2006.

9. Interview date: November 8, 2006.

10. Interview date: October 18, 2006.

11. Interview date: November 13, 2006.

12. Interview date: April 24, 2006.

13. Interview date: October 19, 2006.

14. Interview date: April 20, 2006.

15. Between 1998 and 2006 in Delhi, all categories of violent crime decreased in
    incidence, with the exception of rape, the occurrence of which increased from
    441 to 623 cases, and kidnapping for ransom, which increased from 25 to 32
    cases. The number of murders fell from 649 to 476, robbery from 823 to 541, and
    rioting from 195 to 50. Property crimes fell even more drastically, with burglary
    dropping from 3,764 to 1,101 (source: Rajya Sabha Unstarred Question No. 942,
    dated March 7, 2007). According to the Chief of Police, the increasing incidence
    of rape is likely due to "an increase in reporting." Most cases of rape, he said,
    were "perpetrated by members of the victim's family, or a person known to the

victim." See Police Chief Says Crime in India's Capital under Control, AP *worldstream*, January 6, 2006.

16. Unsafe City—3 Cases a Day in "Rape Capital," *Hindustan Times*, New Delhi, May 1, 2008.

17. R. Bajpai, Verification Drives Not Being Given Weightage. *Hindustan Times*, South Delhi edition, October 1, 2007.

18. Interview with Mr. Ravi Bajpai, *Hindustan Times* office, Delhi, November 6, 2006.

19. Interview with Ms. Uttara Rajinder, *Times Of India* office, Delhi, November 15, 2006.

20. Ayodhya is the former site of the Babri Mosque, which was destroyed by Hindu nationalists in December 1992. This act and the controversy surrounding it fueled a rise in communal politics that led to rioting in numerous cities across India. While the demolition of the mosque was carried out by Hindu activists, the Police Chief seems to be making reference to Muslim extremists in this quote.

21. Bhagidari Thematic Workshop, February 15, 2007.

22. Interview date: January 6, 2007.

23. This aligns with Deshpande's observation that with the advent of the reform era in the early 1990s, the middle class began to claim not just that it represented the ideal nation—what he calls the "proxy" citizen—but "rather that it is itself the nation" (2003, 150).

24. Interview date: April 24, 2006.

25. Interview date: March 3, 2007.

26. Pitampura Sudhar Samiti versus Government of India, CWP No. 4215 of 1995 in the Delhi High Court, final judgment issued on September 27, 2002.

27. Civil Writ Petition No. 593 of 2002 in the Delhi High Court, order dated March 8, 2006.

28. For example, consider the primarily aesthetic function of the 34 million rupee Green Delhi Action Plan, which focuses on roadside landscaping, litter removal, and strategic tree planting without attention to broader sources of resource degradation or deforestation. See Delhi Is Gearing Up for a New Green Revolution. *The Hindu*, New Delhi, July 6, 2008.

29. Yamuna Pollution Issue, Delhi High Court Summons Top Officials, *Hindustan Times*, New Delhi, February 15, 2007.

30. E. Sridharan, Restrict Yamuna with Walls and Develop Low-Lying Areas. *Times Of India*, New Delhi, May 20, 2009.

31. CM Concern for Green Lung, Seeks Expert Panel. *Times Of India*, New Delhi, May 14, 2009.

32. The Delhi Government's Bhagidari scheme issues annual awards for the best RWAs, which are widely celebrated in the media. The top award in 2006 went to an RWA that cleared two slums in its colony.

33. A. Gentleman, In India, Ban on Child Labor to be Tightened. *International Herald Tribune*, New York, October 9, 2006.

References

Anderson, M. R. 1992. Public Nuisance and Private Purpose: Policed Environments in British India, 1860–1947. SOAS Law Department Working Papers, 1. 1–33. London.

Bauman, Z. 2004. *Wasted Lives: Modernity and its Outasts*. London: Polity Press.

Baviskar, A. 2003. Between Violence and Desire: Space, Power, and Identity in the Making of Metropolitan Delhi. *International Social Science Journal*, 55 (1): 89–98.

Bourdieu, P. 1998. *Practical Reason: On the Theory of Action*. Stanford, CA: Stanford University Press.

Caldeira, T. 2001. *City of Walls: Crime, Segregation, and Citizenship in Sao Paulo*. Berkeley, CA: University of California Press.

Chatterjee, P. 2004. *The Politics of the Governed: Reflections on Popular Politics in Most of the World*. New York: Columbia University Press.

Davis, M. 1990. *City of Quartz: Excavating the Future in Los Angeles*. London: Verso.

Deshpande, S. 2003. *Contemporary India: A Sociological View*. New Delhi: Penguin Books.

———. 2006. Mapping the "Middle": Issues in the Analysis of the "Non-Poor" Classes in India. In *Contested Transformations: Changing Economies and Identities in Contemporary India*, ed. M. E. John, P. K. Jha, and S. S. Jodhka. 215–236. New Delhi: Tulika Books.

Douglas, M. 1966. *Purity and Danger: An Analysis of Concepts of Pollution and Taboo*. New York: Praeger.

Eagleton, T. 1990. *The Ideology of the Aesthetic*. Oxford: Basil Blackwell.

Fernandes, L. 2006. *India's New Middle Class: Democratic Politics in an Era of Economic Reform*. Minneapolis, MN: University of Minnesota Press.

Ghertner, D. A. 2008. An Analysis of New Legal Discourse behind Delhi's Slum Demolitions. *Economic and Political Weekly*, 43 (20): 57–66.

———. 2011a. Gentrifying the State, Gentrifying Participation: Elite Governance Programs in Delhi. *International Journal of Urban and Regional Research*, 35 (3): 504–532.

———. 2011b. Rule by Aesthetics: World-Class City Making in Delhi. In *Worlding Cities: Asian Experiments and the Art of Being Global*, ed. A. Roy and A. Ong. 279–306. Oxford: Blackwell.

Gooptu, N. 2005. *The Politics of the Urban Poor in Early Twentieth-Century India*. Cambridge: Cambridge University Press.

Jain, A. K. 2005. *Law and Environment*. Delhi: Ascent.

Kristeva, J. 1982. *Powers of Horror: A Note on Abjection*. New York: Columbia University Press.

Legg, S. 2007. *Spaces of Colonialism: Delhi's Urban Governmentalities*. Oxford: Blackwell.

McClintock, A. 1995. *Imperial Leather: Race, Gender and Sexuality in the Colonial Context*. New York: Routledge.

Moore, D. S., J. Kosek, and A. Pandian. 2003. *Race, Nature and the Politics of Difference.* Durham, NC: Duke University Press.

Nair, J. 2005. *The Promise of the Metropolis: Bangalore's Twentieth Century.* New Delhi: Oxford University Press.

Prakash, G. 1999. *Another Reason: Science and the Imagination of Modern India.* Princeton, NJ: Princeton University Press.

Prashad, V. 2001. The Technology of Sanitation in Colonial Delhi. *Modern Asian Studies,* 35 (1): 113–155.

Sibley, D. 1995. *Geographies of Exclusion.* London: Routledge.

Stallybrass, P. and A. White. 1986. *The Politics and Poetics of Transgression.* Ithaca, NY: Cornell University Press.

Verma, G. D. 2002. *Slumming India: A Chronicle of Slums and their Saviours.* Delhi: Penguin Books.

Index